DANTE'S INFERNO

Dante Alighieri

AF516851

Happy Hour Books

Published by:

HAPPY HOUR BOOKS

www.happyhoursbooks.com

email: happyhourbooks1@gmail.com

First published by Happy Hour Books 2023

Title : **Dante's Inferno**

Paperback ISBN : 9789358480450

Hardback ISBN : 9789358480467

FLORENCE AND DANTE

Dante is himself the hero of the Divine Comedy, and ere many stages of the Inferno have been passed the reader feels that all his steps are being taken in a familiar companionship. When every allowance has been made for what the exigencies of art required him to heighten or suppress, it is still impossible not to be convinced that the author is revealing himself much as he really was—in some of his weakness as well as in all his strength. The poem itself, by many an unconscious touch, does for his moral portraiture what the pencil of Giotto has done for the features of his face. The one likeness answers marvellously to the other; and, together, they have helped the world to recognise in him the great example of a man of genius who, though at first sight he may seem to be austere, is soon found to attract our love by the depth of his feelings as much as he wins our admiration by the wealth of his fancy, and by the clearness of his judgment on everything concerned with the lives and destiny of men. His other writings in greater or less degree confirm the impression of Dante's character to be obtained from the Comedy. Some of them are partly autobiographical; and, studying as a whole all that is left to us of him, we can gain a general notion of the nature of his career—when he was born and what was his condition in life; his early loves and friendships; his studies, military service, and political aims; his hopes and illusions, and the weary purgatory of his exile.

To the knowledge of Dante's life and character which is thus to be acquired, the formal biographies of him have but little to add that is both trustworthy and of value. Something of course there is in the traditional story of his life that has come down from his time with the seal of genuineness; and something that has been ascertained by careful research among Florentine and other documents. But when all that old and modern Lives have to tell us has been sifted, the additional facts regarding him are found to be but few; such at least as are beyond dispute. Boccaccio, his earliest biographer, swells out his Life, as the earlier commentators on the Comedy do their notes, with what are plainly but legendary amplifications of hints supplied by Dante's own words; while more recent and critical writers succeed with infinite pains in little beyond establishing, each to his own satisfaction, what was the order of publication of the poet's works, where he may have travelled to, and when and for how long a time he may have had this or that great lord for a patron.

A very few pages would therefore be enough to tell the events of Dante's life as far as they are certainly known. But, to be of use as an introduction to the study of his great poem, any biographical sketch must contain some account—more or less full—of Florentine affairs before and during his lifetime; for among the actors in these are to be found many of the persons of the Comedy. In reading the poem we are never suffered for long to forget his exile. From one point of view it is an appeal to future ages from Florentine injustice and ingratitude; from another, it is a long and passionate plea with his native town to shake her in her stubborn cruelty. In spite of the worst she can do against him he remains no less her son. In the early copies of it, the Comedy is well described as the work of Dante Alighieri, the Florentine; since not only does he people the other world by preference with Florentines, but it is to Florence that, even when his words are bitter against her, his heart is always feeling back. Among the glories of Paradise he loves to let his memory rest on the church in which he was baptized and the streets he used to tread. He takes pleasure in her stones; and with her towers and palaces Florence stands for the unchanging background to the changing scenes of his mystical pilgrimage.

The history of Florence during the twelfth and thirteenth centuries agrees in general outline with that of most of its neighbours. At the beginning of the period it was a place of but little importance, ranking far below Pisa both in wealth and political influence. Though retaining the names and forms of municipal government, inherited from early times, it was in reality possessed of no effective control over its own affairs, and was subject to its feudal superior almost as completely as was ever any German village planted in the shadow of a castle. To Florence, as to many a city of Northern and Central Italy, the first opportunity of winning freedom came with the contest between Emperor and Pope in the time of Hildebrand. In this quarrel the Church found its best ally in Matilda, Countess of Tuscany. She, to secure the goodwill of her subjects as against the Emperor, yielded first one and then another of her rights in Florence, generally by way of a pious gift—an endowment for a religious house or an increase of jurisdiction to the bishop—these concessions, however veiled, being in effect so many additions to the resources and liberties of the townsmen. She made Rome her heir, and then Florence was able to play off the Papal against the Imperial claims, yielding a kind of barren homage to both Emperor and Pope, and only studious to complete a virtual independence of both. Florence had been Matilda's favourite place of residence; and, benefiting largely as it did by her easy rule, it is no wonder that her name should have been cherished by the Florentines for ages after as a household word.[1] Nor is the greatest Florentine unmindful of her. Foe of the Empire though she was, he only remembers her piety; and it is by Matilda, as representing the active religious life, that Dante is ushered into the presence of Beatrice in the Earthly Paradise.[2]

It was a true instinct which led Florence and other cities to side rather with the Pope than with the Emperor in the long-continued struggle between them for predominance in Italy. With the Pope for overlord they would at least have a master who was an Italian, and one who, his title being imperfect, would in his own interest be led to treatthem with indulgence; while, in the permanent triumph of the Emperor, Italy must have become subject and tributary to Germany, and would have seen new estates carved out of her fertile soil for members of the German garrison. The danger was brought home to many of the youthful commonwealths during the eventful reign of Frederick Barbarossa (1152-1190). Strong in Germany beyond most of his predecessors, that monarch ascended the throne with high prerogative views, in which he was confirmed by the slavish doctrine of some of the new civilians. According to these there couldbe only one master in the world; as far as regarded the things of time, but one source of authority in Christendom. They maintained everything to be the Emperor's that he chose to take. When he descended into Italy to enforce his claims, the cities of the Lombard League met him in open battle. Those of Tuscany, and especially Florence, bent before the blast, temporising as long as they were able, and making the best terms they could when the choice lay between submission and open revolt. Even Florence, it is true, strong in her allies, did once take arms against an Imperial lieutenant; but asa rule she never refused obedience in words, and never yielded it in fact beyond whatcould not be helped. In her pursuit of advantages, skilfully using every opportunity,and steadfast of aim even when most she appeared to waver, she displayed somethingof the same address that was long to be noted as a trait in the character of the individualFlorentine.

The storm was weathered, although not wholly without loss. When, towards the closeof his life, and after he had broken his strength against the obstinate patriotism of Lombardy, Frederick visited Florence in 1185, it was as a master justly displeased with servants who, while they had not openly rebelled against him, had yet proved eminently unprofitable, and whom he was concerned to punish if not to destroy. On the complaint of the neighbouring nobles, that they were oppressed and had been plundered by the city, he gave orders for the restoration to them of their lands and castles. This accomplished, all the territory left to Florence was a narrow belt around the walls. Villani even says that for the four years during which Frederick still lived the Commonwealth was wholly landless. And here, rather than lose ourselves among the endless treaties, leagues, and campaigns which fill so many pages of the chronicles, it may be worth while shortly to glance at the constitution of Florentine society, and especially at the place held in it by the class which found its protector in Barbarossa.

Much about the time at which the Commonwealth was relieved of its feudal trammels, as a result of the favour or the necessities of Matilda, it was beginning to extend its commerce and increase its industry. Starting somewhat late on the career on which Venice, Genoa, and Pisa were already far advanced, Florence was as if strenuous to make up for lost time, and soon displayed a rare comprehension of the nature of the enterprise. It may be questioned if ever, until quite modern times, there has been anywhere so clear an understanding of the truth that public wellbeing is the sum of private prosperity, or such an enlightened perception of what tends to economical progress. Florence had no special command of raw material for her manufactures, no sea-port of her own, and no monopoly unless in the natural genius of her people. She could therefore thrive only by dint of holding open her communications with the worldat large, and grudged no pains either of war or diplomacy to keep at Pisa a free way out and in for her merchandise. Already in the twelfth century she received through that port the rough woollens of Flanders, which, after being skilfully dressed and dyed,were sent out at great profit to every market of Europe. At a somewhat later period the Florentines were to give as strong a proof of their financial capacity as this was of their industrial. It was they who first conducted a large business in bills of exchange, and who first struck a gold coin which, being kept of invariable purity, passed current in every land where men bought and sold—even in countries where the very name of Florence was unknown.[3]

In a community thus devoted to industry and commerce, it was natural that a great place should be filled by merchants. These were divided into six guilds, the members of which, with the notaries and lawyers, who composed a seventh, formed the true body of the citizens. Originally the consuls of these guilds were the only elected officials in the city, and in the early days of its liberty they were even charged with political duties, and are found, for example, signing a treaty of peace with a neighbouring state. In the fully developed commune it was only the wealthier citizens—the members, we may assume, of these guilds—who, along with the nobles,[4] were eligible for and had the right of electing to the public offices. Below them was the great body of the people; all, that is, of servile condition or engaged in the meaner kinds of business. From one

point of view, the liberties of the citizens were only their privileges. But although the labourers and humbler tradesmen were without franchises, their interests were not therefore neglected, being bound up with those of the one or two thousand citizens who shared with the patricians the control of public affairs.

There were two classes of nobles with whom Florence had to reckon as she awoke to life—those within the walls, and those settled in the neighbouring country. In later times it was a favourite boast among the noble citizens—a boast indulged in by Dante—that they were descended from ancient Roman settlers on the banks of the Arno. A safer boast would in many cases have been that their ancestors had come to Italy in the train of Otho and other conquering Emperors. Though settled in the city, in some cases for generations, the patrician families were not altogether of it, being distinguished from the other citizens, if not always by the possession of ancestral landward estates, at least by their delight in war and contempt for honest industry. But with the faults of a noble class they had many of its good qualities. Of these the Republic suffered them to make full proof, allowing them to lead in war and hold civil offices out of all proportion to their numbers.

Like the city itself, the nobles in the country around had been feudally subject to the Marquis of Tuscany. After Matilda's death they claimed to hold direct from the Empire; which meant in practice to be above all law. They exercised absolute jurisdiction over their serfs and dependants, and, when favoured by the situation of their castles, took toll, like the robber barons of Germany, of the goods which passed beneath their walls. Already they had proved to be thorns in the side of the industrious burghers; but at the beginning of the twelfth century their neighbourhood became intolerable, and for a couple of generations the chief political work of Florence was to bring them to reason. Those whose lands came up almost to the city gates were first dealt with, and then in a widening circle the country was cleared of the pest. Year after year, when the days were lengthening out in spring, the roughly organised city militia was mustered, war was declared against some specially obnoxious noble and his fortress was taken by surprise, or, failing that, was subjected to a siege. In the absence of a more definite grievance, it was enough to declare his castle dangerously near the city. These expeditions were led by the nobles who were already citizens, while the country neighbours of the victim looked on with indifference, or even helped to waste the lands or force the stronghold of a rival. The castle once taken, it was either levelled with the ground, or was restored to the owner on condition of his yielding service to the Republic. And, both by way of securing a hold upon an unwilling vassal and of adding a wealthy house and some strong arms to the Commonwealth, he was compelled, along with his family, to reside in Florence for a great part of every year.

With a wider territory and an increasing commerce, it was natural for Florence to assumemore and more the attitude of a sovereign state, ready, when need was, to impose its will upon its neighbours, or to join with them for the common defence of Tuscany. Inthe noble class and its retainers, recruited as has been described, it was possessed of astanding army which, whether from love of adventure or greed of plunder, was never so well pleased as when in active employment. Not that the commons left the fightingwholly to the men of family, for they too, at the summons of the war-bell, had to arm for the field; but at the best they did it from a sense of duty, and, without the aid of professional men-at-arms, they must have failed more frequently in their enterprises, or at any rate have had to endure a greatly prolonged absence from their counters andworkshops. And yet, esteem this advantage as highly as we will, Florence surely lost more than it gained by compelling the crowd of idle gentlemen to come within its walls. In the course of time some of them indeed condescended to engage in trade— sank, as the phrase went, into the ranks of the Popolani, or mere wealthy citizens; butthe great body of them, while their landed property was being largely increased in value in consequence of the general prosperity, held themselves haughtily aloof from honest industry in every form. Each family, or rather each clan of them, lived apart inits own group of houses, from among which towers shot aloft for scores of yards into the air, dominating the humbler dwellings of the common burghers. These, wheneverthey came to the front for a time in the government, were used to decree that all privatetowers were to be lopped down to within a certain distance from the ground.

It is a favourite exercise of Villani and other historians to trace the troubles and revolutions in the state of Florence to chance quarrels between noble families, arisingfrom an angry word or a broken troth. Here, they tell, was sown the seed of the Guelfand Ghibeline wars in Florence; and here that of the feuds of Black and White. Such quarrels and party names were symptoms and nothing more. The enduring source of trouble was the presence within the city of a powerful idle class, constantly eager to recover the privilege it had lost, and to secure itself by every available means, including that of outside help, in the possession of what it still retained; which chafedagainst the curbs put upon its lawlessness, and whose ambitions were all opposed to the general interest. The citizens, for their part, had nothing better to hope for than that Italy should be left to the Italians, Florence to the Florentines. On the occasion of the celebrated Buondelmonti feud (1215), some of the nobles definitely went over to the side of the people, either because they judged it likely[Pg xxviii] to win in the long- run, or impelled unconsciously by the forces that in every society divide ambitious men into two camps, and in one form or another develop party strife. They who made a profession of popular sympathy did it with a view of using rather than of helping the people at large. Both of the noble parties held the same end in sight—control of the Commonwealth; and this would be worth the more the fewer there were to share it. The faction irreconcilable with the Republic on any terms included many of the oldest and proudest houses. Their hope lay in the advent of a strong Emperor, who should depute to them his rights over the money-getting, low-born crowd.

II.

The opportunity of this class might seem to have come when the Hohenstaufen Frederick II., grandson of Barbarossa, ascended the throne, and still more when, on attaining full age, he claimed the whole of the Peninsula as his family inheritance. Other Emperors had withstood the Papal claims, but none had ever proved an antagonist like Frederick. His quarrel seemed indeed to be with the Church itself, with its doctrines and morals as well as with the ambition of churchmen; and he offered the strange spectacle of a Roman Emperor—one of the twin lights in the Christian firmament—whose favour was less easily won by Christian piety, however eminent, than by the learning of the Arab or the Jew. When compelled at last to fulfil a promise extorted from him of conducting a crusade to the Holy Land, he scandalised Christendom by making friends of the Sultan, and by using his presence in the East, not for the deliverance of the Sepulchre, but for the furtherance of learning and commerce. Thrice excommunicated, he had his revenge by proving with how little concern the heaviest anathemas of the Church could be met by one who was armed in unbelief. Literature, art, and manners were sedulously cultivated in his Sicilian court, and among the able ministers whom he selected or formed, the modern idea of the State may be said to have had its birth. Free thinker and free liver, poet, warrior, and statesman, he stood forward against the sombre background of the Middle Ages a figure in every respect so brilliant and original as well to earn from his contemporaries the title of the Wonder of the World.

On the goodwill of Italians Frederick had the claim of being the most Italian of all the Emperors since the revival of the Western Empire, and the only one of them whose throne was permanently set on Italian soil. Yet he never won the popular heart. To the common mind he always appeared as something outlandish and terrible—as the man who had driven a profitable but impious trade in the Sultan's land. Dante, in his childhood, must have heard many a tale of him; and we find him keenly interested in the character of the Emperor who came nearest to uniting Italy into a great nation, in whose court there had been a welcome for every man of intellect, and in whom a great original poet would have found a willing and munificent patron. In the Inferno, by the mouth of Pier delle Vigne, the Imperial Chancellor, he pronounces Frederick to have been worthy of all honour;[5] yet justice requires him to lodge this flower of kings in the burning tomb of the Epicureans, as having been guilty of the arch-heresy of denying the moral government of the world, and holding that with the death of the body all is ended.[6] It was a heresy fostered by the lives of many churchmen, high and low; but the example of Frederick encouraged the profession of it by nobles and learned laymen. On Frederick's character there was a still darker stain than this of religious indifference—that of cold-blooded cruelty. Even in an age which had produced Ezzelino Romano, the Emperor's cloaks of lead were renowned as the highest refinement in torture.[7] But, with all his genius, and his want of scruple in the choice of means, he built nothing politically that was not ere his death crumbling to dust. His enduring work was that of an intellectual reformer under whose protection and with whose personal help his native language was refined, Europe was enriched with a learning new to it or long forgotten, and the minds of men, as they lost their blind reverence for Rome, were prepared for a freer treatment of all the questions with which religion deals. He was thus in some respects a precursor of Dante.

More than once in the course of Frederick's career it seemed as if he might become master of Tuscany in fact as well as in name, had Florence only been as well affected to him as were Siena and Pisa. But already, as has been said, the popular interest had been strengthened by accessions from among the nobles. Others of them, without descending into the ranks of the citizens, had set their hopes on being the first in a commonwealth rather than privates in the Imperial garrison. These men, with their restless and narrow ambitions, were as dangerous to have for allies as for foes, but by throwing their weight into the popular scale they at least served to hold the Imperialist magnates in check, and established something like a balance in the fighting power of Florence; and so, as in the days of Barbarossa, the city was preserved from taking a side too strongly. The hearts of the Florentine traders were in their own affairs—in extending their commerce and increasing their territory and influence in landward Tuscany. As regarded the general politics of Italy, their sympathy was still with the Roman See; but it was a sympathy without devotion or gratitude. For refusing to join in the crusade of 1238 the town was placed under interdict by Gregory IX. The Emperor meanwhile was acknowledged as its lawful overlord, and his vicar received something more than nominal obedience, the choice of the chief magistrates being made subject to his approval. Yet with all this, and although his party was powerful in the city, it was but a grudging service that was yielded to Frederick. More than once fines were levied on the

Florentines; and worse punishments were threatened for their persevering and active enmity to Siena, now dominated by its nobles and held in the Imperial interest. Volunteers from Florence might join the Emperor in his Lombard campaigns; but theywere left equally free by the Commonwealth to join the other side. At last, when he was growing old, and when like his grandfather he had been foiled by the stubborn Lombards, he turned on the Florentines as an easier prey, and sent word to the noblesof his party to seize the city. For months the streets were filled with battle. In January 1248, Frederick of Antioch, the natural son of the Emperor, entered Florence with some squadrons of men-at-arms, and a few days later the nobles that had fought on thepopular side were driven into banishment. This is known in the Florentine annals as the first dispersion of the Guelfs.

Long before they were adopted in Italy, the names of Guelf and Ghibeline had been employed in Germany to mark the partisans of the Bavarian Welf and of the Hohenstaufen lords of Waiblingen. On Italian soil they received an extended meaning: Ghibeline stood for Imperialist; Guelf for anti-Imperialist, Papalist, or simply Nationalist. When the names began to be freely used in Florence, which was towards the close of Frederick's reign and about a century after their first invention, they denoted no new start in politics, but only supplied a nomenclature for parties already in existence. As far as Florence was concerned, the designations were the more convenient that they were not too closely descriptive. The Ghibeline was the Emperor's man, when it served his purpose to be so; while the Guelf, constant only in his enmity to the Ghibelines, was free to think of the Pope as he chose, and to serve him no more than he wished or needed to. Ultimately, indeed, all Florence may be said to have become Guelf. To[Pg xxxiii] begin with, the name distinguished the nobles who sought alliance with the citizens, from the nobles who looked on these as they might have done on serfs newly thriven into wealth. Each party was to come up in turn. Within a period of twenty years each was twice driven into banishment, a measure always accompanied with decrees of confiscation and the levelling of private strongholds in Florence. The exiles kept well together, retreating, as it were in the order of war, to camps of observation they found ready prepared for them in the nearest cities and fortresses held by those of their own way of thinking. All their wits were then bent on how, by dint of some fighting and much diplomacy, they might shake the strength and undermine the credit of their successful rivals in the city, and secure their own return in triumph. It was an art theywere proud to be adepts in.[8]

In a rapid sketch like this it would be impossible to tell half the changes made on the constitution of Florence during the second part of the thirteenth century. Dantein a well-known passage reproaches Florence with the political restlessness which afflicted her like a disease. Laws, he says, made in October were fallen into desuetude ere mid-November.[9] And yet it may be that in this constant readiness to change, lies the best proof of the political capacity of the Florentines. It was to meet new necessities that they made provision of new laws. Especial watchfulness was called for against the encroachments of the grandees, whose constant tendency—whatever their party name—was to weaken legal authority, and play the part of lords and masters of the citizens. But these were no mere weavers and quill-drivers to be plundered at will. Even before the return of the Guelfs, banished in 1248, the citizens, taking advantage of a check suffered in the field by the dominant Ghibelines, had begun to recast the constitution in a popular sense, and to organise the townsmen as a militia on a permanent footing. When, on the death of Frederick in 1250, the Imperialist nobles were left without foreign aid, there began a period of ten years, favourably known in Florentine history as the Government of the Primo Popolo or Popolo Vecchio; that is, of the true body of the citizens, commoners possessed of franchises, as distinguished from the nobles above them and the multitude below. For it is never to be forgotten that Florence, like Athens, and like the other Italian Republics, was far from being a true democracy. The time was yet to come, and it was not far distant, when the ranks of citizenship were to be more widely opened than now to those below, and more closely shut to those above. In the meantime the comparatively small number of wealthy citizens who legally composed the 'People' made good use of their ten years of breathing-time, entering on commercial treaties and widening the possessions of the Commonwealth, now by war, and now by shrewd bargains with great barons. To balance the influence of the Podesta, who had hitherto been the one great officer of State—criminal judge, civil governor, and commander-in-chief all in one—they created the office of Captain of the People. The office of Podesta was not peculiar to Florence. There, as in other cities, in order to secure his impartiality, it was provided that he should be a foreigner, and hold office only for six months. But he was also required to be of gentle birth; and his councils were so composed that, like his own, their sympathies were usually with the nobles. The Captain of the People was therefore created partly as a tribune for the protection of the popular rights, and partly to act as permanent head of the popular forces. Like the Podesta, he had two councils assigned to him; but these were strictly representative of the citizens, and sat to control his conduct as well as to lend to his action the weight of public opinion.

Such of the Ghibelines as had not been banished from Florence on the death of Frederick, lived there on sufferance, as it were, and under a rigid supervision. Once more they were to find a patron and ally in a member of the great house of Hohenstaufen; and with his aid they were again for a few years to become supreme in Florence, and to prove by their abuse of power how well justified was the mistrust the people had of them. In many ways Manfred, one of Frederick's bastards, was a worthy son of his father. Like him he was endowed with great personal charm, and was enamoured of all that opened new regions to intellectual curiosity or gave refinement to sensual pleasure. In his public as well as in his private behaviour, he was reckless of what the Church and its doctrines might promise or threaten; and equally so, his enemies declared, of the dictates of common humanity. Hostile eyes detected in the green clothes which were his favourite dress a secret attachment to Islam; and hostile tongues charged him with the murder of a father and of a brother, and the attempted murder of a nephew. His ambition did not aim at the Empire, but only at being King of Sicily and Naples, lands which the Hohenstaufens claimed as their own through the Norman mother of Frederick. Of these kingdoms he was actual ruler, even while his legitimate brother Conrad lived. On the death of that prince he brushed aside the claims of Conradin, his nephew, and bid boldly for recognition by the Pope, who claimed to be overlord of the southern kingdoms—a recognition refused, or given only to be immediately withdrawn. In the eyes of Rome he was no more than Prince of Tarentum, but by arms and policy he won what seemed a firm footing in the South; and eight years after the rule of the Popolo Vecchio began in Florence he was the acknowledged patron of all in Italy who had been Imperialist—for the Imperial throne was now practically vacant. And Manfred was trusted all the more that he cared nothing for Germany, and stood out even more purely an Italian monarch than his father had ever been. The Ghibelines of Florence looked to him to free them of the yoke under which they groaned.

When it was discovered that they were treating with Manfred, there was an outburst of popular wrath against the disaffected nobles. Some of them were seized and put to death, a fate shared by the Abbot of Vallombrosa, whom neither his priestly office nor his rank as Papal Legate availed to save from torture and[Pg xxxvii] a shameful end.[10] Well accustomed as was the age to violence and cruelty, it was shocked at this free disposal of a great ecclesiastic by a mercantile community; and even to the Guelf chronicler Villani the terrible defeat of Montaperti seemed no more than a just vengeance taken by Heaven upon a crime so heinous.[11] In the meantime the city was laid under interdict, and those concerned in the Abbot's death were excommunicated; while the Ghibelines, taking refuge in Siena, began to plot and scheme with the greater spirit against foes who, in the very face of a grave peril, had offended in the Pope their strongest natural ally.

The leader of the exiles was Farinata, one of the Uberti, a family which, so long ago as 1180, had raised a civil war to force their way into the consulship. Ever since, they had been the most powerful, perhaps, and certainly the most restless, clan in Florence, rich in men of strong character, fiercely tenacious of their purpose. Such was Farinata. To the Florentines of a later age he was to stand for the type of the great Ghibeline gentleman, haughty as Lucifer, a Christian in name though scarcely by profession, and yet almost beloved for his frank excess of pride. It detracted nothing[Pg xxxviii] from the grandeur of his character, in the judgment of his countrymen, that he could be cunning as well as brave. Manfred was coy to afford help to the Tuscan Ghibelines, standing out for an exorbitant price for the loan of his men-at-arms; and to Farinata was attributed the device by which his point of honour was effectually touched.[12] When at last a reinforcement of eight hundred cavalry entered Siena, the exiles and their allies felt themselves more than a match for the militia of Florence, and set themselves to decoy it into the field. Earlier in the same year the Florentines had encamped before Siena, and sought in vain to bring on a general engagement. They were now misled by false messengers, primed by Farinata, into a belief that the Sienese, weary of the arrogance of Provenzano Salvani,[13] then all-powerful in Siena, were ready to betray a gate to them. In vain did Tegghiaio Aldobrandi,[14] one of the Guelf nobles, counsel delay till the German men-at-arms, wearied with waiting on and perhaps dissatisfied with their wages, should be recalled by Manfred. A march in full strength upon the hostile city was resolved on by the eager townsmen.

The battle of Montaperti was fought in September 1260, among the earthy hills washed by the Arbia and its tributary rivulets, a few miles to the east of Siena. It marked the close of the rule of the Popolo Vecchio. Till then no such disastrous day had come to Florence; and the defeat was all the more intolerable that it was counted for a victory to Siena. Yet the battle was far from being a test of the strength of the two rival cities.

Out of the thirty thousand foot in the Guelf army, there were only about five thousand Florentines. In the host which poured out on them from Siena, beside the militia of that city and the Florentine exiles, were included the Ghibelines of Arezzo, the retainers of great lords still unsubdued by any city, and, above all, the German men-at-arms of Manfred.[15] But the worst enemies of Florence were the traitors in her own ranks. She bore it long in mind that it was her merchants and handicraftsmen who stood stubbornly at bay, and tinged the Arbia red with their life-blood; while it was among the men of high degree that the traitors were found. On one of them, Bocca degli Abati, who struck off the right hand of the standard-bearer of the cavalry, and so helped on the confusion and the rout, Dante takes vengeance in his pitiless verse.[16]

The fortifications of Florence had been recently completed and strengthened, and it was capable of a long defence. But the spirit of the people was broken for the time, and the conquerors found the gates open. Then it was that Farinata almost atoned for any wrong he ever did his native town, by withstanding a proposal made by the Ghibelines of the rival Tuscan cities, that Florence should be destroyed, and Empoli advanced to fill her room. 'Alone, with open face I defended her,' Dante makes him say.[17] But the wonder would rather be if he had voted to destroy a city of which he was about to be one of the tyrants. Florence had now a fuller experience than ever of the oppression which it was in the character of the Ghibelines to exercise. A rich booty lay ready to their hands; for in the panic after Montaperti crowds of the best in Florence had fled, leaving all behind them except their wives and children, whom they would not trust to the cruel mercy of the victors. It was in this exile that for the first time the industrious citizen was associated with the Guelf noble. From Lucca, not powerful enough to grant them protection for long, they were driven to Bologna, suffering terribly on the passage of the Apennines from cold and want of food, but safe when the mountains lay between them and the Val d'Arno. While the nobles and young men with a taste for fighting found their livelihood in service against the Lombard Ghibelines, the more sober-minded scattered themselves to seek out their commercial correspondents and increase their acquaintance with the markets of Europe. When at length the way was open for them to return home, they came back educated by travel, as men must always be who travel for a purpose; and from this second exile of the Guelfs dates a vast extension of the commerce of Florence.

Their return was a fruit of the policy followed by the Papal Court The interests of both were the same. The Roman See could have as little independence of action while a hostile monarch was possessed of the southern kingdoms, as the people of Florence could have freedom while the Ghibeline nobility had for patron a military prince, to whom their gates lay open by way of Siena and Pisa. To Sicily and Naples the Pope laid claim by an alternative title—they were either dependent on the See of Rome, or, if they were Imperial fiefs, then, in the vacancy of the Empire, the Pope, as the only head of Christendom, had a right to dispose of them as he would. A champion was needed to maintain the claim, and at length the man was found in Charles of Anjou, brother of St. Louis. This was a prince of intellectual powers far beyond the common, of untiring industry in affairs, pious, 'chaste as a monk,' and cold-hearted as a usurer; gifted with all the qualities, in short, that make a man feared and well served, and with none that make him beloved. He was not one to risk failure for want of deliberation and foresight, and his measures were taken with such prudence that by the time he landed in Italy his victory was almost assured. He found his enemy at Benevento, in the Neapolitan territory (February 1266). In order to get time for reinforcements to come up, Manfred sought to enter into negotiations; but Charles was ready, and knew his advantage. He answered with the splendid confidence of a man sure of a heavenly if he missed an earthly triumph. 'Go tell the Sultan of Lucera,'[18] was his reply, 'that to-day I shall send him to Hell, or he will send me to Paradise.' Manfred was slain, and his body, discovered only after long search, was denied Christian burial. Yet, excommunicated though he was, and suspected of being at heart as much Mohammedan as Christian, he,as well as his great rival, is found by Dante in Purgatory.[19] And, while the Christianpoet pours his invective on the pious Charles,[20] he is at no pains to hide how pitifulappeared to him the fate of the frank and handsome Manfred, all whose followers adored him. He, as more than once it happens in the Comedy to those whose memoryis dear to the poet, is saved from Inferno by the fiction that in the hour of death he sentone thought heavenward—'so wide is the embrace of infinite mercy.'[21]

To Florence Charles proved a useful if a greedy and exacting protector. Under his influence as Pacificator of Tuscany—an office created for him by the Pope—the Guelfs were enabled slowly to return from exile, and the Ghibelines were gradually depressed into a condition of dependence on the goodwill of the citizens over whom they had so lately domineered. Henceforth failure attended every effort they made to lift their heads. The stubbornly irreconcilable were banished or put to death. Elaborateprovisions were enacted in obedience to the Pope's commands, by which the rest were to be at peace with their old foes. Now they were to live in the city, but under disabilities as regarded eligibility to offices; now they were to be represented in the public councils, but so as to be always in a minority. The result of the measures taken,and of the natural drift of things, was that ere many more years had passed there wereno avowed Ghibelines in Florence.

One influence constantly at work in this direction was that of the Parte Guelfa, a Florentine society formed to guard the interests of the Guelfs, and which was possessedof the greater part of the Ghibeline property confiscated after the triumph of Charles had turned the balance of power in Italy. This organisation has been well described asa state within a state, and it seems as if the part it played in the Florentine politics of this period were not yet fully known. This much seems sure, that the members of the Society were mostly Guelf nobles; that its power, derived from the administration of vast wealth to a political end, was so great that the Captain of the Parte Guelfa held a place almost on a level with that of the chief officials of the Commonwealth; and that itmade loans of ready money to Florence and the Pope, on condition of their being usedto the damage of the Ghibelines.[22]

The Commonwealth, busy in resettling its government, was but slightly interested in much that went on around it. The boy Conradin, grandson of Frederick, nephew of Manfred, and in a sense the last of the Hohenstaufens, came to Italy to measure himselfwith Charles, and paid for his audacity upon the scaffold.[23] Charles deputed Guy of Montfort, son of the great Earl Simon, to be his vicar in Florence. The Pope smiled and frowned in turn on the Florentines, as their devotion to him waxed and waned; andso he did on his champion Charles, whose ambition was apt to outrun his piety. All this was of less importance to the Commonwealth than the promotion of its domestic interests. It saw with equanimity a check given to Charles by the election of a new

Emperor in Rudolf of Hapsburg (1273), and a further check by the Sicilian Vespers, which lost him half his kingdom (1283). But Siena and Pisa, Arezzo, and even Pistoia,were the objects of a sleepless anxiety. Pisa was the chief source of danger, being both from sentiment and interest stubbornly Ghibeline. When at length its power was brokenby Genoa, its great maritime rival, in the naval battle of Meloria (1284), there was no longer any city in Tuscany to be compared for wealth and strength with Florence.

III.

It was at this period that Dante, reaching the age of manhood, began to perform the duties that fell to him as a youthful citizen—duties which, till the age of thirty was reached, were chiefly those of military service. The family to which he belonged was abranch of the Elisei, who are included by Villani in the earliest catalogue given by himof the great Florentine houses. Cacciaguida, one of the Elisei, born in 1106, married a daughter of the Aldighieri, a family of Ferrara. Their son was christened Aldighiero, and this was adopted by the family as a surname, afterwards changed to Alighieri. Theson of Aldighiero was Bellincione, father of Aldighiero II., the father of Dante.

It serves no purpose to fill a page of biography with genealogical details when the hero's course in life was in no way affected by the accident of who was his grandfather.In the case of Dante, his position in the State, his political creed, and his whole fashionof regarding life, were vitally influenced by the circumstances of his birth. He knew that his genius, and his genius alone, was to procure him fame; he declares a virtuousand gentle life to be the true proof of nobility: and yet his family pride is always breaking through. In real life, from his family's being decayed in wealth and fallen in consideration compared with its neighbours, he may have been led to put emphasis on his assertion of gentility; and amid the poverty and humiliations of his exile he may have found a tonic in the thought that by birth, not to speak of other things, he was the equal of those who spurned him or coldly lent him aid. However this may be, there is a tacit claim of equality with them in the easy grace with which he encounters great nobles in the world of shades. The bent of his mind in relation to this subject is shown by such a touch as that when he esteems it among the glories of Francis of Assisi not to have been ashamed of his base extraction.[24] In Paradise he meets his great crusading ancestor Cacciaguida, and feigns contrition for the pleasure with which he listens to a declaration of the unmixed purity of their common blood.[25] In Inferno he catches a glimpse, sudden and terrible, of a kinsman whose violent death had remained unavenged; and, for the nonce, the philosopher-poet is nothing but the member of an injured Florentine clan, and winces at the thought of a neglected blood feud.[26] And when Farinata, the great Ghibeline, and haughtiest of all the Florentines of the past generation, asks him, 'Who were thine ancestors?' Dante says with a proud pretence of humility, 'Anxious to obey, I hid nothing, but told him all he demanded.'[27]

Dante was born in Florence in the May of 1265.[28] A brother of his father had been one of the guards of the Florentine Caroccio, or standard-bearing car, at the battle of Montaperti (1260). Whether Dante's father necessarily shared in the exile of his party may be doubted. He is said—on slight authority—to have been a jurisconsult: there is no reason to suppose he was at Montaperti. It is difficult to believe that Florence was quite emptied of its lawyers and merchants as a consequence of the Ghibeline victory. In any case, it is certain that while the fugitive Guelfs were mostly accompanied by their wives, and did not return till 1267, we have Dante's own word for it that he was born in the great city by the Arno,[29] and was baptized in the Baptistery, his beautiful St. John's.[30] At the font he received the name of Durante, shortened, as he bore it, into Dante. It is in this form that it finds a place in the Comedy,[31] once, and only once, written down of necessity, the poet says—the necessity of being faithful in the report of Beatrice's words: from the wider necessity, we may assume, of imbedding in the work itself the name by which the author was commonly known, and by which he desired to be called for all time.

When Dante was about ten years old he lost his father. Of his mother nothing but her Christian name of Bella is known. Neither of them is mentioned in the Comedy,[32] nor indeed are his wife and children. Boccaccio describes the Alighieri as having been in easy though not in wealthy circumstances; and Leonardo Bruni, who in the fifteenth century sought out what he could learn of Dante, says of him that he was possessed ofa patrimony sufficient for an honourable livelihood. That he was so might be inferred from the character of the education he received. His studies, says Boccaccio, werenot directed to any object of worldly profit. That there is no sign of their having been directed by churchmen tends to prove the existence in his native town of a class of cultivated laymen; and[Pg xlviii] that there was such appears from the ease with which, when, passing from boyhood to manhood, he felt a craving for intellectual and congenial society, he found in nobles of the stamp of Guido Cavalcanti men like-minded with himself. It was indeed impossible but that the revival of the study of the civil law, the importation of new learning from the East, and the sceptical spirit fosteredin Italy by the influence of Frederick II. and his court, should all have told on the keen- witted Florentines, of whom a great proportion—even of the common people—couldread; while the class with leisure had every opportunity of knowing what was going on in the world.[33] Heresy, the rough word for intellectual life as well as for religious aspiration, had found in Florence a congenial soil.[34] In the thirteenth century, whichmodern ignorance loves to reckon as having been in a special sense an age of faith, there were many Florentines who, in spite of their outward conformity, had drifted asfar from spiritual allegiance to the Church as the furthest point reached by any of theirdescendants who some two ages later belonged to the school of Florentine Platonists.

Chief among these free-thinkers, and, sooth to say, free-livers—though in this respect they were less distinguished from the orthodox—was Brunetto Latini, for some time Secretary to the Republic, and the foremost Italian man of letters of his day. Meagre though his greatest work, the Tesoro, or Treasure, must seem to any one who now glances over its pages, to his contemporaries it answered the promise of its title and stood for a magazine of almost complete information in the domains of natural history,ethics, and politics. It was written in French, as being a more agreeable language than Italian; and was composed, there is reason to believe, while Latini lived in Paris asan exiled Guelf after Montaperti. His Tesoretto, or Little Treasure, a poem in jingling eight-syllabled Italian verse, has been thought by some to have supplied hints to Dantefor the Comedy.[35] By neither of these works is he evinced a man of strong intellect,or even of good taste. Yet there is the testimony of Villani that he did much to refine the language of his contemporaries, and to apply fixed principles to the conduct of State affairs.[36] Dante meets him in Inferno, and hails him as his intellectual father—as the master who taught him from day to day how fame is to be won.[37] But it is too much to infer from these words that Latini served as his teacher, in the common sense of the word. It is true they imply an intimacy between the veteran scholar and his young townsman; but the closeness of their intercourse is perhaps best accounted for by supposing that Latini had been acquainted with Dante's father, and by the great promise of Dante's boyhood was led to take a warm interest in his intellectual development. Their intimacy, to judge from the tone of their conversation down in Inferno, had lasted till Latini's death. But no tender reminiscence of the days they spent together avails to save him from condemnation at the hands of his severe disciple. By the manners of Brunetto, and the Epicurean heresies of others of his friends, Dante, we may be sure, was never infected or defiled.

Dante describes himself as having begun the serious study of philosophy and theology only at the mature age of twenty-seven. But ere that time he had studied to good effect,and not books alone, but the world around him too, and the world within. The poet was formed before the theologian and philosopher. From his earliest years he was used to write in verse; and he seems to have esteemed as one of his best endowments the easy command of his mother tongue acquired by him while still in boyhood.

Of the poems written in his youth he made a selection, and with a commentary gave them to the world as his first work.[38] All the sonnets and canzoni contained in it bear more or less directly on his love for Beatrice Portinari. This lady, whose name is so indissolubly associated with that of Dante, was the daughter of a rich citizen of good family. When Dante saw her first he was a child of nine, and she a few months younger. It would seem fabulous, he says, if he related what things he did, and of what a passion he was the victim during his boyhood. He seized opportunities of beholding her, but for long never passed beyond a silent worship; and he was eighteen before she spoke to him, and then only in the way of a passing salutation. On this he had a vision, and that inspired him with a sonnet, certainly not the first he had written, but the first he put into circulation. The mode of publication he adopted was the common one of sending copies of it to such other poets as were within reach. The sonnet in itself contains a challenge to interpret his dream. Several poets attempted the riddle—among them the philosopher and poet Guido Cavalcanti. They all failed in the solution; but with some of them he was thus brought into terms of intimacy, and with Cavalcanti of the closest friendship. Some new grace of style in Dante's verse, some art in the presentation of his mystical meaning that escapes the modern reader, may have revealed to the middle-aged man of letters that a new genius had arisen. It was by Guido's advice that the poems of which this sonnet stands the first were some years later collected and published with the explanatory narrative. To him, in a sense, the whole work is addressed; and it agreed with his taste, as well as Dante's own, that it should contain nothing but what was written in the vulgar tongue. Others besides

Guido must have recognised in the little book, as it passed from hand to hand, the masterpiece of Italianprose, as well as of Italian verse. In the simple title of Vita Nuova, or The New Life,[39]we can fancy that a claim is laid to originality of both subject and treatment. Through the body of the work, though not so clearly as in the Comedy, there rings the note of assurance of safety from present neglect and future oblivion.

It may be owing to the free use of personification and symbol in the Vita Nuova that some critics, while not denying the existence of a real Beatrice, have held that sheis introduced only to help out an allegory, and that, under the veil of love for her, the poet would express his youthful passion for truth. Others, going to the opposite extreme, are found wondering why he never sought, or, seeking, failed to win, the hand of Beatrice. To those who would refine the Beatrice of the early work into a beingas purely allegorical as she of the Comedy, it may be conceded that the Vita Nuova is not so much the history of a first love as of the new emotional and intellectual life to which a first love, as Dante experienced it, opens the door. Out of the incidents of their intercourse he chooses only such as serve for motives to the joys and sorrowsof the passionate aspiring soul. On the other hand, they who seek reasons why Dante did not marry Beatrice have this to justify their curiosity, that she did marry another man. But her husband was one of the rich and powerful Bardi; and her father was so wealthy that after providing for his children he could endow a hospital in Florence. The marriage was doubtless arranged as a matter of family convenience, due regard being had to her dower and her husband's fortune; and we may assume that when Dante, too, was married later on, his wife was found for him by the good offices of his friends.[40] Our manners as regards these things are not those of the Italy of the thirteenth century. It may safely be said that Dante never dreamed of Beatrice for his wife; that the expectation of wedding her would have sealed his lips from uttering to the world any word of his love; and that she would have lost something in his esteem if, out of love for him, she had refused the man her father chose for her.

We must not seek in the Vita Nuova what it does not profess to give. There was areal Beatrice Portinari, to a careless glance perhaps not differing much from other Florentine ladies of her age and condition; but her we do not find in Dante's pages. These are devoted to a record of the dreams and visions, the new thoughts and feelingsof which she was the occasion or the object. He worshipped at a distance, and in a single glance found reward enough for months of adoration; he read all heaven into a smile. So high strung is the narrative, that did we come on any hint of loving dallianceit would jar with all the rest She is always at a distance from him, less a woman than an angel.

In all this there is certainly as much of reticence as of exaggeration. When he comes to speak of her death he uses a phrase on which it would seem as if too little valuehad been set. He cannot dwell on the circumstances of her departure, he says, withoutbeing his own panegyrist. Taken along with some other expressions in the Vita Nuova,and the tone of her words to him when they meet in the Earthly Paradise, we may gather from this that not only was she aware of his long devotion, but that, ere she died, he had been given to understand how highly she rated it. And on the occasion ofher death, one described as being her nearest relative by blood and, after Cavalcanti, Dante's chief friend—her brother, no doubt—came to him and begged him to write something concerning her. It would be strange indeed if they had never looked franklyinto one another's faces; and yet, for anything that is directly told in the Vita Nuova, they never did.

The chief value of the Vita Nuova is therefore psychological. It is a mine of materialsillustrative of the author's mental and emotional development, but as regards historicaldetails it is wanting in fulness and precision. Yet, even in such a sketch of Dante'slife as this trics to be, it is necessary to dwell on the turning-points of the narrative contained in the Vita Nuova; the reader always remembering that on one side Dante says more than the fact that so he may glorify his love, and less on another that he may not fail in consideration for Beatrice. She is first a maiden whom no public breath is to disturb in her virgin calm; and afterwards a chaste wife, whose lover is as jealous of her reputation as any husband could be. The youthful lover had begun by propoundingthe riddle of his love so obscurely that even by his fellow-poets it had been found insoluble, adepts though they themselves were in the art of smothering a thought. Then, though all his longing is for Beatrice, lest she become the subject of common talk he feigns that he is in love first with one lady and then with another.[41] He evenpushes his deceit so far that she rebukes him for his fickleness to one of his sham lovesby denying him the customary salutation when they meet—this salutation being the only sign of friendship she has ever shown. It is already some few years since the firstsonnet was written. Now, in a ballad containing a more direct avowal of his love thanhe has yet ventured on,[42] he protests that it was always Beatrice his heart was busy with, and that to her, though his eyes may have seemed to wander, his affection was always true. In the very next poem we find him as if debating with himself whether heshall persevere. He weighs the ennobling influence of a pure love and the sweetness itgives to life, against the pains and self-denial to which it condemns its servant. Here, he tells us in his commentary, he was like a traveller who has come to where the waysdivide. His only means of escape—and he feels it is a poor one—is to throw himself into the arms of Pity.

From internal evidence it seems reasonably certain that the marriage of Beatrice fell at the time when he describes himself as standing at the parting of the ways. Before that he has been careful to write of his love in terms so general as to be understood only by those in possession of the key. Now he makes direct mention of her, and seeks to be in her company; and he even leads us to infer that it was owing to his poems that she became a well-known personage in the streets of Florence. Immediately after the sonnet in which he has recourse to Pity, he tells how he was led by a friend into the house of a lady, married only that day, whom they find surrounded by her lady friends, met to celebrate her home-coming after marriage. It was the fashion for young gentlemen to offer their services at such a feast. On this occasion Dante for one can give no help. A sudden trembling seizes him; he leans for support against the painted wall of the chamber; then, lifting his eyes to see if the ladies have remarked his plight, he is troubled at beholding Beatrice among them, with a smile on her lips, as, leaning towards her, they mock at her lover's weakness. To his friend, who, as he leads him from the chamber, asks what ails him, he replies: 'My feet have reached that point beyond which if they pass they can never return.' It was only matrons that gathered round a bride at her home-coming; Beatrice was therefore by this time a married woman. That she was but newly married we may infer from Dante's confusion on finding her there.[43] His secret has now been discovered, and he must either renounce his love, or, as he is at length free to do, Beatrice being married, declare it openly, and spend his life in loyal devotion to her as the mistress of his imagination and of his heart.[44]

But how is he to pursue his devotion to her, and make use of his new privilege of freer intercourse, when the very sight of her so unmans him? He writes three sonnets explaining what may seem pusillanimity in him, and resolves to write no more. Now comes the most fruitful episode in the history. Questioned by a bevy of fair ladies what is the end of a love like his, that cannot even face the object of its desire, he answers that his happiness lies in the words by which he shows forth the praises of his mistress. He has now discovered that his passion is its own reward. In other words, he has succeeded in spiritualising his love; although to a careless reader it might seem in little need of passing through the process. Then, soon after, as he walks by a crystal brook, he is inspired with the words which begin the noblest poem he had yet produced,[45] and that as the author of which he is hailed by a fellow-poet in Purgatory. It is the first to glorify Beatrice as one in whom Heaven is more concerned than Earth; and in it, too, he anticipates his journey through the other world. She dies,[46] and we are surprised to find that within a year of her death he wavers in his allegiance to her memory. A fair face, expressing a tender compassion, looks down on him from a window as he goes nursing his great sorrow; and he loves the owner of the face because she pities him. Butseeing Beatrice in a vision he is restored, and the closing sonnet tells how his whole desire goes forth to her, and how his spirit is borne above the highest sphere to beholdher receiving honour, and shedding radiance on all around her. The narrative closes with a reference to a vision which he does not recount, but which incites him to severestudy in order that he may learn to write of her as she deserves. And the last sentence of the Vita Nuova expresses a hope—a hope which would be arrogant coming after anything less perfect than the Vita Nuova—that, concerning her, he shall yet say things never said before of any woman. Thus the poet's earliest work contains an earnest of the latest, and his morning makes one day with his evening.

The narrative of the Vita Nuova is fluent and graceful, in this contrasting strongly with the analytical arguments attached to the various poems. Dante treats his readers as if they were able to catch the meaning of the most recondite allegory, and yet were ignorant of the alphabet of literary form. And, as is the case with other poets of the time,the free movement of his fancy is often hampered by the necessity he felt of expressing himself in the language of the popular scholastic philosophy. All this is but to say thathe was a man of his period, as well as a great genius. And even in this his first work he bettered the example of Guido Cavalcanti, Guido of Bologna, and the others whomhe found, but did not long suffer to remain, the masters of Italian verse.[47] These inherited from the Provençal and Sicilian poets much of the cant of which European poetry has been so slow to clear itself; and chiefly that of presenting all human emotionand volition under the figure of love for a mistress, who was often merely a creature offancy, set up to act as Queen of Beauty while the poet ran his intellectual jousts. But Dante dealt in no feigned inspiration, and distinguishes himself from the whole schoolof philosophical and artificial poets as 'one who can only speak as love inspires.'[48]He may deal in allegory and utter sayings dark enough, but the first suggestions of his thoughts are obtained from facts of emotion or of real life. His lady was no creature of fancy, but his neighbour Beatrice Portinari: and she who ends in the Paradiso as the embodied beauty of holiness was, to begin with, a fair Florentine girl.

The instance of Beatrice is the strongest, although others might be adduced, to illustrateDante's economy of actual experience; the skilful use, that is, of real emotions and incidents to serve for suggestion and material of poetical thought. As has been told, towards the close of the Vita Nuova he describes how he found a temporary consolation for the loss of Beatrice in the pity of a fair and noble lady. In his next work,the Convito, or Banquet, she appears as the personification of philosophy. The plan ofthe Convito is that of a commentary on odes which are interpreted as having various meanings—among others the literal as distinguished from the allegorical or essentially true. As far as this lady is concerned, Dante shows some eagerness to pass from the literal meaning; desirous, it may be, to correct the belief that he had ever wavered in his exclusive devotion to Beatrice. That for a time he did transfer his thoughts from Beatrice in Heaven to the fair lady of the window is almost certain, and by the time hewrote the Purgatorio he was able to make confession of such a fault. But at the earlier period at which the Convito[49] was written, he may have come to regard the avowal in the Vita Nuova as an oversight dishonouring to himself as well as to his first love, and so have slurred it over, leaving the fact to stand enveloped in an allegory. At any rate, to his gloss upon this passage in his life we are indebted for an interesting accountof how, at the age of twenty-seven, he put himself to school:—

'After losing the earliest joy of my life, I was so smitten with sorrow that in nothing could I find any comfort. Yet after some time my mind, eager to recover its tone, since nought that I or others could do availed to restore me, directed itself to find how people, being disconsolate, had been comforted. And so I took to reading that little-known book by Boethius, by writing which he, captive and in exile, had obtained relief. Next,hearing that Tully as well had written a book in which, treating of friendship, he had consoled the worthy Laelius on the occasion of the loss of his friend Scipio, I read thattoo. And though at the first I found their meaning hard, at last I comprehended it as faras my knowledge of the language and some little command of mother-wit enabled me to do: which same mother-wit had already helped me to much, as may be seen by the Vita Nuova. And as it often happens that a man goes seeking silver, and lights on gold he is not looking for—the result of chance, or of some divine provision; so I, besides finding the consolation I was in search of to dry my tears, became possessed of wisdom from authors and sciences and books. Weighing this well, I deemed that philosophy, the mistress of these authors, sciences, and books, must be the best of all things. And imagining her to myself fashioned like a great lady, rich in compassion, my admirationof her was so unbounded that I was always delighting myself in her image. And from thus beholding her in fancy I went on to frequent the places where she is to be found in very deed—in the schools of theology, to wit, and the debates of philosophers. So thatin a little time, thirty months or so, I began to taste so much of her sweetness that the love I bore to her effaced or banished every other thought.'[50]

No one would guess from this description of how he grew enamoured of philosophy, that at the beginning of his arduous studies Dante took a wife.

She was Gemma, the daughter of Manetto Donati, but related only distantly, if at all, to the great Corso Donati. They were married in 1292, he being twenty-seven; and in the course of the nine years that elapsed till his exile she bore him five sons and two daughters.[51] From his silence regarding her in his works, and from some words of Boccaccio's which apply only to the period of his exile, it has been inferred that the union was unhappy. But Dante makes no mention in his writings of his parents or children any more than of Gemma.[52] And why should not his wife be included among the things dearest to him which, he tells us, he had to leave behind him on his banishment? For anything we know to the contrary, their wedded life up to the time of his exile may have been happy enough; although most probably the marriage was one of convenience, and almost certainly Dante found little in Gemma's mind that answered to his own.[53] In any case it is not safe to lay stress upon his silence. During the period covered by the Vita Nuova he served more than once in the field, and to this none of his earlier works make any reference. In 1289, Arezzo having warmly espoused the Ghibeline cause, the Florentines, led by Corso Donati and the great merchant Vieri dei Cerchi, took up arms and met the foe in the field of Campaldino, on the edge of the upland region of the Casentino. Dante, as a young man of means and family, fought in the vanguard;[54] and in a letter partly preserved by one of his early biographers[55] he describes himself as being then no tiro in arms, and as having with varying emotions watched the fortunes of the day. From this it is clear that he had served before, probably in an expedition into the Aretine territory made in the previous year, and referred to in the Inferno.[56] In the same year as Campaldino was won he was present at the surrender of Caprona, a fortress belonging to Pisa.[57] But of all this he is silent in his works, or only makes casual mention of it by way of illustration. It is, therefore, a waste of time trying to prove his domestic misery from his silence about his marriage.

IV.

So hard a student was Dante that he now for a time nearly lost the use of his eyes.[58] But he was cured by regimen, and came to see as well as ever, he tells us; which we can easily believe was very well indeed. For his work, as he planned it out, he needed all his powers. The Convito, for example, was designed to admit of a full treatment of all that concerns philosophy. It marks an earlier stage of his intellectual and spiritual life than does the opening of the Inferno. In it we have the fruit of the years during which he was wandering astray from his early ideal, misled by what he afterwards came to count as a vain and profitless curiosity. Most of its contents, as we have it,[59] are only indirectly interesting. It is impossible for most people to care for discussions, conducted with all the nicety of scholastic definition, on such subjects as the system of the universe as it was evolved out of the brains of philosophers; the subject-matter of knowledge; and how we know. But there is one section of it possessed of a very special interest, the Fourth, in which he treats of the nature of nobility. This he affirms to be independent of wealth or ancestry, and he finds every one to be noble who practises the virtues proper to his time of life. 'None of the Uberti of Florence or the Visconti of Milan can say he is noble because belonging to such or such a race; for the Divine seed is sown not in a family but in the individual man.' This amounts, it must be admitted, to no more than saying that high birth is one thing, and nobility of character another; but it is significant of what were the current opinions, that Dante should be at such pains to distinguish between the two qualities. The canzone which supplies the text for the treatise closes with a picture of the noble soul at every stage of life, to which Chaucer may well have been indebted for his description of the true gentleman:[60]—'The soul that is adorned by this grace does not keep it hid, but from the day when soul is wed to body shows it forth even until death. In early life she is modest, obedient, and gentle, investing the outward form and all its members with a gracious beauty: in youth she is temperate and strong, full of love and courteous ways, delighting in loyal deeds: in mature age she is prudent, and just, and apt to liberality, rejoicing to hear of others' good. Then in the fourth stage of life she is married again to God,[61] and contemplates her approaching end with thankfulness for all the past.'[62]

In this passage it is less the poet that is heard than the sober moralist, one with a ripe experience of life, and contemptuous of the vulgar objects of ambition. The calm is on the surface. As has been said above, he was proud of his own birth, the more proud perhaps that his station was but a middling one; and to the close of his life he hated upstarts with their sudden riches, while the Philip Argenti on whom in the Inferno he takes what has much the air of a private revenge may have been only a specimen of the violent and haughty nobles with whom he stood on an uneasy footing.

Yet the impression we get of Dante's surroundings in Florence from the Vita Nuova and other poems, from references in the Comedy, and from some anecdotes more or less true which survive in the pages of Boccaccio and elsewhere, is on the whole a pleasant one. We should mistake did we think of him as always in the guise of absorbed student or tearful lover. Friends he had, and society of various kinds. He tells how in a severe illness he was nursed by a young and noble lady, nearly related to him by blood—his sister most probably; and other ladies are mentioned as watching in his sick-chamber.[63] With Forese and Piccarda Donati, brother and sister of the great Corso Donati, he was on terms of the warmest friendship.[64]

From the Vita Nuova we can gather that, even when his whole heart fainted and failed at the mere sight of Beatrice, he was a favourite with other ladies and conversed familiarly with them. The brother of Beatrice was his dear friend; while among those of the elder generation he could reckon on the friendship of such men as Guido Cavalcanti and Brunetto Latini. Through Latini he would, even as a young man, get the entry of the most lettered and intellectually active society of Florence. The tradition of his intimacy with Giotto is supported by the mention he makes of the painter,[65] and by the fact, referred to in the Vita Nuova, that he was himself a draughtsman. It is to be regretted there are not more anecdotes of him on record like that which tells how one day as he drew an angel on his tablets he was broken in upon by 'certain people of importance.' The musician Casella, whom he 'woes to sing in Purgatory'[66] and Belacqua, the indolent good-humoured lutemaker,[67] are greeted by him in a tone of friendly warmth in the one case and of easy familiarity in the other, which help us to know the terms on which he stood with the quick-witted artist class in Florence.[68] Already he was in the enjoyment of a high reputation as a poet and scholar, and there seemed no limit to the greatness he might attain to in his native town as a man of action as well as a man of thought.

In most respects the Florence of that day was as fitting a home for a man of genius as could well be imagined. It was full of a life which seemed restless only because the possibilities of improvement for the individual and the community seemed infinite. A true measure of its political progress and of the activity of men's minds is supplied by the changes then being made in the outward aspect of the city. The duties of the Government were as much municipal as political, and it would have surprised a Florentine to be told that the one kind of service was of less dignity than the other. The population grew apace, and, to provide the means for extending the city walls, every citizen, on pain of his testament being found invalid, was required to bequeath a part of his estate to the public. Already the banks of the Arno were joined by three bridges of stone, and the main streets were paved with the irregularly-shaped blocks of lava still familiar to the sojourner in Florence. But between the time of Dante's boyhood and the close of the century the other outstanding features of the city were greatly altered, or were in the course of change. The most important churches of Florence, as he first knew it, were the Baptistery and the neighbouring small cathedral church of Santa Reparata; after these ranked the church of the Trinity, Santo Stefano, and some other churches which are now replaced by larger ones, or of which the site alone can be discovered. On the other side of the river, Samminiato with its elegant façade rose as now upon its hill.[69] The only great civic building was the Palace of the Podesta. The Old Market was and had long been the true centre of the city's life.

At the time Dante went into exile Arnolfo was already working on the great new cathedral of St. Mary[Pg lxviii] of the Flowers, the spacious Santa Croce, and the graceful Badia; and Santa Maria Novella was slowly assuming the perfection of form that was later to make it the favourite of Michel Angelo. The Palace of the Signory was already planned, though half a century was to elapse before its tower soared aloft to daunt the private strongholds which bristled, fierce and threatening, all over the city. The bell-tower of Giotto, too, was of later erection—the only pile we can almost regret that Dante never saw. The architect of it was however already adorning the walls of palace and cloister with paintings whose inspiration was no longer, like that of the works they overshadowed, drawn from the outworn motives of Byzantine art, but from the faithful observation of nature.[70] He in painting and the Pisan school in sculpture were furnishing the world with novel types of beauty in the plastic arts, answering to the 'sweet new style' in verse of which it was Dante that discovered the secret.[71]

Florence was now by far the leading city in Tuscany. Its merchants and money-dealerswere in correspondence with every Mediterranean port and with every country ofthe West. Along with bales of goods and letters of exchange new ideas and fresh intelligence were always on the road to Florence. The knowledge of what was going on in the world, and of what men were thinking, was part of the stock-in-trade of the quick-witted citizens, and they were beginning to be employed throughout Europe in diplomatic work, till then almost a monopoly of churchmen. 'These Florentines seem to me to form a fifth element,' said Boniface, who had ample experience of howaccomplished they were.

At home they had full employment for their political genius; and still upon the old problem, of how to curb the arrogance of the class that, in place of being satisfied to share in the general prosperity, sought its profit in the maintenance of privilege. It is necessary, at the cost of what may look like repetition, to revert to the presence and activity of this class in Florence, if we are to form a true idea of the circumstances of Dante's life, and enter into the spirit with which much of the Comedy is informed. Though many of the nobles were now engaged in commerce and figured among the popular leaders, most of the greater houses stood proudly aloof from everything that might corrupt their gentility. These were styled the magnates: they found, as it were, a vocation for themselves in being nobles. Among them the true distinctive spirit of Ghibelinism survived, although none of them would now have dared to describe himselfas a Ghibeline. Their strength lay partly in the unlimited control they retained over theserfs on their landward estates; in the loyalty with which the members of a family held by one another; in their great command of resources as the administrators of the Parte Guelfa; and in the popularity they enjoyed with the smaller people in consequence of their lavish expenditure, and frank if insolent manners. By law scarcely the equals of the full citizens, in point of fact they tyrannised over them. Their houses, set like fortresses in the crowded streets, frequently served as prisons and torture-chambers for the low-born traders or artisans who might offend them.

Measures enough had been passed towards the close of the century with a view to curb the insolence of the magnates; but the difficulty was to get them put in force. At length, in 1294, they, with many additional reforms, were embodied in the celebrated Ordinances of Justice. These for long were counted back to as the Great Charter of Florence—a Great Charter defining the popular rights and the disabilities of the baronage. Punishments of special severity were enacted for nobles who should wrong a plebeian, and the whole of a family or clan was made responsible for the crimes and liabilities of its several members. The smaller tradesmen were conciliated by being admitted to a share in political influence. If serfage was already abolished in the State of Florence, it was the Ordinances which made it possible for the serf to use his liberty.[72] But the greatest blow dealt to the nobles by the new laws was their exclusion, as nobles, from all civil and political offices. These they could hold only by becoming members of one of the trade guilds.[73] And to deprive a citizen of his rights it was enough to inscribe his name in the list of magnates.

It is not known in what year Dante became a member of the Guild of Apothecaries. Without much reason it has been assumed that he was one of the nobles who took advantage of the law of 1294. But there is no evidence that in his time the Alighieri ranked as magnates, and much ground for believing that for some considerable time past they had belonged to the order of full citizens.

It was not necessary for every guildsman to practise the art or engage in the business to which his guild was devoted, and we are not required to imagine Dante as having anything to do with medicine or with the spices and precious stones in which the apothecaries traded. The guilds were political as much as industrial associations, and of the public duties of his membership he took his full share. The constitution of the Republic, jealously careful to limit the power of the individual citizen, provided that the two chief executive officers, the Podesta and the Captain of the People, should always be foreigners. They held office only for six months. To each of them was assigned a numerous Council, and before a law could be abrogated or a new one passed it needed the approval of both these Councils, as well as that of the Priors, and of the heads of the principal guilds. The Priors were six in number, one for each district of the city. With them lay the administration in general of the laws, and the conduct of foreign affairs. Their office was elective, and held for two months.[74] Of one or other of the Councils Dante is known to have been a member in 1295, 1296, 1300, and 1301.[75] In 1299 he is found engaged on a political mission to the little hill-city of San Gemigniano, where in the town-house they still show the pulpit from which he addressed the local senate.[76] From the middle of June till the middle of August 1300 he served as one of the Priors.

At the time when Dante entered on this office, Florence was distracted by the feud of Blacks and Whites, names borrowed from the factions of Pistoia, but fated to become best known from their use in the city which adopted them. The strength of the Blacks lay in the nobles whom the Ordinances of Justice had been designed to depress; both such of them as had retained their standing as magnates, and such as, under the new law, had unwillingly entered the ranks of the citizens. Already they had succeeded in driving into exile Giano della Bella,[78] the chief author of the Ordinances; and their efforts—and those of the citizens who,[Pg lxxiii] fearing the growing power of the lesser guilds, were in sympathy with them—were steadily directed to upset the reforms. An obvious means to this end was to lower in popular esteem the public men whose policy it was to govern firmly on the new lines. The leader of the discontented party was Corso Donati, a man of small fortune, but of high birth; of splendid personal appearance, open-handed, and of popular manners. He and they who went with him affected a violent Guelfism, their chance of recovering the control of domestic affairs being the better the more they could frighten the Florentines with threats of evils like those incurred by the Aretines and Pisans from Ghibeline oppression. It may be imagined what meaning the cry of Ghibeline possessed in days when there was still a class of beggars in Florence—men of good names—whose eyes had been torn out by Farinata and his kind.

One strong claim which Corso Donati had on the goodwill of his fellow-townsmen was that by his ready courage in pushing on the reserves, against superior orders, at the battle of Campaldino,[79] the day had been won to Florence and her allies. As he rode gallantly through the streets he was hailed as the Baron (il Barone), much as in the last generation the victor of Waterloo was sufficiently distinguished as the Duke. At the same battle, Vieri dei Cerchi, the leader of the opposite party of the Whites, had shown no less bravery, but he was ignorant of the art, or despised it, of making political capital out of the performance of his duty. In almost every respect he offered a contrast to Donati. He was of a new family, and his influence depended not on landed possessions, though he had these too, but on wealth derived from commerce.

According to John Villani, a competent authority on such a point,[81] he was at the head of one of the greatest trading houses in the world. The same crowds that cheered Corso as the great Baron sneered at the reticent and cold-tempered merchant as the Ghibeline. It was a strange perversion of ideas, and yet had this of justification, that all the nobles of Ghibeline tendency and all the citizens who, on account of their birth, were suspected of leaning that way were driven into the party of the Whites by the mere fact of the Blacks hoisting so defiantly the Guelf flag, and commanding the resources of the Parte Guelfa. But if Ghibelinism meant, as fifty years previously it did mean, a tendency to exalt privilege as against the general liberties and to court foreign interference in the affairs of Florence, it was the Blacks and not the Whites who had served themselves heirs to Ghibelinism. That the appeal was now taken to the Pope instead of to the Emperor did not matter; or that French soldiers in place of German were called in to settle domestic differences.

The Roman See was at this time filled by Boniface VIII., who six years previously, by violence and fraud, had procured the resignation of Celestine V.—him who made the great refusal.[82] Boniface was at once arrogant and subtle, wholly faithless, and hampered by no scruple either of religion or humanity. But these qualities were too common among those who before and after him filled the Papal throne, to secure him in a special infamy. That he has won from the ruthless hatred which blazes out against him in many a verse of Dante's,[83] and for this hatred he is indebted to his interference in the affairs of Florence, and what came as one of the fruits of it—the poet's exile.

And yet, from the point of view not only of the interest of Rome but also of Italy, there is much to be said for the policy of Boniface. German domination was a just subject of fear, and the Imperialist element was still so strong in Northern and Central Italy, that if the Emperor Albert[84] had been a man of a more resolute ambition, he might—so contemporaries deemed—have conquered Italy at the cost of a march through it. The cities of Romagna were already in Ghibeline revolt, and it was natural that the Pope should seek to secure Florence on the Papal side. It was for the Florentines rather than for him to judge what they would lose or gain by being dragged into the current of general politics. He made a fair beginning with an attempt to reconcile the two parties. The Whites were then the dominant faction, and to them reconciliation meant that their foes would at once divide the government with them, and at the long-run sap the popular liberties, while the Pope's hand would soon be allowed to dip freely into the communal purse. The policy of the Whites was therefore one of steady opposition to all foreign meddling with Florence. But it failed to secure general support, for without being Ghibeline in fact it had the air of being so; and the name of Ghibeline was one that no reasoning could rob of its terrors.[85]

As was usual in Florence when political feeling ran high, the hotter partisans came to blows, and the streets were more than once disturbed by violence and bloodshed. To an onlooker it must have seemed as if the interposition of some external authority was desirable; and almost on the same day as the new Priors, of whom Dante was one and who were all Whites, took office in the June of 1300, the Cardinal Acquasparta entered the city, deputed by the Pope to establish peace. His proposals were declined by the party in power, and having failed in his mission he left the city, and took the priestly revenge upon it of placing it under interdict.[86] Ere many months were passed, the Blacks, at a meeting of the heads of the party, resolved to open negotiations anew with Boniface. For this illegal step some of them, including Corso Donati, were ordered into exile by the authorities, who, to give an appearance of impartiality to their pro[Pglxxvii]ceedings, at the same time banished some of the Whites, and among them Guido Cavalcanti. It was afterwards made a charge against Dante that he had procured the recall of his friend Guido and the other Whites from exile; but to this he could answer that he was not then in office.[87] Corso in the meantime was using his enforced absence from Florence to treat freely with the Pope.

Boniface had already entered into correspondence with Charles of Valois, brother of Philip, the reigning King of France, with the view of securing the services of a strongly-connected champion. It was the game that had been played before by the Roman Court when Charles of Anjou was called to Italy to crush the Hohenstaufens. This second Charles was a man of ability of a sort, as he had given cruel proof in his brother's Flemish wars. By the death of his wife, daughter of his kinsman Charles II. of Naples and so grand-daughter of Charles of Anjou, he had lost the dominions of Maine and Anjou, and had got the nickname of Lackland from his want of a kingdom. He lent a willing ear to Boniface, who presented him with the crown of Sicily on condition that he first wrested it from the Spaniard who wore it.[88] All the Papal influence was exerted to get money for the expenses of the descent on Sicily. Even churchmen were required to contribute, for it was a holy war, and the hope was that when Charles, the champion of the Church, had reduced[Pg lxxviii] Italy to obedience, won Sicily for himself by arms, and perhaps the Eastern Empire by marriage, he would win the Holy Sepulchre for Christendom.

Charles crossed the Alps in August 1301, with five hundred men-at-arms, and, avoiding Florence on his southward march, found Boniface at his favourite residence of Anagni. He was created Pacificator of Tuscany, and loaded with other honours. What better served the purpose of his ambition, he was urged to retrace his steps and justify his new title by restoring peace to Florence. There the Whites were still in power, but they dared not declare themselves openly hostile to the Papal and Guelf interest by refusing him admission to the city. He came with gentle words, and ready to take the most stringent oaths not to tamper with the liberties of the Commonwealth; but once he had gained an entrance (November 1301) and secured his hold on Florence, he threw off every disguise, gave full play to his avarice, and amused himself with looking on at the pillage of the dwellings and warehouses of the Whites by the party of Corso Donati. By all this, says Dante, Charles 'gained no land,' Lackland as he was, 'but only sin and shame.'[89]

There is a want of precise information as to the events of this time. But it seems probable that Dante formed one of an embassy sent by the rulers of Florence to the Pope in the autumn of this year; and that on the occasion of the entrance of Charles he was absent from Florence. What the embassy had to propose which Boniface could be expected to be satisfied with, short of complete submission, is not known and is not easy to guess. It seems clear at least that Dante cannot have been chosen as a person likely to be specially pleasing to the Roman Court. Within the two years preceding he had made himself prominent in the various Councils of which he was a member, by his sturdy opposition to affording aid to the Pope in his Romagnese wars. It is even possible that his theory of the Empire was already more or less known to Boniface, and as that Pontiff claimed Imperial authority over such states as Florence, this would be sufficient to secure him a rough reception.[90] Where he was when the terrible news came to him that for some days there had been no law in Florence, and that Corso Donati was sharing in the triumph of Charles, we do not know. Presageful of worse things to come, he did not seek to return, and is said to have been in Siena when he heard that, on the 27th January 1302, he had been sentenced to a heavy fine and political disabilities for having been guilty of extortion while a Prior, of opposing the coming of Charles, and of crimes against the peace of Florence and the interest of the Parte Guelfa. If the fine was not paid within three days his goods and property were to be confiscated. This condemnation he shared with three others. In the following March he was one of twelve condemned, for contumacy, to be burned alive if ever they fell into the hands of the Florentine authorities. We may perhaps assume that the cruel sentence, as well as the charge of peculation, was uttered only in order to conform to some respectable precedents.

V.

Besides Dante many other Whites had been expelled from Florence.[91] Whether they liked it or not, they were forced to seek aid from the Ghibelines of Arezzo and Romagna. This led naturally to a change of political views, and though at the time of their banishment all of them were Guelfs in various degrees, as months and years went on they developed into Ghibelines, more or less declared. Dissensions, too, would be bred among them out of recriminations touching the past, and charges of deserting the general interest for the sake of securing private advantage in the way of making peace with the Republic. For a time, however, the common desire of gaining a return to Florence held them together. Of the Council constituted to bring this about, Dante was a member. Once only with his associates does he appear to have come the length of formal negotiations with a view to getting back. Charles of Valois had passed away from the temporary scene of his extortions and treachery, upon the futile quest of a crown. Boniface, ere being persecuted to death by his old ally, Philip of France (1303), had vainly attempted to check the cruelty of the Blacks; and Benedict, his successor, sent the Cardinal of Ostia to Florence with powers to reconcile the two parties. Dante is usually credited with the composition of the letter in which Vieri dei Cerchi and his fellow-exiles answered the call of the Cardinal to discuss the conditions of their return home. All that had been done by the banished party, said the letter, had been done for the public good.[92] The negotiations came to nothing; nor were the exiles more fortunate in arms. Along with their allies they did once succeed by a sudden dash in penetrating to the market-place, and Florence lay within their grasp when, seized with panic, they turned and fled from the city, which many of them were never to see again.

Almost certainly Dante took no active part in this attempt, and indeed there is little to show that he was ever heartily associated with the exiles. In his own words, he was compelled to break with his companions owing to their imbecility and wickedness, and to form a party by himself.[93] With the Whites, then, he had little more to do; and the story of their fortunes need not longer detain us. It is enough to say that while, like Dante, the chief men among them were for ever excluded from Florence, the principles for which they had contended survived, and even obtained something like a triumph within its walls. The success of Donati and his party, though won with the help of the people, was too clearly opposed to the popular interest to be permanent. Ere long the inveterate contradiction between magnate and merchant was again to change the[Pg lxxxii] course of Florentine politics; the disabilities against lawless nobles were again to be enforced; and Corso

Donati himself was to be crushed in the collision of passions he had evoked but could not control (1308). Though tenderly attached to members of his family, Dante bore Corso a grudge as having been the chief agent in procuring his exile—a grudge which years could do nothing to wipe out. He places in the mouth of Forese Donati a prophecy of the great Baron's shameful death, expressed in curt and scornful words, terrible from a brother.[94] It is no figure of speech to say that Dante nursed revenge.

For some few years his hopes were set on Henry of Luxemburg, elected Emperor in 1308. A Ghibeline, in the ordinary sense of the term, Dante never was. We have in his De Monarchia a full account of the conception he had formed of the Empire—that of authority in temporal affairs embodied in a just ruler, who, being already supreme, would be delivered from all personal ambition; who should decree justice and be a refuge for all that were oppressed. He was to be the captain of Christian society and the guardian of civil right; as in another sphere the Pope was to be the shepherd of souls and the guardian of the deposit of Divine truth. In Dante's eyes the one great officer was as much God's vicegerent as the other. While the most that a Ghibeline or a moderate Guelf would concede was that there should be a division of power between Pope and Emperor—the Ghibeline leaving it to the Emperor and the Guelf to the Pope to define[Pg lxxxiii] their provinces—Dante held, and in this he stood almost alone among politicians, that they ought to be concerned with wholly different kingdoms, and that Christendom was wronged by the trespass of either upon the other's domain. An equal wrong was done by the neglect by either of his duty, and both, as Dante judged, had been shamefully neglecting it. For more than half a century no Emperor had set foot in Italy; and since the Papal Court had under Clement V. been removed to Avignon (1305), the Pope had ceased to be a free agent, owing to his neighbourhood to France and the unscrupulous Philip.

Dante trusted that the virtuous single-minded Henry VII. would prove a monarch round whom all the best in Italy might gather to make him Emperor in deed as well as in name. His judgment took the colour of his hopes, for under the awful shadow of the Emperor he trusted to enter Florence. Although no Ghibeline or Imperialist in the vulgar sense, he constituted himself Henry's apologist and herald; and in letters addressed to the 'wicked Florentines,' to the Emperor, and to the Princes and Peoples of Italy, he blew as it were a trumpet-blast of triumph over the Emperor's enemies and his own. Henry had crossed the Alps, and was tarrying in the north of Italy, when Dante, with a keen eye for where the key of the situation lay, sharpened by his own wishes, urged him to lose no more time in reducing the Lombard cities to obedience, but to descend on Florence, the rotten sheep which was[Pg lxxxiv] corrupting all the Italian flock. The men of Florence he bids prepare to receive the just reward of their crimes.

The Florentines answered Dante's bitter invective and the Emperor's milder promises by an unwearied opposition with the arms which their increasing command of all that tends to soften life made them now less willing to take up, and by the diplomacy in which they were supreme The exiles were recalled, always excepting the more stubborn or dangerous; and among these was reckoned Dante. Alliances were made on all hands, an art which Henry was notably wanting in the trick of. Wherever he turned he was met and checkmated by the Florentines, who, wise by experience, were set on retaining control of their own affairs. After his coronation at Rome (1312),[96] he marched northwards, and with his Pisan and Aretine allies for six weeks laid fruitless siege to Florence. King Robert of Naples, whose aid he had hoped to gain by means of a family alliance, was joined to the league of Guelfs, and Henry passed away from Florence to engage in an enterprise against the Southern Kingdom, a design cut short by his death (1313). He was the last Emperor that ever sought to take the part in Italian affairs which on Dante's theory belonged to the Imperial office. Well-meaning but weak, he was not the man to succeed in reducing to practice a scheme of government which had broken down even in the strong hands of the two Fredericks, and ere the Commonwealths of Italy had become each as powerful as a Northern kingdom. To explain his failure, Dante finds that his descent into Italy was unseasonable: he came too soon. Rather, it may be said, he came far too late.[97]

When, on the death of Henry, Dante was disappointed in his hopes of a true revival of the Empire, he devoted himself for a time to urging the restoration of the Papal Court to Rome, so that Italy might at least not be left without some centre of authority. In a letter addressed to the Italian Cardinals, he besought them to replace Clement V., who died in 1314,[98] by an Italian Pope. Why should they, he asked, resign this great office into Gascon hands? Why should Rome, the true centre of Christendom, be left deserted and despised? His appeal was fruitless, as indeed it could not fail to be with only six Italian Cardinals in a College of twenty-four; and after a vacancy of two years the Gascon Clement was succeeded by another Gascon. Although Dante's motives in making this attempt were doubtless as purely patriotic as those which inspired Catherine of Siena to similar action a century later, he met, we may be sure, with but little sympathy from his former fellow-citizens. They were intent upon the interests of Florence alone, and even of these they may sometimes have taken a narrow view. His was the wider patriotism of the Italian, and it was the whole Peninsula that he longed to see delivered from French influence and once more provided with a seat of authority in its midst, even if it were only that of spiritual power. The Florentines for their part, desirous of security against the incursions of the northern horde, were rather set on retaining the goodwill of France than on enjoying the neighbourhood of the Pope. In this they were guilty of no desertion of their principles. Their Guelfism had never been more than a mode of minding themselves.

For about three years (1313-1316) the most dangerous foe of Florence was Uguccione de la Faggiuola, a partisan Ghibeline chief, sprung from the mountain-land of Urbino, which lies between Tuscany and Romagna. He made himself lord of Pisa and Lucca, and defeated the Florentines and their allies in the great battle of Montecatini (1315). To him Dante is believed to have attached himself.[99] It would be easy for the Republic to form an exaggerated idea of the part which the exile had in shaping the policy or contributing to the success of his patron; and we are not surprised to find that, although Dante's fighting days were done, he was after the defeat subjected to a thirdcondemnation (November 1315). If caught, he was to lose his head; and hissons, or some of them, were threatened with the same fate. The terms of the sentence may again have been more severe than the intentions of those who uttered it. Howeverthis may be, an amnesty was passed in the course of the following year, and Dante was urged to take advantage of it. He found the conditions of pardon too humiliating.Like a malefactor he would require to walk, taper in hand and a shameful mitre on hishead, to the church of St John, and there make an oblation for his crimes. It was notin this fashion that in his more hopeful hours the exile had imagined his restoration. If ever he trod again the pavement of his beautiful St John's, it was to be proudly, asa patriot touching whom his country had confessed her sins; or, with a poet's more bashful pride, to receive the laurel crown beside the font in which he was baptized. But as he would not enter his well beloved, well hated Florence on the terms imposedby his enemies, so he never had the chance of entering it on his own. The spirit in which he, as it were, turned from the open gates of his native town is well expressed in a letter to a friend, who would seem to have been a churchman who had tried to win his compliance with the terms of the pardon. After thanking his correspondentfor his kindly eagerness to recover him, and referring to the submission required, he says:—'And is it in this glorious fashion that Dante Alighieri, wearied with an almosttrilustral exile, is recalled to his country? Is this the desert of an innocence known to all, and of laborious study[Pg lxxxviii] which for long has kept him asweat?... But, Father, this is no way for me to return to my country by; though if by you or others one can be hit upon through which the honour and fame of Dante will take no hurt, it shall be followed by me with no tardy steps. If by none such Florence is to be entered, I will never enter Florence. What then! Can I not, wherever I may be, behold the sun and stars? Is not meditation upon the sweetness of truth as free to me in one place as another? To enjoy this, no need to submit myself ingloriously and with ignominy to the State and People of Florence! And wherever I may be thrown, in any case I trust at least to find daily bread.'

The cruelty and injustice of Florence to her greatest son have been the subject of much eloquent blame. But, in justice to his contemporaries, we must try to see Dante as they saw him, and bear in mind that the very qualities fame makes so much of—his fervent temper and devotion to great ideas—placed him out of the reach of common sympathy.

Others besides him had been banished from Florence, with as much or as little reason, and had known the saltness of bread which has been begged, and the steepness of strange stairs. The pains of banishment made them the more eager to have it brought to a close. With Dante all that he suffered went to swell the count of grievances for which a reckoning was some day to be exacted. The art of returning was, as he himself knew well, one he was slow to learn.[100] His noble obstinacy, which would stoop to no loss of dignity or sacrifice of principle, must excite[Pg lxxxix] our admiration; it also goes far to account for his difficulty in getting back. We can even imagine that in Florence his refusal to abate one tittle of what was due to him in the way of apology was, for a time, the subject of wondering speculation to the citizens, ere they turned again to their everyday affairs of politics and merchandise. Had they been more used to deal with men in whom a great genius was allied to a stubborn sense of honour, they would certainly have left less room in their treatment of Dante for happier ages to cavil at.

How did the case stand? In the letter above quoted from, Dante says that his innocence was known to all. As far as the charge of corruption in his office-bearing went, his banishment—no one can doubt it for a moment—was certainly unjust; and the political changes in Florence since the death of Corso Donati had taken all the life out of the other charges. But by his eager appeals to the Emperor to chastise the Florentines he had raised fresh barriers against his return. The governors of the Republic could not be expected to adopt his theory of the Empire and share his views of the Imperial claims; and to them Dante must have seemed as much guilty of disloyalty to the Commonwealth in inviting the presence of Henry, as Corso Donati had been in Dante's eyes for his share in bringing Charles of Valois to harry Florence. His political writings since his exile—and all his writings were more or less political—had been such as might well confirm or create an opinion of him as a man difficult to live with, as one whose intellectual arrogance had a ready organ in his unsparing tongue or pen. Rumour would most willingly dwell upon and distort the features of his character and conduct that separated him from the common herd. And to add to all this, even after he had deserted the party of the Whites in exile, and had become a party to himself, he found his friends and patrons—for where else could he find them?—among the foes of Florence.

VI.

History never abhors a vacuum so much as when she has to deal with the life of a great man, and for those who must have details of Dante's career during the nineteen years which elapsed between his banishment and his death, the industry of his biographers has exhausted every available hint, while some of them press into their service much that has only the remotest bearing on their hero. If even one-half of their suppositions were adopted, we should be forced to the conclusion that the Comedy and all the other works of his exile were composed in the intervals of a very busy life. We have his own word for this much, (Convito i. 3,) that since he was cast forth out of Florence—in which he would 'fain rest his wearied soul and fulfil his appointed time'—he had been 'a pilgrim, nay, even a mendicant,' in every quarter of Italy,[101] and had 'been held cheap by many who, because of his fame, had looked to find him come in another guise.' But he gives no journal of his wanderings, and, as will have been observed, says no word of any country but Italy. Keeping close to well-ascertained facts, it seems established that in the earlier period of his exile he sojourned with members of the great family of the Counts Guidi,[102] and that he also found hospitality with the Malaspini,[103] lords of the Val di Magra, between Genoa and Lucca. At a still earlier date (August 1306) he is found witnessing a deed in Padua. It was most probably in the same year that Dante found Giotto there, painting the walls of the Scrovegni Chapel, and was courteously welcomed by the artist, and taken to his house.[104] At some time of his life he studied at Bologna: John Villani says, during his exile.[105] Of his supposed residence in Paris, though it is highly probable, there is a want of proof; of a visit to England, none at all that is worth a moment's consideration. Some of his commentators and biographers seem to think he was so short-witted that he must have been in a place before it could occur to him to name it in his verse.

We have Dante's own word for it that he found his exile almost intolerable. Besides the bitter resentment which he felt at the injustice of it, he probably cherished the conviction that his career had been cut short when he was on the point of acquiring great influence in affairs. The illusion may have been his—one not uncommon among men of a powerful imagination—that, given only due opportunity, he could mould the active life of his time as easily as he moulded and fashioned the creations of his fancy. It was, perhaps, owing to no fault of his own that when a partial opportunity had offered itself, he failed to get his views adopted in Florence; indeed, to judge from the kind of employment in which he was more than once engaged for his patrons, he must have been possessed of no little business tact. Yet, as when his feelings were deeply concerned his words knew no restraint, so his hopes would partake of the largeness of his genius. In the restored Empire, which he was almost alone in longing for as he conceived of it, he may have imagined for himself a place beside Henry like what in Frederick's court had been filled by Pier delle Vigne—the man who held both keys to the Emperor's heart, and opened and shut it as he would.[106]

Thus, as his exile ran on it would grow sadder with the accumulating memories of hopes deferred and then destroyed, and of dreams which had faded away in the light of a cheerless reality. But some consolations he must have found even in the conditions of his exile. He had leisure for meditation, and time enough to spend in that other world which was all his own. With the miseries of a wanderer's life would come not a few of its sweets—freedom from routine, and the intellectual stimulus supplied by change of place. Here and there he would find society such as he cared for—that of scholars, theologians, and men familiar with every court and school of Christendom. And, beyond all, he would get access to books that at home he might never have seen. It was no spare diet that would serve his mind while he was making such ample calls on it for his great work. As it proceeds we seem to detect a growing fulness of knowledge, and it is by reason of the more learned treatment, as well as the loftier theme of the Third Cantica, that so many readers, when once well at sea in the Paradiso, recognise the force of the warning with which it begins.[107]

What amount of intercourse he was able to maintain with Florence during his wanderings is a matter of mere speculation, although of a more interesting kind than that concerned with the chronology of his uneasy travels. That he kept up at least some correspondence with his friends is proved by the letter regarding the terms of his pardon. There is also the well-known anecdote told by Boccaccio as to the discovery and despatch to him of the opening Cantos of the Inferno—an anecdote we may safely accept as founded on fact, although Boccaccio's informants may have failed to note at the time what the manuscript consisted of, and in the course of years may have magnified the importance of their discovery. With his wife he would naturally communicate on subjects of common interest—as, for instance, that of how best to save or recover part of his property—and especially regarding the welfare of his sons, of whom two are found to be with him when he acquires something like a settlement in Verona.

It is quite credible that, as Boccaccio asserts, he would never after his exile was once begun 'go to his wife or suffer her to join him where he was;' although the statement is probably an extension of the fact that she never did join him. In any case it is to make too large a use of the words to find in them evidence, as has frequently been done, of the unhappiness of all his married life, and of his utter estrangement from Gemma during his banishment. The union—marriage of convenience though it was—might be harmonious enough as long as things went moderately well with the pair. Dante was never wealthy, but he seems to have had his own house in Florence and small landed possessions in its neighbourhood.[108] That before his banishment he was considerably in debt appears to be ascertained;[109] but, without knowing the circumstances in which he borrowed, it is impossible to be sure whether he may not only have been making use of his credit in order to put out part of his means to advantage in some of the numerous commercial enterprises in which his neighbours were engaged. In any case his career must have seemed full of promise till he was driven into banishment. When that blow had fallen, it is easy to conceive how what if it was not mutual affection had come to serve instead of it—esteem and forbearance—would be changed into indifference with the lapse of months and years of enforced separation, embittered and filled on both sides with the mean cares of indigence, and,it may be, on Gemma's side with the conviction that her husband had brought her withhimself into disgrace. If all that is said by Boccaccio and some of Dante's enemies as to his temperament and behaviour were true, we could only hope that Gemma's indifference was deep enough to save her from the pangs of jealousy. And on the otherhand, if we are to push suspicion to its utmost length, we may find an allusion to his own experience in the lines where Dante complains of how soon a widow forgets her husband.[110] But this is all matter of the merest speculation. Gemma is known to have been alive in 1314.[111] She brought up her children, says Boccaccio, upon a trifling part of her husband's confiscated estate, recovered on the plea that it was a portion of her dowry. There may have been difficulties of a material kind, insuperable save to an ardent love that was not theirs, in the way of Gemma's joining her husband in any of his cities of refuge.

Complete evidence exists of Dante's having in his later years lived for a longer or shorter time in the three cities of Lucca, Verona, and Ravenna. In Purgatory he meetsa shade from Lucca, in the murmur of whose words he catches he 'knows not whatof Gentucca;'[112] and when he charges the Lucchese to speak plainly out, he is told that Lucca shall yet be found pleasant by him because of a girl not yet grown to womanhood. Uguccione, acting in the interest of Pisa, took possession of Lucca in 1314, and Dante is supposed to have taken up his residence there for some considerable time. What we may certainly infer from his own words in the Purgatorio is that they were written after a stay in Lucca had been sweetened to him by the society of a lady named Gentucca. He cannot well have found shelter there before the city was heldby Uguccione; and research has established that at least two ladies of the uncommon name of Gentucca were resident there in 1314. From the whole tone of his allusion—the mention of her very name and of her innocent girlhood—we may gather that there was nothing in his liking for her of which he had any reason to feel ashamed. In the Inferno he had covered the whole people of Lucca with his scorn.[113] By the time he got thus far with the Purgatorio his thoughts of the place were all softened by his memory of one fair face—or shall we rather say, of one compassionate and womanly soul? That Dante was more than susceptible to feminine charms is coarsely asserted by Boccaccio.[114] But on such a matter Boccaccio is a prejudiced witness, and, in the absence of sufficient proof to the contrary, justice requires us to assume that the tenor of Dante's life was not at variance with that of his writings. He who was so severe a judge of others was not, as we can infer from more than one passage of the Comedy, a lenient judge when his own failings were concerned.[115] That his conduct never fell short of his standard no one will venture to maintain. But what should have hindered him, in his hours of weariness and when even his hold on the future seemed to slacken, in lonely castle or strange town, to seek sympathy from some fair woman who might remind him in something of Beatrice?[116]

When, in 1316, Uguccione was driven out of Lucca and Pisa, that great partisan took military service with Can Grande. It has been disputed whether Dante had earlier enjoyed the hospitality of the Scaligers, or was indebted for his first reception in Verona to the good offices of Uguccione. It is barely credible that by this time in his life he stood in need of any one to answer for him in the court of Can Grande. His fame as a political writer must have preceded him; and it was of a character to commend him to the good graces of the great Imperialist. In his De Monarchia he had, by an exhaustive treatment of propositions which now seem childish or else the mere commonplaces of everyday political argument, established the right of the civil power to independence of Church authority; and though to the Scaliger who aimed at becoming Imperial lieutenant for all the North of Italy he might seem needlessly tender to the spiritual lordship of the Holy Father, yet the drift of his reasoning was all in favour of the Ghibeline position.

[117] Besides this he had written on the need of refining the dialects of Italian, and reducing them to a language fit for general use in the whole of the Peninsula; and this with a novelty of treatment and wealth of illustration

unequalled before or since in any first work on such a subject.[118] And, what would recommend him still more to a youthful prince of lofty taste, he was the poet of the 'sweet new style' of the Vita Nuova, and of sonnets, ballads, and canzoni rich in language and thought beyond the works of all previous poets in the vulgar tongues. Add to this that the Comedy was already written, and published up, perhaps, to the close of the Purgatorio, and that all Italy was eager to find who had a place, and what kind of place, in the strange new world from which the veil was being withdrawn; and it is easy to imagine that Dante's reception at Can Grande's court was rather that of a man both admired and feared for his great genius, than that of a wandering scholar and grumbling exile.

At what time Dante came to Verona, and for how long he stayed, we have no means of fixing with certainty. He himself mentions being there in 1320,[119] and it is usually supposed that his residence covered three years previous to that date; as also that it was shared by his two sons, Piero and Jacopo. One of these was afterwards to find a settlement at Verona in a high legal post. Except some frivolous legends, there is no evidence that Dante met with anything but generous treatment from Can Grande. A passage of the Paradiso, written either towards the close of the poet's residence at Verona, or after he had left it, is full of a praise of the great Scaliger so magnificent[120] as fully to make amends for the contemptuous mention in the Purgatorio of his father and brother.[121] To Can Grande the Paradiso was dedicated by the author in a long epistle containing an exposition of how the first Canto of that Cantica, and, by implication, the whole of the poem, is to be interpreted. The letter is full of gratitude for favours already received, and of expectation of others yet to come. From the terms of the dedication it has been assumed that ere it was made the whole of the Paradiso was written, and that Dante praises the lord of Verona after a long experience of his bounty.

Whether owing to the restlessness of an exile, or to some prospect of attaining a state of greater ease or of having the command of more congenial society, we cannot tell; but from the splendid court of Can Grande he moved down into Romagna, to Ravenna, the city which of all in Italy would now be fixed upon by the traveller as the fittest place for a man of genius, weighed down by infinite sorrows, to close his days in and find a tomb. Some writers on the life of Dante will have it that in Ravenna he spent the greater part of his exile, and that when he is found elsewhere—in Lucca or Verona—he is only on a temporary absence from his permanent home.[123] But this conclusion requires some facts to be ignored, and others unduly dwelt on. In any case his patron there, during at least the last year or two of his life, was Guido Novello of Polenta, lord of Ravenna, the nephew of her who above all the persons of the Comedy lives in the hearts of its readers.

Bernardino, the brother of Francesca and uncle of Guido, had fought on the side of Florence at the battle of Campaldino, and Dante may then have become acquainted with him. The family had the reputation of being moderate Guelfs; but ere this the exile, with his ripe experience of men, had doubtless learned, while retaining intact hisown opinions as to what was the true theory of government, to set good-heartedness and a noble aim in life above political orthodoxy. This Guido Novello—the younger Guido—bears the reputation of having been well-informed, of gentle manners, and fond of gathering around him men accomplished in literature and the fine arts. Onthe death of Dante he made a formal oration in honour of the poet. If his welcome of Dante was as cordial as is generally supposed, and as there is no reason to doubt that itwas, it proved his magnanimity; for in the Purgatorio a family specially hostile to the Polentas had been mentioned with honour,[124] while that to which his wife belongedhad been lightly spoken of. How he got over the condemnation of his kinswoman to Inferno—even under such gentle conditions—it would be more difficult to understandwere there not reason to believe that ere Dante went to Ravenna it had come to be a matter of pride in Italy for a family to have any of its members placed anywhere in thatother world of which Dante held the key.

It seems as if we might assume that the poet's last months or years were soothed by thesociety of his daughter—the child whom he had named after the object of his first andmost enduring love.[125] Whether or not he was acting as Ambassador for Guido to Venice when he caught his last illness, it appears to be pretty well established that he was held in honour by his patron and all around him.[126] For his hours of meditation he had the solemn churches of Ravenna with their storied walls,[127] and the still moresolemn pine forest of Classis, by him first annexed to the world of Romance.[128] For hours of relaxation, when they came, he had neighbours who dabbled in letters and who could at any rate sympathise with him in his love of study. He maintained correspondence with poets and scholars in other cities. In at least one instance this was conducted in the bitter fashion with which the humanists of a century or two later were to make the world familiar;[129] but with the Bolognese scholar, Giovanni del Virgilio, he engaged in a good-humoured, half-bantering exchange of Latin pastoral poems, through the artificial imagery of which there sometimes breaks a natural thought, as when in answer to the pedant's counsel to renounce the vulgar tongue andproduce in Latin something that will entitle him to receive the laurel crown in Bologna, he declares that if ever he is crowned as a poet it will be on the banks of the Arno.

Most of the material for forming a judgment of how Dante stood affected to the religious beliefs of his time is to be gathered from the Comedy, and the place for considering it would rather be in an essay on that work than in a sketch of his life which necessity compels to be swift. A few words may however be here devoted to thesubject, as it is one with some bearing on the manner in which he would be regarded by those around him, and through that on the tenor of his life. That Dante conformed to Church observances, and, except with a few malevolent critics, bore the reputation of a good Catholic, there can be no doubt. It was as a politician and not as a heretic that he suffered persecution; and when he died he was buried in great honour within the Franciscan Church at Ravenna. Some few years after his death, it is true, his De Monarchia was burned as heretical by orders of the Papal Legate in Lombardy, who would gladly, if he could, have had the bones of the author exhumed to share the fate ofhis book. But all this was only because the partisans of Lewis of Bavaria were makingpolitical capital out of the treatise.

Attempts have been made to demonstrate that in spite of his outward conformity Dante was an unbeliever at heart, and that the Comedy is devoted to the promulgation ofa Ghibeline heresy—of which, we may be sure, no Ghibeline ever heard—and tothe overthrow of all that the author professed most devoutly to believe.[130] Other critics of a more sober temper in speculation would find in him a Catholic who held the Catholic beliefs with the same slack grasp as the teaching of Luther was held by Lessing or Goethe.[131] But this is surely to misread the Comedy, which is steeped from beginning to end in a spirit of the warmest faith in the great Christian doctrines. Itwas no mere intellectual perception of these that Dante had—or professed to have—forwhen in Paradise he has satisfied Saint Peter of his being possessed of a just conceptionof the nature of faith, and is next asked if, besides knowing what is the alloy of the coinand the weight of it, he has it in his own purse, he answers boldly, 'Yea, and so shiningand round that of a surety it has the lawful stamp.'[132] And further on, when requiredto declare in what he believes, nothing against the fulness of his creed is to be inferredfrom the fact that he stops short after pronouncing his belief in the existence of God and in the Trinity. This article he gives as implying all the others; it is 'the spark whichspreads out into a vivid flame.'[133]

Yet if the inquiry were to be pushed further, and it were sought to find how much of free thought he allowed himself in matters of religion, Dante might be discovered to have reached his orthodox position by ways hateful to the bigots who then took orderfor preserving the purity of the faith. The office of the Pope he deeply revered, butthe Papal absolution avails nothing in his eyes compared with one tear of heartfelt repentance.[134] It is not on the word of Pope or Council that he rests his faith, but on the Scriptures, and on the evidences of the truth of Christianity, freely examined and weighed.[135] Chief among these evidences, it must however be noted, he esteemed the fact of the existence of the Church as he found it;[136] and in his inquiries he accepted as guides the Scholastic Doctors on whose reasonings the Church had set its seal of approbation. It was a foregone conclusion he reached by stages of his own. Yet that he sympathised at least as much with the honest search for truth as with the arrogant profession of orthodoxy, is shown by his treatment of heretics. He could not condemn severely such as erred only because their reason would not consent to rest like his in the prevalent dogmatic system; and so we find that he makes heresy consist less in intellectual error than in beliefs that tend to vitiate conduct, or to cause schism in societies divinely constituted.[137] For his own part, orthodox although he was, or believed himself to be—which is all that needs to be contended for,—in no sense was he priest-ridden. It was liberty that he went seeking on his great journey;[138] and he gives no hint that it is to be gained by the observance of forms or in submission to sacerdotal authority. He knows it is in his reach only when he has been crowned, and mitred too, lord of himself[139]—subject to Him alone of whom even Popes were servants.

Although in what were to prove his last months Dante might amuse himself with the composition of learned trifles, and in the society and correspondence of men who along with him, if on lines apart from his, were preparing the way for the revival of classical studies, the best part of his mind, then as for long before, was devoted to the Comedy; and he was counting on the suffrages of a wider audience than courts and universities could supply.

Here there is no room to treat at length of that work, to which when we turn our thoughts all else he wrote—though that was enough to secure him fame—seems to fall into the background as if unworthy of his genius. What can hardly be passed over in silence is that in the Comedy, once it was begun, he must have found a refuge for his soul from all petty cares, and a shield against all adverse fortune. We must search its pages, and not the meagre records of his biographers, to find what was the life he lived during the years of his exile; for, in a sense, it contains the true journal of his thoughts, of his hopes, and of his sorrows. The plan was laid wide enough to embrace the observations he made of nature and of man, the fruits of his painful studies, and the intelligence he gathered from those experienced in travel, politics, and war. It was not only his imagination and artistic skill that were spent upon the poem: he gave his life to it. The future reward he knew was sure—an immortal fame; but he hoped for a nearer profit on his venture.

Florence might at last relent, if not because of his innocence and at the spectacle of his inconsolable exile, at least on hearing the rumour of his genius borne to her from every corner of Italy:—

If e'er it comes that this my sacred Lay,

To which both Heaven and Earth have set their hand—

Through which these many years I waste away—

Shall quell the cruelty that keeps me banned

From the fair fold where I, a lamb, was found

Hostile to wolves who 'gainst it violence planned;

With other fleece and voice of other sound,

Poet will I return, and at the font

Where I was christened be with laurel crowned.[141]

But with the completion of the Comedy

Dante's life too came to a close.

He died at Ravenna in the month of September 1321.

FOOTNOTES:

1. Matilda died in 1115. The name Tessa, the contraction of Contessa, was still, longafter her time, sometimes given to Florentine girls. See Perrens, Histoire de Florence.

2. Whether by Matilda the great Countess is meant has been eagerly disputed, and many of the best critics—such as Witte and Scartazzini—prefer to find in her one of the ladies of the Vita Nuova. In spite of their pains it seems as if more can be said for the great Matilda than for any other. The one strong argument against her is, that while she died old, in the poem she appears as young.

3. See note on Inferno xxx. 73.

4. It might, perhaps, be more correct to say that to some offices the nobles were eligible, but did not elect.

5. Inf. xiii. 75.

6. Inf. x. 119.

7. Inf. xxiii. 66.

8. Inf. x. 51.

9. Purg. vi. 144.

10. Dante sets the Abbot among the traitors in Inferno, and says scornfully of him thathis throat was cut at Florence (Inf. xxxii. 119).

11. Villani throws doubt on the guilt of the Abbot. There were some cases of churchmen being Ghibelines, as for instance that of the Cardinal Ubaldini (Inf. x. 120). Twenty years before the Abbot's death the General of the Franciscans had been jeered at in the streets of Florence for turning his coat and joining the Emperor. On the otherhand, many civilians were to be found among the Guelfs.

12. Manfred, says John Villani (Cronica, vi. 74 and 75), at first sent only a hundred men. Having by Farinata's advice been filled with wine before a skirmish in which they were induced to engage, they were easily cut in pieces by the Florentines; and theroyal standard was dragged in the dust. The truth of the story matters less than that it was believed in Florence.

13. Provenzano is found by Dante in Purgatory, which he has been admitted to, in spite of his sins, because of his self-sacrificing devotion to a friend (Purg. xi. 121).

14. For this good advice he gets a word of praise in Inferno (Inf. xvi. 42).

15. These mercenaries, though called Germans, were of various races. There were even Greeks and Saracens among them. The mixture corresponded with the motley civilisation of Manfred's court.

16. Inf. xxxii. 79.

17. Inf. x. 93.

18. Lucera was a fortress which had been peopled with Saracens by Frederick.

19. Manfred, Purg. iii. 112; Charles, Purg. vii. 113.

20. Purg. xx. 67.

21. Purg. iii. 122.

22. For an account of the constitution and activity of the Parte Guelfa at a later period,see Perrens, Hist. de Florence, vol. iv. p. 482.

23. Purg. xx. 68.

24. Parad. xi. 89.

25. Parad. xvi. 40, etc.

26. Inf. xxix. 31.

27. Inf. x. 42. Though Dante was descended from nobles, his rank in Florence

was notthat of a noble or magnate, but of a commoner.

28. The month is indicated by Dante himself, Parad. xxii. 110. The year has recentlybeen disputed. For 1265 we have J. Villani and the earliest biographers; and Dante's own expression at the beginning of the Comedy is in favour of it.

29. Inf. xxiii. 95.

30. Inf. xix. 17; Parad. xxv. 9.

31. Purg. xxx. 55.

32. Inf. viii. 45, where Virgil says of Dante that blessed was she that bore him, can scarcely be regarded as an exception to this statement.

33. In 1326, out of a population of ninety thousand, from eight to ten thousand children were being taught to read; and from five to six hundred were being taught grammar and logic in four high schools. There was not in Dante's time, or till much later, a University in Florence. See J. Villani, xi. 94, and Burckhardt, Cultur der Renaissance,vol. i. p. 76.

34. For an interesting account of Heresy in Florence from the eleventh to the thirteenth centuries, see Perrens, Hist. de Florence, vol. i. livre ii. chap. iii.

35. It opens with Brunetto's being lost in the forest of Roncesvalles, and there are some other features of resemblance—all on the surface—between his experience and Dante's.

36. G. Villani, viii. 10. Latini died in 1294. Villani gives the old scholar a very bad moral character.

37. Inf. xv. 84.

38. We may, I think, assume the Vita Nuova to have been published some time between 1291 and 1300; but the dates of Dante's works are far from being ascertained.

39. So long as even Italian critics are not agreed as to whether the title means New Life, or Youth, I suppose one is free to take his choice; and it seems most naturalto regard it as referring to the new world into which the lover is transported by his passion.

40. As, indeed, Boccaccio, Vita di Dante, expressly says was the case.

41. In this adopting a device frequently used by the love-poets of the period.—Witte,Dante-Forschungen, vol. ii. p. 312.

42. The Vita Nuova contains some thirty poems.

43. See Sir Theodore Martin's Introduction to his Translation of Vita Nuova, page xxi.

44. In this matter we must not judge the conduct of Dante by English customs.

45. Donne, ch' avete intelletto d' amore: Ladies that are acquainted well with love. Quoted in Purg. xxiv. 51.

46. Beatrice died in June 1290, having been born in April 1266.

47. Purg. xi. 98.

48. Purg. xxiv. 52.

49. The date of the Convito is still the subject of controversy, as is that of mostof Dante's works. But it certainly was composed between the Vita Nuova and the Comedy.

There is a remarkable sonnet by Guido Cavalcanti addressed to Dante, reproaching him for the deterioration in his thoughts and habits, and urging him to rid himself of thewoman who has bred the trouble. This may refer to the time after the death of Beatrice.See also Purg. xxx. 124.

50. Convito ii. 13.

51. Some recent writers set his marriage five years later, and reduce the number of his children to three.

52. His sister is probably meant by the 'young and gentle lady, most nearly related to him by blood' mentioned in the Vita Nuova.

53. The difference between the Teutonic and Southern conception of marriage must be kept in mind.

54. He describes the weather on the day of the battle with the exactness of one who had been there (Purg. v. 155).

55. Leonardo Bruni.

56. Inf. xxii. 4.

57. Inf. xxi. 95.

58. Conv. iii. 9, where he illustrates what he has to say about the nature of vision, bytelling that for some time the stars, when he looked at them, seemed lost in a pearly haze.

59. The Convito was to have consisted of fifteen books. Only four were written.

60. Wife of Bath's Tale. In the context he quotes Purg. vii. 121, and takes ideas from the Convito.

61. Dies to sensual pleasure and is abstracted from all worldly affairs and interests.See Convito iv. 28.

62. From the last canzone of the Convito.

63. In the Vita Nuova.

64. Purg. xxiii. 115, xxiv. 75; Parad. iii. 49.

65. Purg. xi. 95.

66. Purg. ii. 91.

67. Purg. iv. 123.

68. Sacchetti's stories of how Dante showed displeasure with the blacksmith and thedonkey-driver who murdered his canzoni are interesting only as showing what kind of legends about him were current in the streets of Florence.—Sacchetti, Novelle, cxiv, cxv.

69. Purg. xii. 101.

70. Purg. xi. 94:—

'In painting Cimabue deemed the field
is own, but now on Giotto goes the cry,
Till by his fame the other's is concealed.'

71. Giotto is often said to have drawn inspiration from the Comedy; but that Dante, on his side, was indebted to the new school of painting and sculpture appears from manya passage of the Purgatorio.

72. Serfage had been abolished in 1289. But doubt has been thrown on the authenticityof the deed of abolition. See Perrens, Hist. de Florence, vol. ii. p. 349.

73. No unusual provision in the industrious Italian cities. Harsh though it may seem,it was probably regarded as a valuable concession to the nobles, for their disaffection appears to have been greatly caused by their uneasiness under disabilities. There is much obscurity on several points. How, for example, came the nobles to be allowed toretain the command of the vast resources of the Parte Guelfa? This made them almostindependent of the Commonwealth.

74. At a later period the Priors were known as the Signory.

75. Fraticelli, Storia della Vita di Dante, page 112 and note.

76. It is to be regretted that Ampère in his charming Voyage Dantesque devoted no chapter to San Gemigniano, than which no Tuscan city has more thoroughly preservedits mediæval character. There is no authority for the assertion that Dante was employed on several Florentine embassies. The tendency of his early biographers is to exaggeratehis political importance and activity.

77. Under the date of April 1301 Dante is deputed by the Road Committee to see to the widening, levelling, and general improvement of a street in the

suburbs.—Witte, Dante-Forschungen, vol. ii. p. 279.

78. Dante has a word of praise for Giano, at Parad. xvi. 127.

79. At which Dante fought. See page lxii.

80. Vieri was called Messer, a title reserved for magnates, knights, and lawyers of a certain rank—notaries and jurisconsults; Dante, for example, never gets it.

81. Villani acted for some time as an agent abroad of the great business house of Peruzzi.

82. Inf. iii. 60.

83. He is 'the Prince of the modern Pharisees' (Inf. xxvii. 85); his place is readyfor him in hell (Inf. xix. 53); and he is elsewhere frequently referred to. In one great passage Dante seems to relent towards him (Purg. xx. 86).

84. Albert of Hapsburg was chosen Emperor in 1298, but was never crowned at Rome.

85. As in the days of Guelf and Ghibeline, so now in those of Blacks and Whites, thecommon multitude of townsmen belonged to neither party.

86. An interdict means that priests are to refuse sacred offices to all in the community,who are thus virtually subjected to the minor excommunication.

87. Guido died soon after his return in 1301. He had suffered in health during his exile. See Inf. x. 63.

88. Charles of Anjou had lost Sicily at the Sicilian Vespers, 1282.

89. Purg. xx. 76.

90. Witte attributes the composition of the De Monarchia to a period before 1301 (Dante-Forschungen, vol. i. Fourth Art.), but the general opinion of critics sets it muchlater.

91. Inf. vi. 66, where their expulsion is prophesied.

92. Dante's authorship of the letter is now much questioned. The drift of recent inquiries has been rather to lessen than to swell the bulk of materials for his biography.

93. Parad. xvii. 61.

94.. Purg. xxiv. 82.

95. See at Purg. xx. 43 Dante's invective against Philip and the Capets in general.

96. Henry had come to Italy with the Pope's approval. He was crowned by the Cardinals who were in Rome as Legates.

97. Parad. xxx. 136. High in Heaven Dante sees an ample chair with a crown on it, and is told it is reserved for Henry. He is to sit among those who are clothed in white.The date assigned to the action of the Comedy, it will be remembered, is the year 1300.

98. Inf. xix. 82, where the Gascon Clement is described as a 'Lawless Pastor from the West.'

99. The ingenious speculations of Troya (Del Veltro Allegorico di Dante) will alwaysmark a stage in the history of the study of Dante, but as is often the case with books on the subject, his shows a considerable gap between the evidence adduced and the conclusions drawn from it. He would make Dante to have been for many years a satellite of the great Ghibeline chief. Dante's temper or pride, however we call it, seems to have been such as to preserve him from ever remaining attached for long to any patron.

100. Inf. x. 81.

101. The Convito is in Italian, and his words are: 'wherever this language is spoken.'

102. His letter to the Florentines and that to the Emperor are dated in 1311, from 'Nearthe sources of the Arno'—that is, from the Casentino, where the Guidi of Romena dwelt. If the letter of condolence with the Counts Oberto and Guido of Romena on thedeath of their uncle is genuine, it has great value for the passage in which he excuses himself for not having come to the funeral:—'It was not negligence or ingratitude, but the poverty into which I am fallen by reason of my exile. This, like a cruel persecutor,holds me as in a prison-house where I have neither horse nor arms; and though I do allI can to free myself, I have failed as yet.' The letter has no date. Like the other ten or twelve epistles attributed to Dante, it is in Latin.

103. There is a splendid passage in praise of this family, Purg. viii. 121. A treaty is onrecord in which Dante acts as representative of the Malaspini in settling the terms of apeace between them and the Bishop of Luni in October 1306.

104. The authority for this is Benvenuto of Imola in his comment on the Comedy (Purg. xi.). The portrait of Dante by Giotto, still in Florence, but ruined by modern bungling restoration, is usually believed to have been executed in 1301 or 1302. But with regard to this, see the note at the end of this essay.

105. It is true that Villani not only says that 'he went to study at Bologna,' but also that 'he went to Paris and many parts of the world' (Cronica, ix. 136), and that Villani,of all contemporary or nearly contemporary writers, is by far the most worthy of credence. But he proves to be more than once in error regarding Dante; making him, e.g., die in a wrong month and be buried in a wrong church at Ravenna. And the 'manyparts of the world' shows that here he is dealing in hearsay of the vaguest sort. Nor can much weight be given to Boccaccio when

he sends Dante to Bologna and Paris. But Benvenuto of Imola, who lectured on the Comedy at Bologna within fifty years of Dante's death, says that Dante studied there. It would indeed be strange if he did not, and at more than one period, Bologna being the University nearest Florence. Proof of Dante's residence in Paris has been found in his familiar reference to the Rue du Fouarre (Parad. x. 137). His graphic description of the coast between Lerici and Turbia (Purg. iii. 49, iv. 25) certainly seems to show a familiarity with the Western as well asthe Eastern Rivieras of Genoa. But it scarcely follows that he was on his way to Pariswhen he visited them.

106. Inf. xiii. 58.

107. 'O ye, who have hitherto been following me in some small craft, ... put not furtherto sea, lest, losing sight of me, you lose yourselves' (Parad. ii. 1). But, to tell the truth,Dante is never so weak as a poet as when he is most the philosopher or the theologian.The following list of books more or less known to him is not given as complete:—The Vulgate, beginning with St. Jerome's Prologue; Aristotle, through the Latin translation then in vogue; Averroes, etc.; Thomas Aquinas and the other Schoolmen; much of theCivil and Canon law; Boethius; Homer only in scraps, through Aristotle, etc.; Virgil, Cicero in part, Livy, Horace, Ovid, Terence, Lucan, and Statius; the works of Brunetto Latini; the poetical literature of Provence, France, and Italy, including the Arthurian Romances—the favourite reading of the Italian nobles, and the tales of Charlemagne and his Peers—equally in favour with the common people. There is little reason to suppose that among the treatises of a scientific and quasi-scientific kind that he fell inwith, and of which he was an eager student, were included the works of Roger Bacon.These there was a conspiracy among priests and schoolmen to keep buried. Dante seems to have set little store on ecclesiastical legends of wonder; at least he gives thema wide berth in his works.

108. In the notes to Fraticelli's Vita di Dante (Florence 1861) are given copies of documents relating to the property of the Alighieri, and of Dante in particular. In 1343 his son Jacopo, by payment of a small fine, recovered vineyards and farms that had been his father's.—Notes to Chap. iii. Fraticelli's admirable Life is now in many respects out of date. He accepts, e.g., Dino Compagni as an authority, and believes inthe romantic story of the letter of Fra Ilario.

109. The details are given by Witte, Dante-Forschungen, vol ii. p. 61. The amount borrowed by Dante and his brother (and a friend) comes to nearly a thousand gold florins. Witte takes this as equivalent to 37,000 francs, i.e. nearly £1500. But the florinbeing the eighth of an ounce, or about ten shillings' worth of gold, a thousand florins would be equal only to £500—representing, of course, an immensely greater sum now-a-days.

110. Purg. viii. 76.

111. See in Scartazzini, Dante Alighieri, 1879, page 552, extract from the will of hermother Maria Donati, dated February 1314. Many of these Florentine dates are subject to correction, the year being usually counted from Lady-Day. 'In 1880 a document was discovered which proves Gemma to have been engaged in a law-suit in 1332.—Il Propugnatore, xiii^a. 156,'—Scheffer-Boichorst, Aus Dantes Verbannung, page 213.

112. Purg. xxiv. 37.

113. Inf. xxi. 40.

114. In questo mirifico poeta trovò ampissimo luego la lussuria; e non solamente ne' giovanili anni, ma ancora ne' maturi.—Boccaccio, La Vita di Dante. After mentioningthat Dante was married, he indulges in a long invective against marriage; confessing, however, that he is ignorant of whether Dante experienced the miseries he describes. His conclusion on the subject is that philosophers should leave marriage to rich fools, to nobles, and to handicraftsmen.

115. In Purgatory his conscience accuses him of pride, and he already seems to feel the weight of the grievous burden beneath which the proud bend as they purge themselves of their sin (Purg. xiii. 136). Some amount of self-accusation seems to be implied in such passages as Inf., v. 142 and Purg. xxvii. 15, etc.; but too much must not be made of it.

116. In a letter of a few lines to one of the Marquises Malaspina, written probably inthe earlier years of his exile, he tells how his purpose of renouncing ladies' society andthe writing of love-songs had been upset by the view of a lady of marvellous beauty who 'in all respects answered to his tastes, habits, and circumstances.' He says he sends with the letter a poem containing a fuller account of his subjection to this new passion. The poem is not found attached to the copy of the letter, but with good reason it is guessed to be the Canzone beginning Amor, dacchè convien, which describes howhe was overmastered by a passion born 'in the heart of the mountains in the valleyof that river beside which he had always been the victim of love.' This points to the Casentino as the scene. He also calls the Canzone his 'mountain song.' The passion it expresses may be real, but that he makes the most of it appears from the close, which is occupied by the thought of how the verses will be taken in Florence.

117. However early the De Monarchia may have been written, it is difficult to think that it can be of a later date than the death of Henry.

118. The De Vulgari Eloquio is in Latin. Dante's own Italian is richer and more elastic than that of contemporary writers. Its base is the Tuscan dialect, as refined by the example of the Sicilian poets. His Latin, on the contrary, is I believe regarded as being somewhat barbarous, even for the period.

119. In his Quæstio de Aqua et Terra. In it he speaks of having been in Mantua. The thesis was maintained in Verona, but of course he may, after a prolonged absence, have returned to that city.

120. Parad. xvii. 70.

121. Purg. xviii. 121.

122. But in urgent need of more of it.—He says of 'the sublime Cantica, adorned with the title of the Paradiso', that 'illam sub præsenti epistola, tamquam sub epigrammate proprio dedicatam, vobis adscribo, vobis offero, vobis denique recommendo.' But it may be questioned if this involves that the Cantica was already finished.

123. As, for instance, Herr Scheffer-Boichorst in his Aus Dantes Verbannung, 1882.

124. The Traversari (Purg. xiv. 107). Guido's wife was of the Bagnacavalli (Purg.xiv. 115). The only mention of the Polenta family, apart from that of Francesca, is at Inf. xxvii. 41.

125. In 1350 a sum of ten gold florins was sent from Florence by the hands of Boccaccio to Beatrice, daughter of Dante; she being then a nun at Ravenna.

126. The embassy to Venice is mentioned by Villani, and there was a treaty concludedin 1321 between the Republic and Guido. But Dante's name does not appear in it among those of the envoys from Ravenna. A letter, probably apocryphal, to Guido from Dante in Venice is dated 1314. If Dante, as is maintained by some writers, was engaged in tuition while in Ravenna, it is to be feared that his pupils would find in himan impatient master.

127. Not that Dante ever mentions these any more than a hundred other churches in which he must have spent thoughtful hours.

128. Purg. xxviii. 20.

129. A certain Cecco d'Ascoli stuck to him like a bur, charging him, among other things, with lust, and a want of religious faith which would one day secure him a placein his own Inferno. Cecco was himself burned in Florence, in 1327, for making too much of evil spirits, and holding that human actions are necessarily affected by the position of the stars. He had been at one time a professor of astronomy.

130. Gabriel Rossetti, Comment on the Divina Commedia, 1826, and Aroux, Dante, Hérétique, Révolutionnaire et Socialiste, 1854.

131. Scartazzini, Dante Alighieri, Seine Zeit, etc., 1879, page 268.

132. Parad. xxiv. 86.

133. Parad. xxiv. 145.

134. Inf. xxvii. 101; Purg. iii. 118.

135. Parad. xxiv. 91.

136. Parad. xxiv. 106.

137. Inf. x. and xxviii. There is no place in Purgatory where those who in their lives had once held heretical opinions are purified of the sin; leaving us to infer that it could be repented of in the world so as to obliterate the stain. See also Parad. iv. 67.

138. Purg. i. 71.

139. Purg. xxvii. 139.

140. Purg. xix. 134.

141. Parad. xxv. 1.

GIOTTO'S PORTRAIT OF DANTE.[142]

Vasari, in his Lives of the Painters, tells that in his day the portrait of Dante by Giotto was still to be seen in the chapel of the Podesta's palace in Florence. Writers of an earlier date had already drawn attention to this work.[143] But in the course of an age when Italians cared little for Dante, and less for Giotto, it was allowed to be buried out of sight; and when at length there came a revival of esteem for these great men, the alterations in the interior arrangement of the palace were found to have been so sweeping that it was even uncertain which out of many chambers had formerly served as the chapel. Twenty years after a fruitless attempt had been made to discover whether or not the portrait was still in existence, Signor Aubrey Bezzi, encouraged by Mr. Wilde and Mr. Kirkup, took the first step in a search (1839) which was to end by restoring to the world what is certainly the most interesting of all portraits, if account be taken of its beauty, as well as of who was its author and who its subject.

On the removal from it of a layer of lime, one of the end walls of what had been the chapel was found to be covered by a fresco painting, evidently the work of Giotto, and representing a Paradise—the subject in which Dante's portrait was known to occur. As is usual in such works, from the time of Giotto downwards, the subject is treated so as to allow of the free introduction of contemporary personages. Among these was a figure in a red gown, which there was no difficulty in recognising as the portrait of Dante. It shows him younger and with a sweeter expression than does Raphael's Dante, or Masaccio's,[144] or that in the Cathedral of Florence,[145] or that of the mask said to have been taken after his death. But to all of them it bears a strong resemblance.

The question of when this portrait was painted will easily be seen to be one of much importance in connection with Dante's biography. The fresco it belongs to is found to contain a cardinal, and a young man, who, because he wears his hair long and has a coronet set on his cap, is known to be meant for a French prince.[146] If, as is usually assumed, this prince is Charles of Valois, then the date of the event celebrated in the fresco is 1301 or 1302. With regard to when the work was executed, Messrs Crowe and Cavalcaselle, in their valuable book, say as follows:[147]—

'All inferences to be deduced from the subject and form of these frescos point to the date of 1301-2. It may be inquired whether they were executed by Giotto at the time, and this inquiry can only be satisfied approximatively. It may be inferred that Dante's portrait would hardly have been introduced into a picture so conspicuously visible as this, had not the poet at the time been influent in Florence. Dante's age in the fresco corresponds with the date of 1302, and is that of a man of thirty-five. He had himself enjoyed the highest office of Florence from June to August 1300.[148] In the fresco he does not wear the dress of the "Priori," but he holds in the ranks of those near Charles of Valois an honourable place. It may be presumed that the frescos were executed previous[149] to Dante's exile, and this view is confirmed by the technical and artistic progress which they reveal. They exhibit, indeed, the master in a higher sphere of development than at Assisi and Rome.'

This account of the subject of the work and the probable date of its execution may, I think, be accepted as containing all that is to be said in favour of the current opinion on the matter. That writer after writer has adopted that opinion without a sign of doubtas to its credibility must surely have arisen from failure to observe the insuperable difficulties it presents.

Both Charles of Valois and the Cardinal Acquasparta were in Florence during part of the winter of 1301-1302; but the circumstances under which they were there make it highly improbable that the Commonwealth was anxious to do them honour beyond granting them the outward show of respect which it would have been dangerous to refuse. Earlier in the year 1301 the Cardinal Acquasparta, having failed in gainingthe object which brought him to Florence, had, as it were, shaken the dust of the city from off his feet and left the people of it under interdict. While Charles of Valois was in Florence the Cardinal returned to make a second attempt to reconcile the opposing parties, failed a second time, and again left the city under an interdict—if indeed the first had ever been raised. On the occasion of his first visit, the Whites, who were thenin power, would have none of his counsels; on his second, the Blacks in their turn despised them.[150] There would therefore have been something almost satirical in the compliment, had the Commonwealth resolved to give him a place in a triumphal picture.

As for Charles of Valois, though much was expected from an alliance with him whilehe was still at a distance, the very party that invited his presence was soon disgusted with him owing to his faithlessness and greed. The earlier part of his stay was disturbed by pillage and bloodshed. Nor is it easy to imagine how, at any time duringhis residence of five months, the leading citizens could have either the time or the wish to arrange for honouring him in a fashion he was not the man to care for. His onecraving was for money, and still more money; and any leisure the members of public bodies had to spare from giving heed to their own interests and securing vengeance upon their opponents, was devoted to holding the common purse shut as tightly as they could against their avaricious Pacificator. When he at last delivered the city from his presence no one would have the heart to revive the memory of his disastrous visit.

But if, in all this confusion of Florentine affairs, Giotto did receive a commission to paint in the palace of the Podesta, yet it remains incredible that he should have been suffered to assign to Dante, of all men, a place of honour in the picture. No citizen had more stubbornly opposed the policy which brought Charles of Valois to Florence, and that Charles was in the city was reason enough for Dante to keep out of it. In his absence, he was sentenced in January 1302 to pay a ruinously heavy fine, and in the following March he was condemned to be put to death if ever he was caught. On fuller acquaintance his fellow-citizens liked the Frenchman as little as he, but this had no effect in softening their dislike or removing their fear of Dante. We may be sure that any friends he may still have had in Florence, as their influence could not protect his goods from confiscation or him from banishment, would hardly care to risk their own safety by urging, while his condemnation was still fresh, the admission of his portrait among those of illustrious Florentines.[151] It is true that there have been instances of great artists having reached so high a pitch of fame as to be able to dictate terms to patrons, however exalted. In his later years Giotto could perhaps have made such a point a matter of treaty with his employers, but in 1301 he was still young,[152] and great although his fame already was, he could scarcely have ventured to insist on the Republic's confessing its injustice to his friend; as it would have done had it consented that Dante, newly driven into exile, should obtain a place of honour in a work painted at the public cost.

These considerations seem to make it highly improbable that Giotto's wall-painting was meant to do honour to Charles of Valois and the Cardinal Acquasparta. But if it should still be held that it was painted in 1302, we must either cease to believe, in spite of all that Vasari and the others say, that the portrait is meant for Dante; or else confess it to be inexplicable how it got there. A way out of the difficulty begins to open up as soon as we allow ourselves some latitude in speculating as to when Giotto may have painted the fresco. The order in which that artist's works were produced is very imperfectly settled; and it may easily be that the position in Vasari's pages of the mention made by him of this fresco has given rise to a misunderstanding regarding the date of it. He speaks of it at the very beginning of his Life of Giotto. But this he does because he needs an illustration of what he has been saying in his opening sentences about the advance that painter made on Cimabue. Only after making mention of Dante's portrait does he begin his chronological list of Giotto's works; to the portrait he never returns, and so, as far as Vasari is concerned, it is without a date. Judging ofit by means of Mr. Kirkup's careful and beautiful sketch—and unfortunately we havenow no other means of knowing what the original was like—it may safely be asserted to be in Giotto's ripest style.[153] Everything considered, it is therefore allowable to search the Florentine chronicles lower down for an event more likely to be the subjectof Giotto's fresco than that usually fixed upon.

We read in John Villani that in the middle of the year 1326 the Cardinal Gianni Orsinicame to Florence as Papal Legate and Pacificator of Tuscany. The city was greatly pleased at his coming, and as an earnest of gratitude for his services presented him witha cup containing a thousand florins.[154] A month later there arrived Charles Duke ofCalabria, the eldest son of King Robert of Naples, and great-grandson of Charles of Anjou. He came as Protector of the Commonwealth, which office—an extraordinary one, and with a great salary attached to it—he had been elected to hold for five years. Never before had a spectacle like that of his entry been offered to Florence. Villani gives a long list of the barons who rode in his train, and tells that in his squadrons of men-at-arms there were no fewer than two hundred knights. The chronicler pauses to bid the reader note how great an enterprise his fellow-citizens had shown in bringing to sojourn among them, and in their interest, not only such a powerful lord as the Dukeof Calabria was, but a Papal Legate as well. Italy counted it a great thing, he says, andhe deems that the whole world ought to know of it.[155] Charles took up his abode in the Podesta's palace. He appears to have gained a better place in the hearts of the Florentines than what they were used to give to strangers and princes. When a son wasborn to him, all the city rejoiced, and it mourned with him when, in a few weeks, he lost the child. After seventeen months' experience of his rule the citizens were sorry to lose him, and bade him a farewell as hearty as their welcome had been. To some ofthem, it is true, the policy seemed a dangerous one which bore even the appearance of subjecting the Republic to the Royal House of Naples; and some of them could have wished that he 'had shown more vigour in civil and military affairs. But he was a gentle lord, popular with the townsfolk, and in the course of his residence he greatly improved the condition of things in Florence, and brought to a close many feuds.'[156]

They felt that the nine hundred thousand gold florins spent on him and his men had, on the whole, been well laid out.

One detail of the Duke's personal appearance deserves remark. We have seen that theprince in the fresco has long hair. John Villani had known the Duke well by sight, andwhen he comes to record his death and[Pg cxviii] describe what kind of man he was tolook upon, he specially says that 'he wore his hair loose.'[157]

A subject worthy of Giotto's pencil, and one likely to be offered to him if he was thenin Florence, we have therefore found in this visit of the Duke and the Cardinal. But thatGiotto was in Florence at that time is certain. He painted a portrait[158] of the Duke in the Palace of the Signory; and through that prince, as Vasari tells, he was invitedby King Robert to go down to work in Naples. All this, in the absence of evidence of any value in favour of another date, makes it, at the very least, highly probable that thefresco was a work of 1326 or 1327.

In 1326 Dante had been dead for five years. The grudge his fellow-townsmen had nourished against him for so long was now worn out. We know that very soon after his death Florence began to be proud of him; and even such of his old enemies as stillsurvived would be willing that Giotto should set him in a place of honour among the great Florentines who help to fill the fresco of the Paradise. That he was already dead would be no hindrance to his finding room alongside of Charles of Calabria; for the age was wisely tolerant of such anachronisms.[159] Had Dante been still living the painterwould have been less at liberty to create, out of the records he doubtless possessed of the features of the friend who had paid him beforehand with one immortal line, the face which, as we look into it, we feel to be a glorified transcript of what it was in theflesh. It is the face of one who has wellnigh forgotten his earthly life, instead of havingthe worst of it still before him; of one who, from that troubled Italy which like his ownSapia he knew but as a pilgrim, has passed to the 'true city,' of which he remains for evermore a citizen—the city faintly imaged by Giotto upon the chapel wall.

FOOTNOTES:

142. It is best known, and can now be judged of only through the lithograph after a tracing made by Mr. Seymour Kirkup before it was restored and ruined:published bythe Arundel Society.

143. Antonio Pucci, born in 1300, in his Centiloquio, describes the figure of Dante asbeing clothed in blood-red. Philip Villani also mentions it. He wrote towards the closeof the fourteenth century; Vasari towards the middle of the sixteenth.

144. In the Munich collection of drawings, and ascribed to Masaccio, but with how much reason I do not know.

145. Painted by Domenico Michelino in 1465, after a sketch by Alessio

Baldovinetto.

146. 'Wearing over the long hair of the Frenchmen of the period a coroneted cap.'— Crowe and Cavalcaselle, History of Painting in Italy (1864), i. 264.

147. Vol. i. p. 269.

148. The Priorate was the highest office to which a citizen could aspire, but by no means the highest in Florence.

149. I suppose the meaning is 'immediately previous.'

150. John Villani, Cronica, viii. 40 and 49; and Perrens, Hist. de Florence, under dateof 1301. Charles entered Florence on the 1st of November of that year, and left it in the following April.

151. Who the other Florentines in the fresco are does not greatly affect the present question. Villani says that along with Dante Giotto painted Corso Donati and BrunettoLatini.

152. Only twenty-five, if the commonly accepted date of his birth is correct. In any case, he was still a young man.

153. It is true that, on technical grounds, it has been questioned if it is Giotto's at all; but there is more than sufficient reason to think it is. With such doubts however we arescarcely here concerned. Even were it proved to be by a pupil, everything in the text that applies to the question of date would still remain in point.

154. J. Villani, ix. 353.

155. J. Villani, x. 1.

156. Ibid. x. 49.

157. J. Villani, x. 107.

158. Long since destroyed.

159. An anachronism of another kind would have been committed by Giotto, if, before the Comedy was even begun, he had represented Dante as holding the closed book and cluster of three pomegranates—emblematical of the three regions describedby him and of the completion of his work.—I say nothing of the Inferno found on another wall of the chapel, since there seems good reason to doubt if it is by Giotto.

THE INFERNO.

CANTO I.

In middle[160] of the journey of our days
I found that I was in a darksome wood[161]—
The right road lost and vanished in the maze.
Ah me! how hard to make it understood
How rough that wood was, wild, and terrible:
By the mere thought my terror is renewed.
More bitter scarce were death. But ere I tell
At large of good which there by me was found,
I will relate what other things befell.
Scarce know I how I entered on that ground,
So deeply, at the moment when I passed
From the right way, was I in slumber drowned.
But when beneath a hill[162] arrived at last,
Which for the boundary of the valley stood,
That with such terror had my heart harassed,
I upwards looked and saw its shoulders glowed,
Radiant already with that planet's[163] light
Which guideth surely upon every road.
A little then was quieted by the sight
The fear which deep within my heart had lain
Through all my sore experience of the night.
And as the man, who, breathing short in pain,
Hath 'scaped the sea and struggled to the shore,
Turns back to gaze upon the perilous main;

Even so my soul which fear still forward bore
Turned to review the pass whence I egressed,
And which none, living, ever left before.
My wearied frame refreshed with scanty rest,
I to ascend the lonely hill essayed;
The lower foot[164] still that on which I pressed.
And lo! ere I had well beginning made,
A nimble leopard,[165] light upon her feet,
And in a skin all spotted o'er arrayed:
Nor ceased she e'er me full in the face to meet,
And to me in my path such hindrance threw
That many a time I wheeled me to retreat.
It was the hour of dawn; with retinue
Of stars[166] that were with him when Love Divine
In the beginning into motion drew
Those beauteous things, the sun began to shine;
And I took heart to be of better cheer
Touching the creature with the gaudy skin,
Seeing 'twas morn,[167] and spring-tide of the year;
Yet not so much but that when into sight
A lion[168] came, I was disturbed with fear.
Towards me he seemed advancing in his might,
Rabid with hunger and with head high thrown:
The very air was tremulous with fright.
A she-wolf,[169] too, beheld I further on;
All kinds of lust seemed in her leanness pent:
Through her, ere now, much folk have misery known.
By her oppressed, and altogether spent
By the terror breathing from her aspect fell,

I lost all hope of making the ascent.
And as the man who joys while thriving well,
When comes the time to lose what he has won
In all his thoughts weeps inconsolable,
So mourned I through the brute which rest knows none:
She barred my way again and yet again,
And thrust me back where silent is the sun.
And as I downward rushed to reach the plain,
Before mine eyes appeared there one aghast,
And dumb like those that silence long maintain.
When I beheld him in the desert vast,
'Whate'er thou art, or ghost or man,' I cried,
'I pray thee show such pity as thou hast.'
'No man,[170] though once I was; on either side
Lombard my parents were, and both of them
For native place had Mantua,' he replied.
'Though late, sub Julio,[171] to the world I came,
And lived at Rome in good Augustus' day,
While yet false gods and lying were supreme.Poet
I was, renowning in my lay
Anchises' righteous son, who fled from Troy
What time proud Ilion was to flames a prey.
But thou, why going back to such annoy?
The hill delectable why fear to mount,
The origin and ground of every joy?'
'And thou in sooth art Virgil, and the fount
Whence in a stream so full doth language flow?
Abashed, I answered him with humble front.
'Of other poets light and honour thou!

Let the long study and great zeal I've shown
In searching well thy book, avail me now!
My master thou, and author[172] thou, alone!
From thee alone I, borrowing, could attain
The style[173] consummate which has made me known
.Behold the beast which makes me turn again:
Deliver me from her, illustrious Sage;
Because of her I tremble, pulse and vein.'
'Thou must attempt another pilgrimage,'
Observing that I wept, he made reply,
'If from this waste thyself thou 'dst disengage.
Because the beast thou art afflicted by
Will suffer none along her way to pass,
But, hindering them, harasses till they die.
So vile a nature and corrupt she has,
Her raging lust is still insatiate,
And food but makes it fiercer than it was.
Many a creature[174] hath she ta'en for mate,
And more she'll wed until the hound comes forth
To slay her and afflict with torment great.
He will not batten upon pelf or earth;
But he shall feed on valour, love, and lore;
Feltro and Feltro[175] 'tween shall be his birth.
He will save humbled Italy, and restore,
For which of old virgin Camilla[176] died;
Turnus, Euryalus, Nisus, died of yore.
Her through all cities chasing far and wide,
He at the last to Hell will thrust her down,
Whence envy[177] first unloosed her. I decide

Therefore and judge that thou hadst best come on
With me for guide;[178] and hence I'll lead thee where
A place eternal shall to thee be shown.
There shalt thou hear the howlings of despair
In which the ancient spirits make lament,
All of them fain the second death to share.
Next shalt thou them behold who are content,
Because they hope some time, though now in fire,
To join the blessed they will win consent.
And if to these thou later wouldst aspire,
A soul[179] shall guide thee, worthier far than I;
When I depart thee will I leave with her.
Because the Emperor[180] who reigns on high
Wills not, since 'gainst His laws I did rebel,[181]
That to His city I bring any nigh.
O'er all the world He rules, there reigns as well;
There is His city and exalted seat:
O happy whom He chooses there to dwell!'
And I to him: 'Poet, I thee entreat,
Even by that God who was to thee unknown,
That I may 'scape this present ill, nor meet
With worse, conduct me whither thou hast shown,
That I may see Saint Peter's gate,[182] and those
Whom thou reportest in such misery thrown.'
He moved away; behind him held I close.

FOOTNOTES:

160. Middle: In his Convito , comparing human life to an arch, Dante says thatat the age of thirty-five a man has reached the top and begins to go down. As he was born in 1265 that was his own age in 1300, the year in which the action of the poemis laid.

161. Darksome wood: A state of spiritual darkness or despair into which he has gradually drifted, not without fault of his own.

162. A hill: Lower down this hill is termed 'the origin and cause of all joy.' It is symbolical of spiritual freedom—of the peace and security that spring from the practice of virtue. Only, as it seems, by gaining such a vantage-ground can he escape from the wilderness of doubt—the valley of the shadow of death—in which he is lost.

163. That planet: On the Ptolemaic system, which, as perfected by the Arabian astronomers, and with some Christian additions, was that followed by Dante, the sun is reckoned as one of the seven planets; all the others as well as the earth and the fixedstars deriving their light from it. Here the sunlight may signify the Divine help grantedto all men in their efforts after virtue.

164. The lower foot, etc.: This describes a cautious, slow ascent.

165. A nimble leopard: The leopard and the lion and wolf that come with it are suggested by Jeremiah v. 6: 'A lion out of the forest shall slay them,' etc. We have Dante's own authority for it, in his letter to Can Grande, that several meanings are often hidden under the incidents of the Comedy. But whatever else the beasts may signify, their chief meaning is that of moral hindrances. It is plain that the lion and wolf are the sins of others—pride and avarice. If the leopard agrees with them in this, itmost probably stands for the envy of those among whom Dante lived: at Inf. vi. 74 wefind envy, pride, and avarice classed together as the sins that have corrupted Florence. But from Inf. xvi. 106 it appears that Dante hoped to get the better of the leopard by means of a cord which he wore girt about his loins. The cord is emblematical of self- control; and hence the leopard seems best to answer the idea of sensual pleasure in the sense of a temptation that makes difficult the pursuit of virtue. But it will be observedthat this hindrance Dante trusts to overcome.

166. Stars, etc.: The sun being then in Aries, as it was believed to have been at the creation.

167. Morn, etc.: It is the morning of Friday the 25th of March in the year 1300, and by the use of Florence, which began the year on the anniversary of the incarnation, it is the first day of the New Year. The Good Friday of 1300 fell a fortnight later; but the25th of March was held to be the true anniversary of the crucifixion as well as of the incarnation and of the creation of the world. The date of the action is fixed by. The day was of good omen for success in the struggle with his lower self.

168. A lion: Pride or arrogance; to be taken in its widest sense of violent opposition to all that is good.

169. A she-wolf: Used elsewhere in the Comedy to represent avarice. Dante may havehad specially in his mind the greed and worldly ambition of the Pope and the Court ofRome, but it is plain from line 110 that the wolf stands primarily for a sin, and not fora person or corporate body.

170. No man: Brunetto Latini, the friend and master of Dante, says 'the soul is the life of man, but without the body is not man.'

171. Sub Julio: Julius was not even consul when Virgil was born. But Dante reckonedJulius as the founder of the Empire, and therefore makes the time in which he flourished his. Virgil was only twenty-five years of age when Cæsar was slain; and thus it was under Augustus that his maturer life was spent.

172. Author: Dante defines an author as 'one worthy to be believed and obeyed' (Convito iv. 6). For a guide and companion on his great pilgrimage he chooses Virgil,not only because of his fame as a poet, but also because he had himself described a descent to the Shades—had been already there. The vulgar conception of Virgil was that of a virtuous great magician.

173. The style, etc.: Some at least of Dante's minor works had been given to the world before 1300, certainly the Vita Nuova and others of his poems. To his study of Virgil he may have felt himself indebted for the purity of taste that kept him superior to the frigid and artificial style of his contemporaries, He prided himself on suiting hislanguage to his theme, as well as on writing straight from the heart.

174. Many a creature, etc.: Great men and states, infected with avarice in its extendedsense of encroachment on the rights of others.

175. Feltro and Feltro, etc.: Who the deliverer was that Dante prophesies the coming of is not known, and perhaps never can be. Against the claims of Can Grande of Verona the objection is that, at any date which can reasonably be assigned for the publicationof the Inferno, he had done nothing to justify such bright hopes of his future career. There seems proof, too, that till the Paradiso was written Dante entertained no great respect for the Scala family (Purg. xvi. 118, xviii. 121). Neither is Verona, or the widest territory over which Can Grande ever ruled, at all described by saying it lay between Feltro and Feltro.—I have preferred to translate nazi-one as birth rather than as nation or people. 'The birth of the deliverer will be found to have been between feltro and feltro.' Feltro, as Dante wrote it, would have no capital letter; and according to an old gloss the deliverer is to be of humble birth; feltro being the name of a poor sort of cloth. This interpretation I give as a curiosity more than anything else; for the most competent critics have decided against it, or ignored it.—Henry of Luxemburg, chosen Emperor in November 1308, is an old claimant for the post of the allegorical veltro or greyhound. On him Dante's hopes were long set as the man who should 'save Italy;' and it seems not out of place to draw attention to what is said of him by John Villani, the contemporary and fellow-townsman of Dante: 'He was of a magnanimous nature, though, as regarded his family, of poor extraction' (Cronica, ix. 1). Whatever may be made of the Feltros, the description in the text of the deliverer as one superior to all personal ambition certainly answers better to Dante's ideal of a righteous Emperor than to the character of a partisan leader like Uguccione della Faggiuola, or an ambitious prince like Can Grande.

176. Camilla, etc.: All persons of the Æneid.

177. Envy: That of Satan.

178. Thou hadst best, etc.: As will be seen from the next Canto, Virgil has been sent to the relief of Dante; but how that is to be wrought out is left to his own judgment. He might secure a partial deliverance for his ward by conducting him up the Delectable Mount—the peaceful heights familiar to himself, and which are to be won by the practice of natural piety. He chooses the other course, of guiding Dante through the regions of the future state, where the pilgrim's trust in the Divine government will be strengthened by what he sees, and his soul acquirc a largcr peace.

179. A soul: Beatrice.

180. The Emperor: The attribution of this title to God is significant of Dante's lofty conception of the Empire.

181 'Gainst his laws, etc.: Virgil was a rebel only in the sense of being ignorant of the Christian revelation

182.Saint Peter's gate: Virgil has not mentioned Saint Peter. Dante names him as if to proclaim that it is as a Christian, though under heathen guidance, that he makes the pilgrimage. Here the gate seems to be spoken of as if it formed the entrance to Paradise, as it was popularly believed to do, and as if it were at that point Virgil would cease to guide him. But they are to find it nearer at hand, and after it has been passed Virgil is to act as guide through Purgatory.

CANTO II.

It was the close of day;[183] the twilight brown
All living things on earth was setting free
From toil, while I preparing was alone[184]
To face the battle which awaited me,
As well of ruth as of the perilous quest,
Now to be limned by faultless memory.
Help, lofty genius! Muses,[185] manifest
Goodwill to me! Recording what befell,
Do thou, O mind, now show thee at thy best!
I thus began: 'Poet, and Guide as well,
Ere trusting me on this adventure wide,
Judge if my strength of it be capable.
Thou say'st that Silvius' father,[186] ere he died,
Still mortal to the world immortal went,
There in the body some time to abide.
Yet that the Foe of evil was content
That he should come, seeing what high effect,
And who and what should from him claim descent,
No room for doubt can thoughtful man detect:
For he of noble Rome, and of her sway
Imperial, in high Heaven grew sire elect.
And both of these,[187] the very truth to say,
Were founded for the holy seat, whereon
The Greater Peter's follower sits to-day.
Upon this journey, praised by thee, were known
And heard things by him, to the which he owed

His triumph, whence derives the Papal gown.[188]

That path the Chosen Vessel[189] later trod

So of the faith assurance to receive,

Which is beginning of salvation's road.

But why should I go? Who will sanction give?

For I am no Æneas and no Paul;

Me worthy of it no one can believe,

Nor I myself. Hence venturing at thy call,

I dread the journey may prove rash.

But vain For me to reason; wise, thou know'st it all.'

Like one no more for what he wished for fain,

Whose purpose shares mutation with his thought

Till from the thing begun he turns again;

On that dim slope so grew I all distraught,

Because, by brooding on it, the design

I shrank from, which before I warmly sought.

'If well I understand these words of thine,'

The shade of him magnanimous made reply, '

Thy soul 'neath cowardice hath sunk supine,

Which a man often is so burdened by,

It makes him falter from a noble aim,

As beasts at objects ill-distinguished shy.

To loose thee from this terror, why I came,

And what the speech I heard, I will relate,

When first of all I pitied thee. A dame[190]

Hailed me where I 'mongst those in dubious state[191]

Had my abode: so blest was she and fair,

Her to command me I petitioned straight.

Her eyes were shining brighter than the star;[192]

And she began to say in accents sweet
And tuneable as angel's voices are:
"O Mantuan Shade, in courtesy complete,
Whose fame survives on earth, nor less shall grow
Through all the ages, while the world hath seat;
A friend of mine, with fortune for his foe,
Has met with hindrance on his desert way,
And, terror-smitten, can no further go,
But turns; and that he is too far astray,
And that I rose too late for help, I dread,
From what in Heaven concerning him they say.
Go, with thy speech persuasive him bestead,
And with all needful help his guardian prove,
That touching him I may be comforted.
Know, it is Beatrice seeks thee thus to move.
Thence come I where I to return am fain:
My coming and my plea are ruled by love.
When I shall stand before my Lord again,
Often to Him I will renew thy praise."
And here she ceased, nor did I dumb remain:
"O virtuous Lady, thou alone the race
Of man exaltest 'bove all else that dwell
Beneath the heaven which wheels in narrowest space.[193]
To do thy bidding pleases me so well,
Though 'twere already done 'twere all too slow;
Thy wish at greater length no need to tell.
But say, what tempted thee to come thus low,
Even to this centre, from the region vast,[194]
Whither again thou art on fire to go?"

"This much to learn since a desire thou hast,"
She answered, "briefly thee I'll satisfy,
How, coming here, I through no terrors passed.
We are, of right, such things alarmèd by,
As have the power to hurt us; all beside
Are harmless, and not fearful. Wherefore I—
Thus formed by God, His bounty is so wide—
Am left untouched by all your miseries,
And through this burning[195] unmolested glide.
A noble lady[196] is in Heaven, who sighs
O'er the obstruction where I'd have thee go,
And breaks the rigid edict of the skies.
Calling on Lucia,[197] thus she made her know
What she desired: 'Thy vassal[198] now hath need
Of help from thee; do thou then helpful show.'
Lucia, who hates all cruelty, in speed
Rose, and approaching where I sat at rest,
To venerable Rachel[199] giving heed,
Me: 'Beatrice, true praise of God,' addressed;
'Why not help him who had such love for thee,
And from the vulgar throng to win thee pressed?
Dost thou not hear him weeping pitiably,
Nor mark the death now threatening him upon
A flood[200] than which less awful is the sea?'
Never on earth did any ever run,
Allured by profit or impelled by fear,
Swifter than I, when speaking she had done,
From sitting 'mong the blest descended here,
My trust upon thy comely rhetoric cast,

Which honours thee and those who lend it ear."
When of these words she spoken had the last,
She turned aside bright eyes which tears[201] did fill,
And I by this was urged to greater haste.
And so it was I joined thee by her will,
And from that raging beast delivered thee,
Which barred the near way up the beauteous hill.
What ails thee then? Why thus a laggard be?
Why cherish in thy heart a craven fear?
Where is thy franchise, where thy bravery,
When three such blessed ladies have a care
For thee in Heaven's court, and these words of mine
Thee for such wealth of blessedness prepare?'
As flowers, by chills nocturnal made to pine
And shut themselves, when touched by morning bright
Upon their stems arise, full-blown and fine;
So of my faltering courage changed the plight,
And such good cheer ran through my heart, it spurred
Me to declare, like free-born generous wight:
'O pitiful, who for my succour stirred!
And thou how full of courtesy to run,
Alert in service, hearkening her true word!
Thou with thine eloquence my heart hast won
To keen desire to go, and the intent
Which first I held I now no longer shun.
Therefore proceed; my will with thine is blent:
Thou art my Guide, Lord, Master;[202] thou alone!'
Thus I; and with him, as he forward went,
The steep and rugged road I entered on.

FOOTNOTES:

183. Close of day: The evening of the Friday. It comes on us with something of a surprise that a whole day has been spent in the attempt to ascend the hill, and inconference with Virgil.

184. Alone: Of earthly creatures, though in company with Virgil, a shade. In these words is to be found the keynote to the Canto. With the sense of deliverance from immediate danger his enthusiasm has died away. After all, Virgil is only a shade;and his heart misgives him at the thought of engaging, in the absence of all human companionship, upon a journey so full of terrors. He is not reassured till Virgil has displayed his commission.

185. Muses: The invocation comes now, the First Canto being properly an introduction. Here it may be pointed out, as illustrating the refinement of Dante's art, that the invocation in the Purgatorio is in a higher strain, and that in the Paradiso in a nobler still.

186. Silvius' father: Æneas, whose visit to the world of shades is described in the Sixth Æneid. He finds there his father Anchises, who foretells to him the fortunes of his descendants down to the time of Augustus.

187. Both of these: Dante uses language slightly apologetic as he unfolds to Virgil, the great Imperialist poet, the final cause of Rome and the Empire. But while he thus exaltsthe Papal office, making all Roman history a preparation for its establishment, Dante throughout his works is careful to refuse any but a spiritual or religious allegianceto the Pope, and leaves himself free, as will be frequently seen in the course of the Comedy, to blame the Popes as men, while yielding all honour to their great office. Inthis emphatic mention of Rome as the divinely-appointed seat of Peter's Chair may beimplied a censure on the Pope for the transference of the Holy See to Avignon, whichwas effected in 1305, between the date assigned to the action of the poem and the period when it was written.

188. Papal gown: 'The great mantle' Dante elsewhere terms it; the emblem of the Papal dignity. It was only in Dante's own time that coronation began to take the placeof investiture with the mantle.

189. Chosen Vessel: Paul, who like Æneas visited the other world, though not the same region of it. Throughout the poem instances drawn from profane history, and even poetry and mythology, are given as of authority equal to those from Christian sources.

190. A dame: Beatrice, the heroine of the Vita Nuova, at the close of which Dante promises some day to say of her what was never yet said of any woman. She died in 1290, aged twenty-four. In the Comedy she fills different parts: she is the glorified Beatrice Portinari whom Dante first knew as a fair Florentine girl;

but she also represents heavenly truth, or the knowledge of it—the handmaid of eternal life. Theology is too hard and technical a term to bestow on her. Virgil, for his part, represents the knowledge that men may acquire of Divine law by the use of their reason, helped by such illumination as was enjoyed by the virtuous heathen. In other words, he is the exponent of the Divine revelation involved in the Imperial system—for the Empire was never far from Dante's thoughts. To him it meant the perfection of just rule, in which due cognisance is taken of every right and of every duty. The relation Dante bears to these two is that of erring humanity struggling to the light. Virgil leads him as far as he can, and then commits him to the holier rule of Beatrice. But the poem would lose its charm if the allegorical meaning of every passage were too closely insisted on. And, worse than that, it cannot always be found.

191. Dubious state: The limbo of the virtuous heathen (Canto iv.).

192. The star: In the Vita Nuova Dante speaks of the star in the singular when he means the stars.

193. In narrowest space: The heaven of the moon, on the Ptolemaic system the lowest of the seven planets. Below it there is only the heaven of fire, to which all the flames of earth are attracted. The meaning is, above all on earth.

194. The region vast: The empyrean, or tenth and highest heaven of all. It is an addition by the Christian astronomers to the heavens of the Ptolemaic system, and extends above the primum mobile, which imparts to all beneath it a common motion, while leaving its own special motion to each. The empyrean is the heaven of Divine rest.

195. Burning: 'Flame of this burning,' allegorical, as applied to the limbo where Virgil had his abode. He and his companions suffer only from unfulfilled but lofty desire (Inf. iv. 41).

196. A noble lady: The Virgin Mary, of whom it is said (Parad. xxxiii. 16) that her 'benignity not only succours those who ask, but often anticipates their demand;' as here. She is the symbol of Divine grace in its widest sense. Neither Christ nor Mary is mentioned by name in the Inferno.

197. Lucia: The martyr saint of Syracuse. Witte (Dante-Forschungen, vol. ii. 30) suggests that Lucia Ubaldini may be meant, a thirteenth-century Florentine saint, and sister of the Cardinal (Inf. x. 120). The day devoted to her memory was the 30th of May. Dante was born in May, and if it could be proved that he was born on the 30th of the month the suggestion would be plausible. But for the greater Lucy is to be said that she was especially helpful to those troubled in their eyesight, as Dante was at one time of his life. Here she is the symbol of illuminating grace.

198. Thy vassal: Saint Lucy being held in special veneration by Dante; or only that he was one that sought light. The word fedele may of course, as it usually is, be read in itsprimary sense of 'faithful one;' but it is old Italian for vassal; and to take the referenceto be to the duty of the overlord to help his dependant in need seems to give force to the appeal.

199. Rachel: Symbol of the contemplative life.

200. A flood, etc.: 'The sea of troubles' in which Dante is involved.

201. Tears: Beatrice weeps for human misery—especially that of Dante—though unaffected by the view of the sufferings of Inferno.

202. My Guide, etc.: After hearing how Virgil was moved to come, Dante accepts him not only for his guide, as he did at the close of the First Canto, but for his lord andmaster as well.

CANTO III.

Through me to the city dolorous lies the way,
Who pass through me shall pains eternal prove,
Through me are reached the people lost for aye.'
Twas Justice did my Glorious Maker move;
I was created by the Power Divine,[203]
The Highest Wisdom, and the Primal Love.
No thing's creation earlier was than mine,
If not eternal;[204] I for aye endure:
Ye who make entrance, every hope resign!
These words beheld I writ in hue obscure
On summit of a gateway; wherefore I:
'Hard[205] is their meaning, Master.' Like one sure
Beforehand of my thought, he made reply:'
Here it behoves to leave all fears behind;
All cowardice behoveth here to die.
For now the place I told thee of we find,
Where thou the miserable folk shouldst see
Who the true good[206] of reason have resigned.'
Then, with a glance of glad serenity,
He took my hand in his, which made me bold,
And brought me in where secret things there be.
There sighs and plaints and wailings uncontrolled
The dim and starless air resounded through;
Nor at the first could I from tears withhold.
The various languages and words of woe,
The uncouth accents,[207] mixed with angry cries

And smiting palms and voices loud and low,
Composed a tumult which doth circling rise
For ever in that air obscured for aye;
As when the sand upon the whirlwind flies.
And, horror-stricken,[208] I began to say:
'Master, what sound can this be that I hear,
And who the folk thus whelmed in misery?'
And he replied: 'In this condition drear
Are held the souls of that inglorious crew
Who lived unhonoured, but from guilt kept clear.
Mingled they are with caitiff angels, who,
Though from avowed rebellion they refrained,
Disloyal to God, did selfish ends pursue.
Heaven hurled them forth, lest they her beauty stained;
Received they are not by the nether hell,
Else triumph[209] thence were by the guilty gained.'
And I: 'What bear they, Master, to compel
Their lamentations in such grievous tone?'
He answered: 'In few words I will thee tell.
No hope of death is to the wretches known
;So dim the life and abject where they sigh
They count all sufferings easier than their own.
Of them the world endures no memory;
Mercy and justice them alike disdain.
Speak we not of them: glance, and pass them by.'
I saw a banner[210] when I looked again,
Which, always whirling round, advanced in haste
As if despising steadfast to remain.
And after it so many people chased

In long procession, I should not have said
That death[211] had ever wrought such countless waste.
Some first I recognised, and then the shade
I saw and knew of him, the search to close,
Whose dastard soul the great refusal[212] made.
Straightway I knew and was assured that those
Were of the tribe of caitiffs,[213] even the race
Despised of God and hated of His foes.
The wretches, who when living showed no trace
Of life, went naked, and were fiercely stung
By wasps and hornets swarming in that place.
Blood drawn by these out of their faces sprung
And, mingled with their tears, was at their feet
Sucked up by loathsome worms it fell among.
Casting mine eyes beyond, of these replete,
People I saw beside an ample stream,
Whereon I said: 'O Master, I entreat,
Tell who these are, and by what law they seem
Impatient till across the river gone;
As I distinguish by this feeble gleam.'
And he: 'These things shall unto thee be known
What time our footsteps shall at rest be found
Upon the woful shores of Acheron.'
Then with ashamèd eyes cast on the ground,
Fearing my words were irksome in his ear,
Until we reached the stream I made no sound.
And toward us, lo, within a bark drew near
A veteran[214] who with ancient hair was white,
Shouting: 'Ye souls depraved, be filled with fear

.Hope never more of Heaven to win the sight;
I come to take you to the other strand,
To frost and fire and everlasting night.
And thou, O living soul, who there dost stand,
From 'mong the dead withdraw thee.'
Then, awareThat not at all I stirred at his command,
'By other ways,[215] from other ports thou'lt fare;
But they will lead thee to another shore,
And 'tis a skiff more buoyant must thee bear.'
And then my leader: 'Charon, be not sore,
For thus it has been willed where power ne'er came
Short of the will; thou therefore ask no more.'
And hereupon his shaggy cheeks grew tame
Who is the pilot of the livid pool,
And round about whose eyes glowed wheels of flame.
But all the shades, naked and spent with dool,
Stood chattering with their teeth, and changing hue
Soon as they heard the words unmerciful.
God they blasphemed, and families whence they grew;
Mankind, the time, place, seed in which began
Their lives, and seed whence they were born.
Then drewThey crowding all together, as they ran,
Bitterly weeping, to the accursed shore
Predestinate for every godless man.
The demon Charon, with eyes evermore
Aglow, makes signals, gathering them all;
And whoso lingers smiteth with his oar.
And as the faded leaves of autumn fall
One after the other, till at last the bough

Sees on the ground spread all its coronal;
With Adam's evil seed so haps it now:
At signs each falls in turn from off the coast,
As fowls[216] into the ambush fluttering go.
The gloomy waters thus by them are crossed,
And ere upon the further side they land,
On this, anew, is gathering a host.
'Son,' said the courteous Master,[217] 'understand,
All such as in the wrath of God expire,
From every country muster on this strand.
To cross the river they are all on fire;
Their wills by Heavenly justice goaded on
Until their terror merges in desire.
This way no righteous soul has ever gone;
Wherefore[218] of thee if Charon should complain,
Now art thou sure what by his words is shown.'
When he had uttered this the dismal plain
Trembled[219] so violently, my terror past
Recalling now, I'm bathed in sweat again.
Out of the tearful ground there moaned a blast
Whence lightning flashed forth red and terrible,
Which vanquished all my senses; and, as cast
In sudden slumber, to the ground I fell.

FOOTNOTES:

203. Power Divine, etc.: The Persons of the Trinity, described by their attributes.

204. If not eternal: Only the angels and the heavenly spheres were created before Inferno. The creation of man came later. But from Inf. xxxiv. 124 it appears that Inferno was hollowed out of the earth; and at Parad. vii. 124 the earth is declared to be 'corruptible and enduring short while;' therefore not eternal.

205. Hard, etc.: The injunction to leave all hope behind makes Dante hesitate to enter. Virgil anticipates the objection before it is fully expressed, and reminds him that the passage through Inferno is to be only one stage of his journey. Not by this gate will heseek to quit it.

206. True good, etc.: Truth in its highest form—the contemplation of God.

207. Uncouth accents: 'Like German,' says Boccaccio.

208. Horror-stricken: 'My head enveloped in horror.' Some texts have 'error,' and this yields a better meaning—that Dante is amazed to have come full into the crowd ofsuffering shades before he has even crossed Acheron. If with the best texts 'horror' beread, the meaning seems to be that he is so overwhelmed by fear as to lose his presenceof mind. They are not yet in the true Inferno, but only in the vestibule or forecourt of it—the flat rim which runs round the edge of the pit.

209. Else triumph, etc.: The satisfaction of the rebel angels at finding that they endured no worse punishment than that of such as remained neutral.

210. A banner: Emblem of the instability of those who would never take a side.

211. That death, etc.: The touch is very characteristic of Dante. He feigns astonishmentat finding that such a proportion of mankind can preserve so pitiful a middle course between good and evil, and spend lives that are only 'a kind of—as it were.'

212. The great refusal: Dante recognises him, and so he who made the great refusal must have been a contemporary. Almost beyond doubt Celestine V. is meant, who was in 1294 elected Pope against his will, and resigned the tiara after wearing it a few months; the only Pope who ever resigned it, unless we count Clement I. As he was notcanonized till 1326, Dante was free to form his own judgment of his conduct. It has been objected that Dante would not treat with contumely a man so devout as Celestine. But what specially fits him to be the representative caitiff is just that, being himself virtuous, he pusillanimously threw away the greatest opportunity of doing good. By his resignation Boniface VIII. became Pope, to whose meddling in Florentine affairs it was that Dante owed his banishment. Indirectly, therefore, he owed it to the resignation of Celestine; so that here we have the first of many private scores to be paid off in the course of the Comedy. Celestine's resignation is referred to (Inf. xxvii. 104).—Esau and the rich young man in the Gospel have both been suggested in place of Celestine. To either of them there lies the objection that Dante could not have recognised him. And, besides, Dante's contemporaries appear at once to have discovered Celestine in him who made the great refusal. In Paradise the poet is told by his ancestor Cacciaguida that his rebuke is to be like the wind, which strikes most fiercely on the loftiest summits (Parad. xvii. 133); and it agrees well with such a profession, that the first stroke he deals in the Comedy is at a Pope.

213. Caitiffs: To one who had suffered like Dante for the frank part he took in affairs,neutrality may well have seemed the unpardonable sin in politics; and no doubt but that his thoughts were set on the trimmers in Florence when he wrote, 'Let us not speakof them!'

214. A veteran: Charon. In all this description of the passage of the river by the shades, Dante borrows freely from Virgil. It has been already remarked on Inf. ii. 28 that he draws illustrations from Pagan sources. More than that, as we begin to find, he boldly introduces legendary and mythological characters among the persons of his drama. With Milton in mind, it surprises, on a first acquaintance with the Comedy, todiscover how nearly independent of angels is the economy invented by Dante for the other world.

215. Other ways, etc.: The souls bound from earth to Purgatory gather at the mouth ofthe Tiber, whence they are wafted on an angel's skiff to their destination (Purg. ii. 100).It may be here noted that never does Dante hint a fear of one day becoming a denizenof Inferno. It is only the pains of Purgatory that oppress his soul by anticipation. So here Charon is made to see at a glance that the pilgrim is not of those 'who make descent to Acheron.'

216. As fowls, etc.: 'As a bird to its lure'—generally interpreted of the falcon when called back. But a witness of the sport of netting thrushes in Tuscany describes them as 'flying into the vocal ambush in a hurried, half-reluctant, and very remarkable manner.'

217. Courteous Master: Virgil here gives the answer promised at line 76; and Dante by the epithet he uses removes any impression that his guide had been wanting in courtesy when he bade him wait.

218. Wherefore: Charon's displeasure only proves that he feels he has no hold on Dante.

219. Trembled, etc.: Symbolical of the increase of woe in Inferno when the doomed souls have landed on the thither side of Acheron. Hell opens to receive them. Conversely, when any purified soul is released from Purgatory the mountain of purification trembles to its base with joy (Purg. xxi. 58).

CANTO IV.

Resounding thunder broke the slumber deep
That drowsed my senses, and myself
I shookLike one by force awakened out of sleep.
Then rising up I cast a steady look,
With eyes refreshed, on all that lay around,
And cognisance of where I found me took
.In sooth, me on the valley's brink I found
Of the dolorous abyss, where infinite
Despairing cries converge with thundering sound.[220]
Cloudy it was, and deep, and dark as night;
So dark that, peering eagerly to find
What its depths held, no object met my sight.'
Descend we now into this region blind,'
Began the Poet with a face all pale;
'I will go first, and do thou come behind.'
Marking the wanness on his cheek prevail,
I asked, 'How can I, seeing thou hast dread,
My wonted comforter when doubts assail?'
'The anguish of the people,' then he said,
'Who are below, has painted on my face
Pity,[221] by thee for fear interpreted.
Come! The long journey bids us move apace.'
Then entered he and made me enter too
The topmost circle girding the abyss.
Therein, as far as I by listening knew,
There was no lamentation save of sighs,

Whence throbbed the air eternal through and through.
This, sorrow without suffering made arise
From infants and from women and from men,
Gathered in great and many companies.
And the good Master: 'Wouldst thou[222] nothing then
Of who those spirits are have me relate?
Yet know, ere passing further, although when
On earth they sinned not, worth however great
Availed them not, they being unbaptized—
Part[223] of the faith thou holdest. If their fate
Was to be born ere man was Christianised,
God, as behoved, they never could adore:
And I myself am with this folk comprised.
For such defects—our guilt is nothing more—
We are thus lost, suffering from this alone
That, hopeless, we our want of bliss deplore.'
Greatly I sorrowed when he made this known,
Because I knew that some who did excel
In worthiness were to that limbo[224] gone.
'Tell me, O Sir,' I prayed him, 'Master,[225] tell,'
—That I of the belief might surety win,
Victorious every error to dispel—
'Did ever any hence to bliss attain
By merit of another or his own?'
And he, to whom my hidden drift[226] was plain:
'I to this place but lately[227] had come down,
When I beheld one hither make descent;
A Potentate[228] who wore a victor's crown.
The shade of our first sire forth with him went,

And his son Abel's, Noah's forth he drew,
Moses' who gave the laws, the obedient
Patriarch Abram's, and King David's too;
And, with his sire and children, Israel,
And Rachel, winning whom such toils he knew;
And many more, in blessedness to dwell.
And I would have thee know, earlier than these
No human soul was ever saved from Hell.'
While thus he spake our progress did not cease
,But we continued through the wood to stray;
The wood, I mean, with crowded ghosts for trees.
Ere from the summit far upon our way
We yet had gone, I saw a flame which glowed,
Holding a hemisphere[229] of dark at bay.
'Twas still a little further on our road,
Yet not so far but that in part I guessed
That honourable people there abode.
'Of art and science Ornament confessed!
Who are these honoured in such high degree,
And in their lot distinguished from the rest?'
He said: 'For them their glorious memory,
Still in thy world the subject of renown,
Wins grace[230] by Heaven distinguished thus to be.'
Meanwhile I heard a voice: 'Be honour shown
To the illustrious poet,[231] for his shade
Is now returning which a while was gone.'
When the voice paused nor further utterance made,
Four mighty shades drew near with one accord,
In aspect neither sorrowful nor glad.

‘Consider that one, armèd with a sword,’[232]
Began my worthy Master in my ear,
‘Before the three advancing like their lord;
For he is Homer, poet with no peer:
Horace the satirist is next in line,
Ovid comes third, and Lucan in the rear.
And ’tis because their claim agrees with mine
Upon the name they with one voice did cry,
They to their honour[233] in my praise combine.’
Thus I beheld their goodly company—
The lords[234] of song in that exalted style
Which o’er all others, eagle-like, soars high.
Having conferred among themselves a while
They turned toward me and salutation made,
And, this beholding, did my Master smile.[235]
And honour higher still to me was paid,
For of their company they made me one;
So I the sixth part ’mong such genius played.
Thus journeyed we to where the brightness shone,
Holding discourse which now ’tis well to hide,
As, where I was, to hold it was well done.
At length we reached a noble castle’s[236] side
Which lofty sevenfold walls encompassed round,
And it was moated by a sparkling tide.
This we traversed as if it were dry ground;
I through seven gates did with those sages go;
Then in a verdant mead people we found
Whose glances were deliberate and slow.
Authority was stamped on every face;

Seldom they spake, in tuneful voices low.
We drew apart to a high open space
Upon one side which, luminously serene,
Did of them all a perfect view embrace.
Thence, opposite, on the enamel green
Were shown me mighty spirits; with delight
I still am stirred them only to have seen.
With many more, Electra was in sight;
'Mong them I Hector and Æneas spied,
Cæsar in arms,[237] his eyes, like falcon's, bright.
And, opposite, Camilla I descried;
Penthesilea too; the Latian King
Sat with his child Lavinia by his side. Brutus[238]
I saw, who Tarquin forth did fling;Cornelia,
Marcia,[239] Julia, and Lucrece.
Saladin[240] sat alone. Considering
What lay beyond with somewhat lifted eyes,
The Master[241] I beheld of those that know, '
Mong such as in philosophy were wise.
All gazed on him as if toward him to show
Becoming honour; Plato in advance
With Socrates: the others stood below.
Democritus[242] who set the world on chance;
Thales, Diogenes, Empedocles,
Zeno, and Anaxagoras met my glance;
Heraclitus, and Dioscorides,
Wise judge of nature. Tully, Orpheus, were
With ethic Seneca and Linus.[243] These,
And Ptolemy,[244] too, and Euclid, geometer,

Galen, Hippocrates, and Avicen,[245]

Averroes,[246] the same who did prepare

The Comment, saw I; nor can tell again

The names of all I saw; the subject wide

So urgent is, time often fails me.

Then Into two bands the six of us divide;

Me by another way my Leader wise

Doth from the calm to air which trembles, guide.

I reach a part[247] which all benighted lies.

FOOTNOTES:

220. Thundering sound: In a state of unconsciousness, Dante, he knows not how, has been conveyed across Acheron, and is awakened by what seems like the thunder-peal following the lightning-flash which made him insensible. He now stands on the brink of Inferno, where the sounds peculiar to each region of it converge and are reverberated from its rim. These sounds are not again to be heard by him except in their proper localities. No sooner does he actually pass into the First Circle than he hears only sighs.—As regards the topography of Inferno, it is enough, as yet, to note that it consists of a cavity extending from the surface to the centre of the earth; narrowing to its base, and with many circular ledges or terraces, of great width in the case of the upper ones, running round its wall—that is, round the sides of the pit. Each terrace or circle is thus less in circumference than the one above it. From one circle to the next there slopes a bank of more or less height and steepness. Down the bank which falls to the comparatively flat ground of the First Circle they are now about to pass.—To put it otherwise, the Inferno is an inverted hollow cone.

221. Pity: The pity felt by Virgil has reference only to those in the circle they are about to enter, which is his own. See also Purg. iii. 43.

222. Wouldst thou, etc.: He will not have Dante form a false opinion of the character of those condemned to the circle which is his own.

223. Part: parte, altered by some editors into porta; but though baptism is technically described as the gate of the sacraments, it never is as the gate of the faith. A tenet of Dante's faith was that all the unbaptized are lost. He had no choice in the matter.

224. Limbo: Border, or borderland. Dante makes the First Circle consist of the two limbos of Thomas Aquinas: that of unbaptized infants, limbus puerorum, and that of the fathers of the old covenant, limbus sanctorum patrum. But the second he finds is now inhabited only by the virtuous heathen.

225. Sir—Master: As a delicate means of expressing sympathy, Dante redoubles hiscourtesy to Virgil.

226. Hidden drift: to find out, at first hand as it were, if the article in the creed is truewhich relates to the Descent into Hell; and, perhaps, to learn if when Christ descendedHe delivered none of the virtuous heathen.

227. Lately: Virgil died about half a century before the crucifixion.

228. A Potentate: The name of Christ is not mentioned in the Inferno.

229. A hemisphere, etc.: An elaborate way of saying that part of the limbo was clearly lit. The flame is symbolical of the light of genius, or of virtue; both in Dante's eyes being modes of worth.

230. Wins grace, etc.: The thirst for fame was one keenly felt and openly confessed by Dante. See, e.g. De Monarchia, i. 1. In this he anticipated the humanists of the followingcentury. Here we find that to be famous on earth helps the case of disembodied souls.

231. Poet: Throughout the Comedy, with the exception of Parad. i. 29, and xxv. 8, the term 'poet' is confined to those who wrote in Greek and Latin. In Purg. xxi. 85 the name of poet is said to be that 'which is most enduring and honourable.'

232. A sword: Because Homer sings of battles. Dante's acquaintance with his workscan have been but slight, as they were not then translated into Latin, and Dante knew little or no Greek.

233. To their honour: 'And in that they do well:' perhaps as showing themselves freefrom jealousy. But the remark of Benvenuto of Imola is: 'Poets love and honour one another, and are never envious and quarrelsome like those who cultivate the other arts and sciences.'—I quote with misgiving from Tamburini's untrustworthy Italian translation. Benvenuto lectured on the Comedy in Bologna for some years about 1370.It is greatly to be wished that his commentary, lively and full of side-lights as it is, should be printed in full from the original Latin.

234. The lords, etc.: Not the company of him—Homer or Virgil—who is lord of the great song, and soars above all others; but the company of the great masters, whose verse, etc.

235. Did my Master smile: To see Dante made free of the guild of great poets; or, it may be, to think they are about to discover in him a fellow poet.

236. A noble castle: Where the light burns, and in which, as their peculiar seat, the shades of the heathen distinguished for virtue and genius reside. The seven walls are in their number symbolical of the perfect strength of the castle; or, to take it more pedantically, may mean the four moral virtues and the three speculative. The gates will then stand for the seven liberal arts of grammar, rhetoric, etc. The moat may be eloquence, set outside the castle to signify that only as reflected in the eloquent wordsof inspired men can the outside world get to know wisdom. Over the stream Dante passes easily, as being an adept in learned speech. The castle encloses a spacious mead enamelled with eternal green.

237. Cæsar in arms, etc.: Suetonius says of Cæsar that he was of fair complexion, but had black and piercing eyes. Brunetto Latini, Dante's teacher, says in his Tesoro (v. 11), of the hawk here mentioned—the grifagno—that its eyes 'flame like fire.'

238. Brutus: Introduced here that he may not be confounded with the later Brutus, forwhom is reserved the lowest place of all in Inferno.

239. Marcia: Wife of Cato; mentioned also in Purg. i. Julia: daughter of Cæsar and wife of Pompey.

240. Saladin: Died 1193. To the thirteenth and fourteenth centuries he supplied the ideal of a just Mohammedan ruler. Here are no other such. 'He sits apart, because notof gentle birth,' says Boccaccio; which shows what even a man of genius risks when he becomes a commentator.

241. The Master: Aristotle, often spoken of by Dante as the Philosopher, and reverenced by him as the genius to whom the secrets of nature lay most open.

242. Democritus, etc.: According to whom the world owes its form to a chance arrangement of atoms.

243. Linus: Not Livy, into which some have changed it. Linus is mentioned by Virgilalong with Orpheus, Egl. iv.

244. Ptolemy: Greek geographer of the beginning of the second century, and author of the system of the world believed in by Dante, and freely used by him throughout the poem.

245. Avicenna: A physician, born in Bokhara, and died at Ispahan, 1037. His MedicalCanon was for centuries used as a text-book in Europe.

246. Averroes: A Mohammedan philosopher of Cordova, died 1198. In his great Commentary on Aristotle he gives and explains every sentence of that philosopher's works. He was himself ignorant of Greek, and made use of Arabic versions. Out of his Arabic the Commentary was translated into Hebrew, and thence into Latin. The presence of the three Mohammedans in this honourable place greatly puzzles the earlycommentators.

247. A part, etc.: He passes into the darkness of the Limbo out of the brightly-lit, fortified enclosure. It is worth remarking, as one reads, how vividly he describes his first impression of a new scene, while when he comes to leave it a word is all he speaks.

CANTO V.

From the First Circle thus I downward went
Into the Second,[248] which girds narrower space,
But greater woe compelling loud lament.
Minos[249] waits awful there and snarls, the case
Examining of all who enter in;
And, as he girds him, dooms them to their place.
I say, each ill-starred spirit must begin
On reaching him its guilt in full to tell;
And he, omniscient as concerning sin,
Sees to what circle it belongs in Hell;
Then round him is his tail as often curled
As he would have it stages deep to dwell.
And evermore before him stand a world
Of shades; and all in turn to judgment come,
Confess and hear, and then are downward hurled.[250]
'O thou who comest to the very home
Of woe,' when he beheld me Minos cried,
Ceasing a while from utterance of doom,
'Enter not rashly nor in all confide;
By ease of entering be not led astray.'
'Why also[251] growling?' answered him my Guide;
'Seek not his course predestinate to stay;
For thus 'tis willed[252] where nothing ever fails
Of what is willed. No further speech essay.'
And now by me are agonising wails
Distinguished plain; now am I come outright

Where grievous lamentation me assails.
Now had I reached a place devoid of light,
Raging as in a tempest howls the sea
When with it winds, blown thwart each other, fight.
The infernal storm is raging ceaselessly,
Sweeping the shades along with it, and them
It smites and whirls, nor lets them ever be.
Arrived at the precipitous extreme,[253]
In shrieks and lamentations they complain,
And even the Power Divine itself blaspheme.
I understood[254] that to this mode of pain
Are doomed the sinners of the carnal kind,
Who o'er their reason let their impulse reign.
As starlings in the winter-time combined
Float on the wing in crowded phalanx wide,
So these bad spirits, driven by that wind,
Float up and down and veer from side to side
;Nor for their comfort any hope they spy
Of rest, or even of suffering mollified.
And as the cranes[255] in long-drawn company
Pursue their flight while uttering their song,
So I beheld approach with wailing cry
Shades lifted onward by that whirlwind strong.
'Master, what folk are these,'[256] I therefore said,
'Who by the murky air are whipped along?'
'She, first of them,' his answer thus was made,
'Of whom thou wouldst a wider knowledge win
,O'er many tongues and peoples, empire swayed.
So ruined was she by licentious sin

That she decreed lust should be uncontrolled,

To ease the shame that she herself was in.

She is Semiramis, of whom 'tis told

She followed Ninus, and his wife had been.

Hers were the realms now by the Sultan ruled.

The next[257] is she who, amorous and self-slain,

Unto Sichæus' dust did faithless show:

Then lustful Cleopatra.' Next was seen

Helen, for whom so many years in woe

Ran out; and I the great Achilles knew,

Who at the last[258] encountered love for foe.Paris

I saw and Tristram.[259] In review

A thousand shades and more, he one by one

Pointed and named, whom love from life withdrew

.And after I had heard my Teacher run

O'er many a dame of yore and many a knight,

I, lost in pity, was wellnigh undone.

Then I: 'O Poet, if I only might

Speak with the two that as companions hie,

And on the wind appear to be so light!'[260]

And he to me: 'When they shall come more nigh

Them shalt thou mark, and by the love shalt pray

Which leads them onward, and they will comply.'

Soon as the wind bends them to where we stayI lift my voice:

'O wearied souls and worn!

Come speak with us if none[261] the boon gainsay.'

Then even as doves,[262] urged by desire, return

On outspread wings and firm to their sweet nest

As through the air by mere volition borne,

From Dido's[263] band those spirits issuing pressed
Towards where we were, athwart the air malign;
My passionate prayer such influence possessed.
'O living creature,[264] gracious and benign,
Us visiting in this obscurèd air,
Who did the earth with blood incarnadine;
If in the favour of the King we were
Who rules the world, we for thy peace[265] would pray,
Since our misfortunes thy compassion stir.
Whate'er now pleases thee to hear or say
We listen to, or tell, at your demand;[266]
While yet the wind, as now, doth silent stay.
My native city[267] lies upon the strand
Where to the sea descends the river Po
For peace, with all his tributary band.
Love, in a generous heart set soon aglow,
Seized him for the fair form was mine above;
And still it irks me to have lost it so.[268]
Love, which absolves[269] no one beloved from love,
So strong a passion for him in me wrought
That, as thou seest, I still its mastery prove.
Love led us where we in one death were caught.
For him who slew us waits Caïna[270] now.'
Unto our ears these words from them were brought.
When I had heard these troubled souls, my brow
I downward bent, and long while musing stayed,
Until the Poet asked: 'What thinkest thou?'
And when I answered him, 'Alas!' I said,
'Sweet thoughts how many, and what strong desire,

These to their sad catastrophe betrayed!'

Then, turned once more to them, I to inquireBegan:

'Francesca, these thine agonies

Me with compassion unto tears inspire.

But tell me, at the season of sweet sighs

What sign made love, and what the means he chose

To strip your dubious longings of disguise?'

And she to me: 'The bitterest of woesIs to remember in the midst of pain

A happy past; as well thy teacher[271] knows.

Yet none the less, and since thou art so fain

The first occasion of our love to hear,

Like one I speak that cannot tears restrain.

As we for pastime one day reading were

How Lancelot[272] by love was fettered fast—

All by ourselves and without any fear—

Moved by the tale our eyes we often cast

On one another, and our colour fled;

But one word was it, vanquished us at last.

When how the smile, long wearied for, we read

Was kissed by him who loved like none before,

This one, who henceforth never leaves me, laid

A kiss on my mouth, trembling the while all o'er.

The book was Galahad,[273] and he as well

Who wrote the book. That day we read no more.'

And while one shade continued thus to tell,

The other wept so bitterly, I swooned

Away for pity, and as dead I fell:

Yea, as a corpse falls, fell I on the ground.

FOOTNOTES:

248. The Second: The Second Circle of the Inferno, and the first of punishment. The lower the circle, the more rigorous the penalty endured in it. Here is punished carnal sin.

249. Minos: Son of Jupiter and King of Crete, so severely just as to be made after death one of the judges of the under world. He is degraded by Dante, as many other noble persons of the old mythology are by him, into a demon. Unlike the fallen angelsof Milton, Dante's devils have no interest of their own. Their only function is to help in working out human destinies.

250. Downward hurled: Each falls to his proper place without lingering by the way. All through Inferno there is an absence of direct Divine interposition. It is ruled, as it were, by a course of nature. The sinners, compelled by a fatal impulse, advance to heartheir doom, just as they fall inevitably one by one into Charon's boat. Minos by a sortof devilish instinct sentences each sinner to his appropriate punishment. In Inf. xxvii. 127 we find the words in which Minos utters his judgment. In Inf. xxi. 29 a devil bearsthe sinner to his own place.

251. Why also, etc.: Like Charon. If Minos represents conscience, as some would have it, Dante is here again assailed by misgivings as to his enterprise, and is quieted by reason in the person of Virgil.

252. Thus 'tis willed, etc.: These two lines are the same as those to Charon, Inf. iii.95, 96.

253. Precipitous extreme: Opinions vary as to what is meant by ruina. As Dante is certainly still on the outer edge of the Second Circle or terrace, and while standing there hears distinctly the words the spirits say when they reach the ruina, it most likely denotes the steep slope falling from the First to the Second Circle. The spirits, driven against the wall which hems them in, burst into sharp lamentations against theirirremediable fate.

254. I understood, etc.: From the nature of the punishment, which, like all the othersinvented by Dante, bears some relation to the sin to which it is assigned. They who onearth failed to exercise self-restraint are beaten hither and thither by every wind that blows; and, as once they were blinded by passion, so now they see nothing plainly in that dim and obscure place. That Dante should assign the least grievous punishment of all to this sin throws light upon his views of life. In his eyes it had more than any other the excuse of natural bent, and had least of malice. Here, it must be remarked, areno seducers. For them a lower depth is reserved (Inf. xviii. See also Purg. xxvii. 15).

255. The cranes: 'The cranes are a kind of bird that go in a troop, as cavaliers go to battle, following one another in single file. And one of them goes always in front as their gonfalonier, guiding and leading them with its voice' (Brunetto

Latini, Tesoro, v. 27).

256. What folk are these: The general crowd of sinners guilty of unlawful love are described as being close packed like starlings. The other troop, who go in single file like cranes, are those regarding whom Dante specially inquires; and they prove to be the nobler sort of sinners—lovers with something tragic or pathetic in their fate.

257. The next: Dido, perhaps not named by Virgil because to him she owed her fame. For love of Æneas she broke the vow of perpetual chastity made on the tomb of her husband.

258. At the last, etc.: Achilles, when about to espouse Polyxena, and when off his guard, was slain.

259. Paris ... and Tristram: Paris of Troy, and the Tristram of King Arthur's Table.

260. So light: Denoting the violence of the passion to which they had succumbed.

261. If none: If no Superior Power.

262. Doves: The motion of the tempest-driven shades is compared to the flight of birds—starlings, cranes, and doves. This last simile prepares us for the tenderness of Francesca's tale.

263. Dido: Has been already indicated, and is now named. This association of the twolovers with Virgil's Dido is a further delicate touch to engage our sympathy; for her love, though illicit, was the infirmity of a noble heart.

264. Living creature: 'Animal.' No shade, but an animated body.

265. Thy peace: Peace from all the doubts that assail him, and which have compelledhim to the journey: peace, it may be, from temptation to sin cognate to her own. Evenin the gloom of Inferno her great goodheartedness is left her—a consolation, if not a grace.

266. Your demand: By a refinement of courtesy, Francesca, though addressing only Dante, includes Virgil in her profession of willingness to tell all they care to hear. Butas almost always, he remains silent. It is not for his good the journey is being made.

267. Native city: Ravenna. The speaker is Francesca, daughter of Guido of Polenta, lord of Ravenna. About the year 1275 she was married to Gianciotto (Deformed John)Malatesta, son of the lord of Rimini; the marriage, like most of that time in the class towhich she belonged, being one of political convenience. She allowed her affections tosettle on Paolo, her husband's handsome brother; and Gianciotto's suspicions having been aroused, he surprised the lovers and slew them on the spot. This happened at Pesaro. The association of Francesca's

name with Rimini is merely accidental. The date of her death is not known. Dante can never have set eyes on Francesca; but at the battle of Campaldino in 1289, where he was present, a troop of cavaliers from Pistoia fought on the Florentine side under the command of her brother Bernardino; and in the following year, Dante being then twenty-five years of age, her father, Guido, was Podesta in Florence. The Guido of Polenta, lord of Ravenna, whom Dante had for his last and most generous patron, was grandson of that elder Guido, and nephew of Francesca.

268. To have lost it so: A husband's right and duty were too well defined in the prevalent social code for her to complain that Gianciotto avenged himself. What she does resent is that she was left no breathing-space for repentance and farewells.

269. Which absolves, etc.: Which compels whoever is beloved to love in return. Here is the key to Dante's comparatively lenient estimate of the guilt of Francesca's sin. See line 39, and Inf. xi. 83. The Church allowed no distinctions with regard to the lost. Dante, for his own purposes, invents a scale of guilt; and in settling the degrees of it he is greatly influenced by human feeling—sometimes by private likes and dislikes. The vestibule of the caitiffs, e.g., is his own creation.

270. Caïna: The Division of the Ninth and lowest Circle, assigned to those treacherous to their kindred (Inf. xxxii. 58). Her husband was still living in 1300.—May not the words of this line be spoken by Paolo? It is as a fratricide even more than as the slayer of his wife that Gianciotto is to find his place in Caïna. The words are more in keeping with the masculine than the feminine character. They certainly jar somewhat with the gentler censure of line 102. And, immediately after, Dante speaks of what the 'souls' have said.

271. Thy teacher: Boethius, one of Dante's favourite authors (Convito ii. 13), says in his De Consol. Phil., 'The greatest misery in adverse fortune is once to have been happy.' But, granting that Dante found the idea in Boethius, it is clearly Virgil that Francesca means. She sees that Dante's guide is a shade, and gathers from his grave passionless aspect that he is one condemned for ever to look back with futile regret upon his happier past.

272. Lancelot: King Arthur's famous knight, who was too bashful to make his love for Queen Guinivere known to her. Galahad, holding the secret of both, persuaded the Queen to make the first declaration of love at a meeting he arranged for between them. Her smile, or laugh, as she 'took Lancelot by the chin and kissed him,' assured her lover of his conquest. The Arthurian Romances were the favourite reading of the Italian nobles of Dante's time.

273. Galahad: From the part played by Galahad, or Galeotto, in the tale of Lancelot, his name grew to be Italian for Pander. The book, says Francesca, was that which tells of Galahad; and the author of it proved a very Galahad to us. The early editions of the Decameron bear the second title of 'The Prince Galeotto.'

CANTO VI.

When I regained my senses, which had fled
At my compassion for the kindred two,
Which for pure sorrow quite had turned my head,
New torments and a crowd of sufferers new
I see around me as I move again,[274]
Where'er I turn, where'er I bend my view.
In the Third Circle am I of the rain
Which, heavy, cold, eternal, big with woe,
Doth always of one kind and force remain.
Large hail and turbid water, mixed with snow,
Keep pouring down athwart the murky air;
And from the ground they fall on, stenches grow.
The savage Cerberus,[275] a monster drear,
Howls from his threefold throat with canine cries
Above the people who are whelmèd there.
Oily and black his beard, and red his eyes,
His belly huge: claws from his fingers sprout.
The shades he flays, hooks, rends in cruel wise.
Beat by the rain these, dog-like, yelp and shout,
And shield themselves in turn with either side;
And oft[276] the wretched sinners turn about.
When we by Cerberus, great worm,[277] were spied,
He oped his mouths and all his fangs he showed,
While not a limb did motionless abide.
My Leader having spread his hands abroad,
Filled both his fists with earth ta'en from the ground,

And down the ravening gullets flung the load.
Then, as sharp set with hunger barks the hound,
But is appeased when at his meat he gnaws,
And, worrying it, forgets all else around;
So with those filthy faces there it was
Of the fiend Cerberus, who deafs the crowd
Of souls till they from hearing fain would pause
.We, travelling o'er the spirits who lay cowed
And sorely by the grievous showers harassed,
Upon their semblances[278] of bodies trod.
Prone on the ground the whole of them were cast
,Save one of them who sat upright with speed
When he beheld that near to him we passed.
'O thou who art through this Inferno led,[279]
Me if thou canst,' he asked me, 'recognise;
For ere I was dismantled thou wast made.'
And I to him: 'Thy present tortured guise
Perchance hath blurred my memory of thy face,
Until it seems I ne'er on thee set eyes.
But tell me who thou art, within this place
So cruel set, exposed to such a pain,
Than which, if greater, none has more disgrace.'
And he: 'Thy city, swelling with the bane
Of envy till the sack is running o'er,
Me in the life serene did once contain.
As Ciacco[280] me your citizens named of yore;
And for the damning sin of gluttony
I, as thou seest, am beaten by this shower.
No solitary woful soul am I,

For all of these endure the selfsame doom
For the same fault.' Here ended his reply.
I answered him, 'O Ciacco, with such gloom
Thy misery weighs me, I to weep am prone;
But, if thou canst, declare to what shall come
The citizens[281] of the divided town.
Holds it one just man? And declare the cause
Why 'tis of discord such a victim grown.'
Then he to me: 'After[282] contentious pause
Blood will be spilt; the boorish party[283] then
Will chase the others forth with grievous loss.
The former it behoves to fall again
Within three suns, the others to ascend,
Holpen[284] by him whose wiles ere now are plain.
Long time, with heads held high, they'll make to bend
The other party under burdens dire,
Howe'er themselves in tears and rage they spend.
There are two just[285] men, at whom none inquire.
Envy, and pride, and avarice, even these
Are the three sparks have set all hearts on fire.'
With this the tearful sound he made to cease:
And I to him, 'Yet would I have thee tell—
And of thy speech do thou the gift increase—
Tegghiaio[286] and Farinata, honourable,
James Rusticucci,[287] Mosca, Arrigo,
With all the rest so studious to excel
In good; where are they? Help me this to know;
Great hunger for the news hath seizèd me;
Delights them Heaven, or tortures Hell below?'

He said: 'Among the blackest souls they be;
Them to the bottom weighs another sin.
Shouldst thou so far descend, thou mayst them see.
But when[288] the sweet world thou again dost win
,I pray thee bring me among men to mind;
No more I tell, nor new reply begin.'
Then his straightforward eyes askance declined;
He looked at me a moment ere his head
He bowed; then fell flat 'mong the other blind
.'Henceforth he waketh not,' my Leader said,
'Till he shall hear the angel's trumpet sound,
Ushering the hostile Judge.
By every shadeIts dismal sepulchre shall then be found,
Its flesh and ancient form it shall resume,
And list[289] what echoes in eternal round.'
So passed we where the shades and rainy spume
Made filthy mixture, with steps taken slow;
Touching a little on the world to come.[290]
Wherefore I said: 'Master, shall torments grow
After the awful sentence hath been heard,
Or lesser prove and not so fiercely glow?'
'Repair unto thy Science,'[291] was his word
;'Which tells, as things approach a perfect state
To keener joy or suffering they are stirred.
Therefore although this people cursed by fate
Ne'er find perfection in its full extent,
To it they then shall more approximate
Than now.'[292] Our course we round the circle bent,
Still holding speech, of which I nothing say,

Until we came where down the pathway went:

There found we Plutus, the great enemy.

FOOTNOTES:

274. As I move again: In his swoon he has been conveyed from the Second Circle down to the Third.

275. Cerberus: In the Greek mythology Cerberus is the watch-dog of the under world.By Dante he is converted into a demon, and with his three throats, canine voracity, and ugly inflamed bulk, is appropriately set to guard the entrance to the circle of the gluttonous and wine-bibbers.

276. And oft, etc.: On entering the circle the shades are seized and torn by Cerberus;once over-nice in how they fed, they are now treated as if they were food for dogs. But their enduring pain is to be subjected to every kind of physical discomfort. Their senses of hearing, touch, and smell are assailed by the opposite of what they were most used to enjoy at their luxurious feasts.

277. Great worm: Though human in a monstrous form, Cerberus is so called as beinga disgusting brute.

278. Semblances, etc.: 'Emptiness which seems to be a person.' To this conception of the shades as only seeming to have bodies, Dante has difficulty in remaining true. For instance, at line 101 they mix with the sleet to make a sludgy mass; and cannot therefore be impalpable.

279. Ciacco at once perceives by the weight of Dante's tread that he is a living man.

280. Ciacco: The name or nickname of a Florentine wit, and, in his day, a great diner- out. Boccaccio, in his commentary, says that, though poor, Ciacco associated with men of birth and wealth, especially such as ate and drank delicately. In the Decameron, ix. 8, he is introduced as being on such terms with the great Corso Donati as to be ableto propose himself to dinner with him. Clearly he was not a bad fellow, and his pitifulcase, perhaps contrasted with the high spirits and jovial surroundings in which he waslast met by Dante, almost, though not quite, win a tear from the stern pilgrim.

281. The citizens, etc.: Dante eagerly confers on Florentine politics with the first Florentine he encounters in Inferno.

282. After, etc.: In the following nine lines the party history of Florence for two yearsafter the period of the poem (March 1300) is roughly indicated. The city was divided into two factions—the Whites, led by the great merchant Vieri dei

Cerchi, and the Blacks, led by Corso Donati, a poor and turbulent noble. At the close of 1300 there wasa bloody encounter between the more violent members of the two parties. In May 1301 the Blacks were banished. In the autumn of that year they returned in triumph to the city in the train of Charles of Valois, and got the Whites banished in April 1302, withinthree years, that is, of the poet's talk with Ciacco. Dante himself was associated with the Whites, but not as a violent partisan; for though he was a strong politician no partyquite answered his views. From the middle of June till the middle of August 1300 he was one of the Priors. In the course of 1301 he is believed to have gone on an embassy to Rome to persuade the Pope to abstain from meddling in Florentine affairs. He never entered Florence again, being condemned virtually to banishment in January 1302.

283. The boorish party: la parte selvaggia. The Whites; but what is exactly meant byselvaggia is not clear. Literally it is 'woodland,' and some say it refers to the Cerchi having originally come from a well-wooded district; which is absurd. Nor, takingthe word in its secondary meaning of savage, does it apply better to one party than another—not so well, perhaps, to the Whites as to the Blacks. Villani also terms the Cerchi salvatichi (viii. 39), and in a connection where it may mean rude, ill-mannered.I take it that Dante here indulges in a gibe at the party to which he once belonged, butwhich, ere he began the Comedy, he had quite broken with. In Parad. xvii. 62 he termsthe members of it 'wicked and stupid.' The sneer in the text would come well enoughfrom the witty and soft-living Ciacco.

284. Holpen, etc.: Pope Boniface, already intriguing to gain the preponderance in Florence, which for a time he enjoyed, with the greedy and faithless Charles of Valois for his agent.

285. Two just: Dante and another, unknown. He thus distinctly puts from himself any blame for the evil turn things had taken in Florence. How thoroughly he had broken with his party ere he wrote this is proved by his exclusion of the irresolute butrespectable Vieri dei Cerchi from the number of the just men. He, in Dante's judgment,was only too much listened to.—It will be borne in mind that, at the time assigned to the action of the Comedy, Dante was still resident in Florence.

286. Tegghiaio: See Inf. xvi. 42. Farinata: Inf. x. 32.

287. Rusticucci: Inf. xvi. 44. Mosca: Inf. xxviii. 106. Arrigo: Cannot be identified. All these distinguished Florentines we may assume to have been hospitable patrons of Ciacco's.

288. But when, etc.: In the Inferno many such prayers are addressed to Dante. The shades in Purgatory ask to have their friends on earth stirred to offer up petitions for their speedy purification and deliverance; but the only alleviation possible for the doomed spirits is to know that they are not yet forgotten up in

the 'sweet world.' A double artistic purpose is served by representing them as feeling thus. It relieves the mind to think that in such misery there is any source of comfort at all. And by making thembe still interested on their own account in the thoughts of men, the eager colloquies inwhich they engage with Dante on such unequal terms gain in verisimilitude.

289. . And list, etc.: The final sentence against them is to echo, in its results, through all eternity.

290. The world to come: The life after doomsday.

291. Thy Science: To Aristotle. In the Convito, iv. 16, he quotes 'the Philosopher' as teaching that 'everything is then at its full perfection when it thoroughly fulfils its special functions.'

292. Than now: Augustine says that 'after the resurrection of the flesh the joys of theblessed and the sufferings of the wicked will be enhanced.' And, according to Thomas Aquinas, 'the soul, without the body, is wanting in the perfection designed for it by Nature.'

CANTO VII.

Pape[293] Satan! Pape Satan! Aleppe!
Plutus[294] began in accents rough and hard:
And that mild Sage, all-knowing, said to me,
For my encouragement: 'Pay no regard
Unto thy fear; whatever power he sways
Thy passage down this cliff shall not be barred.'
Then turning round to that inflamèd face
He bade: 'Accursed wolf,[295] at peace remain;
And, pent within thee, let thy fury blaze.
Down to the pit we journey not in vain:
So rule they where by Michael in Heaven's height
On the adulterous pride[296] was vengeance ta'en.'
Then as the bellied sails, by wind swelled tight,
Suddenly drag whenever snaps the mast;
Such, falling to the ground, the monster's plight
.To the Fourth Cavern so we downward passed,
Winning new reaches of the doleful shore
Where all the vileness of the world is cast.
Justice of God! which pilest more and more
Pain as I saw, and travail manifold!
Why will we sin, to be thus wasted sore?
As at Charybdis waves are forward rolled
To break on other billows midway met,
The people here a counterdance must hold.
A greater crowd than I had seen as yet,
With piercing yells advanced on either track,

Rolling great stones to which their chests were set
.They crashed together, and then each turned back
Upon the way he came, while shouts arise,
'Why clutch it so?' and 'Why to hold it slack?'
In the dark circle wheeled they on this wise
From either hand to the opposing part,
Where evermore they raised insulting cries.
Thither arrived, each, turning, made fresh start
Through the half circle[297] a new joust to run;
And I, stung almost to the very heart,
Said, 'O my Master, wilt thou make it known
Who the folk are? Were these all clerks[298] who go
Before us on the left, with shaven crown?'
And he replied: 'All of them squinted so
In mental vision while in life they were,
They nothing spent by rule. And this they show,
And with their yelping voices make appear
When half-way round the circle they have sped,
And sins opposing them asunder tear.
Each wanting thatch of hair upon his head
Was once a clerk, or pope, or cardinal,
In whom abound the ripest growths of greed.'
And I: 'O Master, surely among all
Of these I ought[299] some few to recognise,
Who by such filthy sins were held in thrall.'
And he to me: 'Vain thoughts within thee rise;
Their witless life, which made them vile, now mocks—
Dimming[300] their faces still—all searching eyes.
Eternally they meet with hostile shocks;

These rising from the tomb at last shall stand
With tight clenched fists, and those with ruined locks.[301]
Squandering or hoarding, they the happy land[302]
Have lost, and now are marshalled for this fray;
Which to describe doth no fine words demand.
Know hence, my Son, how fleeting is the play
Of goods at the dispose of Fortune thrown,
And which mankind to such fierce strife betray.
Not all the gold which is beneath the moon
Could purchase peace, nor all that ever was,
To but one soul of these by toil undone.'
'Master,' I said, 'tell thou, ere making pause,
Who Fortune is of whom thou speak'st askance,
Who holds all worldly riches in her claws.'[303]'
O foolish creatures, lost in ignorance!'
He answer made. 'Now see that the reply
Thou store, which I concerning her advance.
He who in knowledge is exalted high,
Framing[304] all Heavens gave such as should them guide,
That so each part might shine to all; whereby
Is equal light diffused on every side:
And likewise to one guide and governor,
Of worldly splendours did control confide,
That she in turns should different peoples dower
With this vain good; from blood should make it pass
To blood, in spite of human wit. Hence, power,
Some races failing,[305] other some amass,
According to her absolute decree
Which hidden lurks, like serpent in the grass.

Vain 'gainst her foresight yours must ever be
.She makes provision, judges, holds her reign,
As doth his power supreme each deity.
Her permutations can no truce sustain;
Necessity[306] compels her to be swift,
So swift they follow who their turn must gain.
And this is she whom they so often[307] lift
Upon the cross, who ought to yield her praise;
And blame on her and scorn unjustly shift.
But she is blest nor hears what any says,
With other primal creatures turns her sphere,
Jocund and glad, rejoicing in her ways.
To greater woe now let us downward steer.
The stars[308] which rose when I began to guide
Are falling now, nor may we linger here.'
We crossed the circle to the other side,
Arriving where a boiling fountain fell
Into a brooklet by its streams supplied.
In depth of hue the flood did perse[309] excel,
And we, with this dim stream to lead us on,
Descended by a pathway terrible.
A marsh which by the name of Styx is known,
Fed by this gloomy brook, lies at the base
Of threatening cliffs hewn out of cold grey stone.
And I, intent on study of the place,[310]
Saw people in that ditch, mud-smeared. In it
All naked stood with anger-clouded face.
Nor with their fists alone each fiercely hit
The other, but with feet and chest and head,

And with their teeth to shreds each other bit.
'Son, now behold,' the worthy Master said,
'The souls of those whom anger made a prize;
And, further, I would have thee certified
That 'neath the water people utter sighs,
And make the bubbles to the surface come;
As thou mayst see by casting round thine eyes.
Fixed in the mud they say: "We lived in gloom[311]
In the sweet air made jocund by the day,
Nursing within us melancholy fume.
In this black mud we now our gloom display."
This hymn with gurgling throats they strive to sound,
Which they in speech unbroken fail to say.'
And thus about the loathsome pool we wound
For a wide arc, between the dry and soft,
With eyes on those who gulp the filth, turned round.
At last we reached a tower that soared aloft.

FOOTNOTES:

293. Pape, etc.: These words have exercised the ingenuity of many scholars, who onthe whole lean to the opinion that they contain an appeal to Satan against the invasionof his domain. Virgil seems to have understood them, but the text leaves it doubtful whether Dante himself did. Later on, but there with an obvious purpose, we find a lineof pure gibberish (Inf. xxxi. 67).

294. Plutus: The god of riches; degraded here into a demon. He guards the Fourth Circle, which is that of the misers and spendthrifts.

295. Wolf: Frequently used by Dante as symbolical of greed.

296. Pride: Which in its way was a kind of greed—that of dominion. Similarly, the avarice represented by the wolf of Canto i. was seen to be the lust of aggrandisement. Virgil here answers Plutus's (supposed) appeal to Satan by referring to the higher Power, under whose protection he and his companion come.

297. The half circle: This Fourth Circle is divided half-way round between the misers and spendthrifts, and the two bands at set periods clash against one another in their vain effort to pass into the section belonging to the opposite party. Their condition is emblematical of their sins while in life. They were one-sided in their use of wealth; so here they can never complete the circle. The monotony of their employment andof their cries represents their subjection to one idea, and, as in life, so now, their displeasure is excited by nothing so much as by coming into contact with the failing opposite to their own. Yet they are set in the same circle because the sin of both arose from inordinate desire of wealth, the miser craving it to hoard, and the spendthrift to spend. In Purgatory also they are placed together (see Purg. xxii. 40). So, on Dante's scheme, liberality is allied to and dependent on a wise and reasonable frugality.— There is no hint of the enormous length of the course run by these shades. Far lower down, when the circles of the Inferno have greatly narrowed, the circuit is twenty-twomiles (Inf. xxix. 9).

298. Clerks: Churchmen. The tonsure is the sign that a man is of ecclesiastical condition. Many took the tonsure who never became priests.

299. I ought, etc.: Dante is astonished that he can pick out no greedy priest or friar ofhis acquaintance, when he had known so many.

300. Dimming, etc.: Their original disposition is by this time smothered by the predominance of greed. Dante treats these sinners with a special contemptuous bitterness. Scores of times since he became dependent on the generosity of others he must have watched how at a bare hint the faces of miser and spendthrift fell, while theireyes travelled vaguely beyond him, and their voices grew cold.

301. Ruined locks: 'A spendthrift will spend his very hair,' says an Italian proverb.

302. The happy land: Heaven.

303. Her claws: Dante speaks of Fortune as if she were a brutal and somewhat malicious power. In Virgil's answer there is a refutation of the opinion of Fortune given by Dante himself, in the Convito (iv. 11). After describing three ways in whichthe goods of Fortune come to men he says: 'In each of these three ways her injustice is manifest.' This part of the Convito Fraticelli seems almost to prove was written in 1297.

304. Framing, etc.: According to the scholastic theory of the world, each of the nine heavens was directed in its motion by intelligences, called angels by the vulgar, and by the heathen, gods (Convito ii. 5). As these spheres and the influences they exercise onhuman affairs are under the guidance of divinely-appointed ministers, so, Virgil says, is the distribution of worldly wealth ruled by Providence through Fortune.

305. Some races failing: It was long believed, nor is the belief quite obsolete, that one community can gain only at the expense of another. Sir Thomas Browne says: 'All cannot be happy at once; for because the glory of one state depends upon the ruin of another, there is a revolution and vicissitude of their greatness, and all must obey the swing of that wheel, not moved by intelligences, but by the hand of God, whereby all states arise to their zeniths and vertical points according to their predestinated periods.'—Rel. Med. i. 17.

306. Necessity, etc.: Suggested, perhaps, by Horace's Te semper anteit sæva necessitas (Od. i. 35). The question of how men can be free in the face of necessity, here associated with Fortune, more than once emerges in the Comedy. Dante's belief on the subject was substantially that of his favourite author Boethius, who holds that ultimately 'it is Providence that turns the wheel of all things;' and who says, that 'if you spread your sails to the wind you will be carried, not where you would, but whither you are driven by the gale: if you choose to commit yourself to Fortune, you must endure the manners of your mistress.'

307. Whom they so often, etc.: Treat with contumely.

308. The stars, etc.: It is now past midnight, and towards the morning of Saturday, the 26th of March 1300. Only a few hours have been employed as yet upon the journey.

309. Perse: 'Perse is a colour between purple and black, but the black predominates' (Conv. iv. 20). The hue of the waters of Styx agrees with the gloomy temper of the sinners plunged in them.

310. The place: They are now in the Fifth Circle, where the wrathful are punished.

311. In gloom: These submerged spirits are, according to the older commentators, the slothful—those guilty of the sin of slackness in the pursuit of good, as, e.g. neglect of the means of grace. This is, theologically speaking, the sin directly opposed to the active grace of charity. By more modern critics it has been ingeniously sought to find in this circle a place not only for the slothful but for the proud and envious as well. To each of these classes of sinners—such of them as have repented in this life—a terrace of Purgatory is assigned, and at first sight it does seem natural to expect that the impenitent among them should be found in Inferno. But, while in Purgatory souls purge themselves of every kind of mortal sin, Inferno, as Dante conceived of it, contains only such sinners as have been guilty of wicked acts. Drift and bent of heart and mind are taken no account of. The evil seed must have borne a harvest, and the guilt of every victim of Justice must be plain and open. Now, pride and envy are sins indeed, but sins that a man may keep to himself. If they have betrayed the subject of them into the commission of crimes, in those crimes they are punished lower down, as is indicated at xii. 49. And so we find

that Lucifer is condemned as a traitor, thoughhis treachery sprang from envy: the greater guilt includes the less. For sluggishness in the pursuit of good the vestibule of the caitiffs seems the appropriate place.—There are two kinds of wrath. One is vehement, and declares itself in violent acts; the other does not blaze out, but is grudging and adverse to all social good—the wrath that is nursed. One as much as the other affects behaviour. So in this circle, as in the preceding, we have represented the two excesses of one sin.—Dante's theory of sins is ably treated of in Witte's Dante-Forschungen,

CANTO VIII.

I say, continuing,[312] that long before
To its foundations we approachèd nigh
Our eyes went travelling to the top of the tower;
For, hung out there, two flames[313] we could espy.
Then at such distance, scarce our eyesight made
It clearly out, another gave reply.
And, to the Sea of Knowledge turned,
I said: 'What meaneth this? and what reply would yield
That other light, and who have it displayed?'
'Thou shouldst upon the impure watery field,'
He said, 'already what approaches know,
But that the fen-fog holds it still concealed.'
Never was arrow yet from sharp-drawn bow
Urged through the air upon a swifter flight
Than what I saw a tiny vessel show,
Across the water shooting into sight;
A single pilot served it for a crew,
Who shouted: 'Art thou come, thou guilty sprite?'[314]
'O Phlegyas, Phlegyas,[315] this thy loud halloo!
For once,' my Lord said, 'idle is and vain0
Thou hast us only till the mud we're through.'
And, as one cheated inly smarts with pain
When the deceit wrought on him is betrayed,
His gathering ire could Phlegyas scarce contain.
Into the bark my Leader stepped, and made
Me take my place beside him; nor a jot,

Till I had entered, was it downward weighed.
Soon as my Guide and I were in the boat,
To cleave the flood began the ancient prow,
Deeper[316] than 'tis with others wont to float.
Then, as the stagnant ditch we glided through,
One smeared with filth in front of me arose
And said: 'Thus coming ere thy period,[317] who
Art thou?' And I: 'As one who forthwith goes
I come; but thou defiled, how name they thee?'
'I am but one who weeps,'[318] he said. 'With woes,'
I answered him, 'with tears and misery,
Accursèd soul, remain; for thou art known
Unto me now, all filthy though thou be.'
Then both his hands were on the vessel thrown;
But him my wary Master backward heaved, Saying:
'Do thou 'mong the other dogs be gone!'
Then to my neck with both his arms he cleaved,
And kissed my face, and, 'Soul disdainful,'[319] said,
'O blessed she in whom thou wast conceived!
He in the world great haughtiness displayed.
No deeds of worth his memory adorn;
And therefore rages here his sinful shade.
And many are there by whom crowns are worn
On earth, shall wallow here like swine in mire,
Leaving behind them names o'erwhelmed[320] in scorn.'
And I: 'O Master, I have great desire
To see him well soused in this filthy tide,
Ere from the lake we finally retire.'
And he: 'Or ever shall have been descried

The shore by thee, thy longing shall be met;
For such a wish were justly gratified.'
A little after in such fierce onset
The miry people down upon him bore,
I praise and bless God for it even yet.
'Philip Argenti![321] at him!' was the roar;
And then that furious spirit Florentine
Turned with his teeth upon himself and tore.
Here was he left, nor wins more words of mine.
Now in my ears a lamentation rung,
Whence I to search what lies ahead begin.
And the good Master told me: 'Son, ere long
We to the city called of Dis[322] draw near,
Where in great armies cruel burghers[323] throng.'
And I: 'Already, Master, I appear
Mosques[324] in the valley to distinguish well,
Vermilion, as if they from furnace were
Fresh come.' And he: 'Fires everlasting dwell
Within them, whence appear they glowing hot,
As thou discernest in this lower hell.'
We to the moat profound at length were brought,
Which girds that city all disconsolate;
The walls around it seemed of iron wrought.
Not without fetching first a compass great,
We came to where with angry cry at last:
'Get out,' the boatman yelled; 'behold the gate!'[325]
More than a thousand, who from Heaven[326] were cast,
I saw above the gates, who furiously
Demanded: 'Who, ere death on him has passed,

Holds through the region of the dead his way?'
And my wise Master made to them a sign
That he had something secretly to say.
Then ceased they somewhat from their great disdain,
And said: 'Come thou, but let that one be gone
Who thus presumptuous enters on this reign.
Let him retrace his madcap way alone,
If he but can; thou meanwhile lingering here,
Through such dark regions who hast led him down.
'Judge, reader, if I was not filled with fear,
Hearing the words of this accursèd threat;
For of return my hopes extinguished were.
'Beloved Guide, who more than seven times[327] set
Me in security, and safely brought
Through frightful dangers in my progress met,
Leave me not thus undone;' I him besought:
'If further progress be to us denied,
Let us retreat together, tarrying not.'
The Lord who led me thither then replied:
'Fear not: by One so great has been assigned
Our passage, vainly were all hindrance tried.
Await me here, and let thy fainting mind
Be comforted and with good hope be fed
,Not to be left in this low world behind.'
Thus goes he, thus am I abandonèd
By my sweet Father. I in doubt remain,
With Yes and No[328] contending in my head
.I could not hear what speech he did maintain,
But no long time conferred he in that place,

Till, to be first, all inward raced again.
And then the gates were closed in my Lord's face
By these our enemies; outside stood he;
Then backward turned to me with lingering pace,
With downcast eyes, and all the bravery
Stripped from his brows; and he exclaimed with sighs;
'Who dare[329] deny the doleful seats to me!'
And then he said: 'Although my wrath arise,
Fear not, for I to victory will pursue,
Howe'er within they plot, the enterprise.
This arrogance of theirs is nothing new;
They showed it[330] once at a less secret door
Which stands unbolted since. Thou didst it view,
And saw the dark-writ legend which it bore.
Thence, even now, is one who hastens down
Through all the circles, guideless, to this shore,
And he shall win us entrance to the town.'

FOOTNOTES:

312. Continuing: The account of the Fifth Circle, begun in the preceding Canto, is continued in this. It is impossible to adopt Boccaccio's story of how the first seven Cantos were found among a heap of other papers, years after Dante's exile began;and that 'continuing' marks the resumption of his work. The word most probably suggested the invention of the incident, or at least led to the identification of some manuscript that may have been sent to Dante, with the opening pages of the Comedy. If the tale were true, not only must Ciacco's prophecy (Inf. vi.) have been interpolated,but we should be obliged to hold that Dante began the poem while he was a prosperouscitizen.—Boccaccio himself in his Comment on the Comedy points out the difficulty of reconciling the story with Ciacco's prophecy.

313. Two flames: Denoting the number of passengers who are to be conveyed acrossthe Stygian pool. It is a signal for the ferryman, and is answered by a light

hung out onthe battlements of the city of Dis.

314. Guilty sprite: Only one is addressed; whether Virgil or Dante is not clear.

315. Phlegyas: Who burnt the temple of Apollo at Delphi in revenge for the violationof his daughter by the god.

316. Deeper, etc.: Because used to carry only shades.

317. Ere thy period: The curiosity of the shade is excited by the sinking of the boat in the water. He assumes that Dante will one day be condemned to Inferno. Neither Francesca nor Ciacco made a like mistake.

318. One who weeps: He is ashamed to tell his name, and hopes in his vile disguise to remain unknown by Dante, whose Florentine speech and dress, and perhaps whosefeatures, he has now recognised.

319. Soul disdainful: Dante has been found guilty of here glorying in the same sin which he so severely reprobates in others. But, without question, of set purpose he herecontrasts righteous indignation with the ignoble rage punished in this circle. With his quick temper and zeal so often kindling into flame, he may have felt a special personalneed of emphasising the distinction.

320. Names o'erwhelmed, etc.: 'Horrible reproaches.'

321. Philip Argenti: A Florentine gentleman related to the great family of the Adimari, and a contemporary of Dante's. Boccaccio in his commentary describes him as a cavalier, very rich, and so ostentatious that he once shod his horse with silver, whencehis surname. In the Decameron (ix. 8) he is introduced as violently assaulting—tearingout his hair and dragging him in the mire—the victim of a practical joke played by the Ciacco of Canto vi. Some, without reason, suppose that Dante shows such severity tohim because he was a Black, and so a political opponent of his own.

322. Dis: A name of Pluto, the god of the infernal regions.

323. Burghers: The city of Dis composes the Sixth Circle, and, as immediately appears, is populated by demons. The sinners punished in it are not mentioned at all in this Canto, and it seems more reasonable to apply burghers to the demons than to the shades. They are called gravi, generally taken to mean sore burdened, and the description is then applicable to the shades; but grave also bears the sense of cruel, andmay describe the fierceness of the devils. Though the city is inhabited by the subjectsof Dis, he is found as Lucifer at the very bottom of the pit. By some critics the whole of the lower Inferno, all that lies beyond this point, is regarded as being the city of Dis. But it is the Sixth Circle, with its minarets, that is the city; its walls, however, serving as bulwarks for all the lower Inferno. The shape of the city is, of course, that of a circular belt. Here it may be noted that the Fifth and Sixth Circles are on the samelevel; the water of Styx, which as a marsh covers the Fifth, is gathered into a moat to surround

the walls of the Sixth.

324. Mosques: The feature of an Infidel city that first struck crusader and pilgrim.

325. The gate: They have floated across the stagnant marsh into the deeper waters of the moat, and up to the gate where Phlegyas is used to land his passengers. It may be aquestion whether his services are required for all who are doomed to the lower Inferno,or only for those bound to the city.

326. From Heaven: 'Rained from Heaven.' Fallen angels.

327. Seven times: Given as a round number.

328. .Yes and No: He will return—He will not return. The demons have said that Virgil shall remain, and he has promised Dante not to desert him.

329. Who dare, etc.: Virgil knows the hindrance is only temporary, but wonders what superior devilish power can have incited the demons to deny him entrance. The incident displays the fallen angels as being still rebellious, and is at the same time skilfully conceived to mark a pause before Dante enters on the lower Inferno.

330. They showed it, etc.: At the gate of Inferno, on the occasion of Christ's descentto Limbo. The reference is to the words in the Missal service for Easter Eve: 'This is the night in which, having burst the bonds of death, Christ victoriously ascended fromHell.'

CANTO IX.

The hue which cowardice on my face did paint
When I beheld my guide return again,
Put his new colour[331] quicker 'neath restraint.
Like one who listens did he fixed remain;
For far to penetrate the air like night,
And heavy mist, the eye was bent in vain.
'Yet surely we must vanquish in the fight;'
Thus he, 'unless[332]—but with such proffered aid—
O how I weary till he come in sight!'
Well I remarked how he transition made,1
Covering his opening words with those behind,
Which contradicted what at first he said.
Nath'less his speech with terror charged my mind,
For, haply, to the word which broken fell
Worse meaning than he purposed,
I assigned.Down to this bottom[333] of the dismal shell
Comes ever any from the First Degree,[334]
Where all their pain is, stripped of hope to dwell?
To this my question thus responded he:
'Seldom it haps to any to pursue
The journey now embarked upon by me.
Yet I ere this descended, it is true,
Beneath a spell of dire Erichtho's[335] laid,
Who could the corpse with soul inform anew.
Short while my flesh of me was empty made
When she required me to o'erpass that wall,

From Judas' circle[336] to abstract a shade.
That is the deepest, darkest place of all,
And furthest from the heaven[337] which moves the skies
;I know the way; fear nought that can befall.
These fens[338] from which vile exhalations rise
The doleful city all around invest,
Which now we reach not save in angry wise.'
Of more he spake nought in my mind doth rest,
For, with mine eyes, my every thought had been
Fixed on the lofty tower with flaming crest,
Where, in a moment and upright, were seen
Three hellish furies, all with blood defaced,
And woman-like in members and in mien.
Hydras of brilliant green begirt their waist;
Snakes and cerastes for their tresses grew,
And these were round their dreadful temples braced.
That they the drudges were, full well he knew,
Of her who is the queen of endless woes,
And said to me: 'The fierce Erynnyes[339] view!
Herself upon the left Megæra shows;
That is Alecto weeping on the right;
Tisiphone's between.' Here made he close.
Each with her nails her breast tore, and did smite
Herself with open palms. They screamed in tone
So fierce, I to the Poet clove for fright.
'Medusa,[340] come, that we may make him stone!'
All shouted as they downward gazed; 'Alack!
Theseus[341] escaped us when he ventured down.'
'Keep thine eyes closed and turn to them thy back

,For if the Gorgon chance to be displayed
And thou shouldst look, farewell the upward track!'
Thus spake the Master, and himself he swayed
Me round about; nor put he trust in mine
But his own hands upon mine eyelids laid.
O ye with judgment gifted to divine
Look closely now, and mark what hidden lore
Lies 'neath the veil of my mysterious line![342]
Across the turbid waters came a roar
And crash of sound, which big with fear arose:
Because of it fell trembling either shore.
The fashion of it was as when there blows
A blast by cross heats made to rage amain,
Which smites the forest and without repose
The shattered branches sweeps in hurricane;
In clouds of dust, majestic, onward flies,
Wild beasts and herdsmen driving o'er the plain.
'Sharpen thy gaze,' he bade—and freed mine eyes—
'Across the foam-flecked immemorial lake,
Where sourest vapour most unbroken lies.'
And as the frogs before the hostile snake
Together of the water get them clear,
And on the dry ground, huddling, shelter take;
More than a thousand ruined souls in fear Beheld
I flee from one who, dry of feet,
Was by the Stygian ferry drawing near.
Waving his left hand he the vapour beat
Swiftly from 'fore his face, nor seemed he spent
Save with fatigue at having this to meet.

Well I opined that he from Heaven[343] was sent,
And to my Master turned. His gesture taught
I should be dumb and in obeisance bent.
Ah me, how with disdain appeared he fraught!
He reached the gate, which, touching with a rod,[344]
He oped with ease, for it resisted not.
'People despised and banished far from God,'
Upon the awful threshold then he spoke,
'How holds in you such insolence abode?
Why kick against that will which never broke
Short of its end, if ever it begin,
And often for you fiercer torments woke?
Butting 'gainst fate, what can ye hope to win?
Your Cerberus,[345] as is to you well known,
Still bears for this a well-peeled throat and chin.'
Then by the passage foul he back was gone,
Nor spake to us, but like a man was he
By other cares[346] absorbed and driven on
Than that of those who may around him be.
And we, confiding in the sacred word,
Moved toward the town in all security.
We entered without hindrance, and I, spurred
By my desire the character to know
And style of place such strong defences gird,Entering,
begin mine eyes around to throw,
And see on every hand a vast champaign,
The teeming seat of torments and of woe.
And as at Arles[347] where Rhone spreads o'er the plain,
Or Pola,[348] hard upon Quarnaro sound

Which bathes the boundaries Italian,
The sepulchres uneven make the ground;
So here on every side, but far more dire
And grievous was the fashion of them found.
For scattered 'mid the tombs blazed many a fire,
Because of which these with such fervour burned
No arts which work in iron more require.
All of the lids were lifted. I discerned
By keen laments which from the tombs arose
That sad and suffering ones were there inurned
.I said: 'O Master, tell me who are those
Buried within the tombs, of whom the sighs
Come to our ears thus eloquent of woes?'
And he to me: 'The lords of heresies[349]
With followers of all sects, a greater band
Than thou wouldst think, these sepulchres comprise.
To lodge them like to like the tombs are planned.
The sepulchres have more or less of heat.'[350]
Then passed we, turning to the dexter hand,[351] '
Tween torments and the lofty parapet.

FOOTNOTES:

331. New colour: Both have changed colour, Virgil in anger and Dante in fear.

332. Unless: To conceal his misgiving from Dante, Virgil refrains from expressing all his thought. The 'unless' may refer to what the lying demons had told him or threatened him with; the 'proffered aid,' to that involved in Beatrice's request.

333.This bottom: The lower depths of Inferno. How much still lies below him is unknown to Dante.

334. First Degree: The limbo where Virgil resides. Dante by an indirect question, seeks to learn how much experience of Inferno is possessed by his guide.

335. Erichtho: A Thessalian sorceress, of whom Lucan (Pharsalia vi.) tells that she evoked a shade to predict to Sextus Pompey the result of the war between his father and Cæsar. This happened thirty years before the death of Virgil.

336. Judas' circle: The Judecca, or very lowest point of the Inferno. Virgil's death preceded that of Judas by fifty years. He gives no hint of whose the shade was that hewent down to fetch; but Lucan's tale was probably in Dante's mind. In the Middle Ages the memory of Virgil was revered as that of a great sorcerer, especially in the neighbourhood of Naples.

337. The heaven, etc.: The Primum Mobile; but used here for the highest heaven. SeeInf. ii. 83, note.

338. These fens, etc.: Virgil knows the locality. They have no choice, but must remainwhere they are, for the same moat and wall gird the city all around.

339. Erynnyes: The Furies. The Queen of whom they are handmaids is Proserpine,carried off by Dis, or Pluto, to the under world.

340. Medusa: Onc of the Gorgons. Whoever looked on the head of Medusa was turned into stone.

341. Theseus: Who descended into the infernal regions to rescue Proserpine, and escaped by the help of Hercules.

342. Mysterious line: 'Strange verses:' That the verses are called strange, as Boccaccioand others of the older commentators say, because treating of such a subject in the vulgar tongue for the first time, and in rhyme, is difficult to believe. Rather they are strange because of the meaning they convey. What that is, Dante warns the reader of superior intellect to pause and consider. It has been noted (Inf. ii. 28) how he uses thecharacters of the old mythology as if believing in their real existence. But this is for his poetical ends. Here he bids us look below the surface and seek for the truth hiddenunder the strange disguise.—The opposition to their progress offered by the powers of Hell perplexes even Virgil, while Dante is reduced to a state of absolute terror,and is afflicted with still sharper misgivings than he had at the first as to the issue of his adventure. By an indirect question he seeks to learn how much Virgil really knows of the economy of the lower world; but he cannot so much as listen to all of his Master's reassuring answer, terrified as he is by the sudden appearance of the Furies upon the tower, which rises out of the city of unbelief. These symbolise the trouble ofhis conscience, and, assailing him with threats, shake his already trembling faith in the Divine government. How, in the face of such foes, is he to find the peace and liberty ofsoul of which he is in search? That this is the city of unbelief he has not yet been told,and without knowing it he is standing under the very walls of Doubting

Castle. And now, if he chance to let his eyes rest on the Gorgon's head, his soul will be petrified by despair; like the denizens of Hell, he will lose the 'good of the intellect,' and will pass into a state from which Virgil—or reason—will be powerless to deliver him. But Virgil takes him in time, and makes him avert his eyes; which may signify that the only safe course for men is to turn their backs on the deep and insoluble problem of how the reality of the Divine government can be reconciled with the apparent triumph of evil.

343. From Heaven: The messenger comes from Heaven, and his words are holy. Against the obvious interpretation, that he is a good angel, there lies the objection that no other such is met with in Inferno, and also that it is spoken of as a new sight for him when Dante first meets with one in Purgatory. But the obstruction now to be overcome is worthy of angelic interference; and Dante can hardly be said to meet the messenger, who does not even glance in his direction. The commentators have made this angel mean all kind of outlandish things.

344. A rod: A piece of the angelic outfit, derived from the caduceus of Mercury.

345. Cerberus: Hercules, when Cerberus opposed his entrance to the infernal regions, fastened a chain round his neck and dragged him to the gate. The angel's speech answers Dante's doubts as to the limits of diabolical power.

346. By other cares, etc.: It is not in Inferno that Dante is to hold converse with celestial intelligences. The angel, like Beatrice when she sought Virgil in Limbo, is all on fire to return to his own place.

347. Arles: The Alyscampo (Elysian Fields) at Arles was an enormous cemetery, of which ruins still exist. It had a circumference of about six miles, and contained numerous sarcophagi dating from Roman times.

348. Pola: In Istria, near the Gulf of Quarnaro, said to have contained many ancient tombs.

349. Lords of heresies: 'Heresiarchs.' Dante now learns for the first time that Dis is the city of unbelief. Each class of heretics has its own great sepulchre.

350. More or less of heat: According to the heinousness of the heresy punished in each. It was natural to associate heretics and punishment by fire in days when Dominican monks ruled the roast.

351. Dexter hand: As they move across the circles, and down from one to the other, their course is usually to the left hand. Here for some reason Virgil turns to the right, so as to have the tombs on the left as he advances. It may be that a special proof of his knowledge of the locality is introduced when most needed—after the repulse by the demons—to strengthen Dante's confidence in him as a guide; or, as some subtly think, they being now about to enter the abode of heresy, the movement to the right signifies the importance of the first step in forming opinion. The only other occasion on which their course is taken to the right hand is at Inf. xvii. 31.

CANTO X.

And now advance we by a narrow track
Between the torments and the ramparts high,
My Master first, and I behind his back.
'O mighty Virtue,[352] at whose will am I
Wheeled through these impious circles,' then I said,
'Speak, and in full my longing satisfy.
The people who within the tombs are laid,
May they be seen? The coverings are all thrown
Open, nor is there[353] any guard displayed.'
And he to me: 'All shall be fastened down
When hither from Jehoshaphat[354] they come
Again in bodies which were once their own.
All here with Epicurus[355] find their tomb
Who are his followers, and by whom 'tis held
That the soul shares the body's mortal doom.
Things here discovered then shall answer yield,
And quickly, to thy question asked of me;
As well as[356] to the wish thou hast concealed.'
And I: 'Good Leader, if I hide from thee
My heart, it is that I may little say;
Nor only now[357] learned I thus dumb to be.'
'O Tuscan, who, still living, mak'st thy way,
Modest of speech, through the abode of flame,
Be pleased[358] a little in this place to stay.
The accents of thy language thee proclaim
To be a native of that state renowned

Which I, perchance, wronged somewhat.' Sudden came
These words from out a tomb which there was found '
Mongst others; whereon I, compelled by fright,
A little toward my Leader shifted ground.
And he: 'Turn round, what ails thee? Lo! upright
Beginneth Farinata[359] to arise;
All of him 'bove the girdle comes in sight.'
On him already had I fixed mine eyes.
Towering erect with lifted front and chest,
He seemed Inferno greatly to despise.
And toward him I among the tombs was pressed
By my Guide's nimble and courageous hand,
While he, 'Choose well thy language,' gave behest.
Beneath his tomb when I had ta'en my stand
Regarding me a moment, 'Of what house
Art thou?' as if in scorn, he made demand.
To show myself obedient, anxious,
I nothing hid, but told my ancestors;
And, listening, he gently raised his brows.[360]
'Fiercely to me they proved themselves adverse
,And to my sires and party,' then he said;
'Because of which I did them twice disperse.'[361]
I answered him: 'And what although they fled!
Twice from all quarters they returned with might,
An art not mastered yet by these you[362] led.'
Beside him then there issued into sight
Another shade, uncovered to the chin,
Propped on his knees, if I surmised aright
.He peered around as if he fain would win

Knowledge if any other was with me;
And then, his hope all spent, did thus begin,Weeping:
'By dint of genius if it be
Thou visit'st this dark prison, where my son?
And wherefore not found in thy company?'
And I to him: 'I come not here alone:
He waiting yonder guides me: but disdain
Of him perchance was by your Guido[363] shown.'
The words he used, and manner of his pain,
Revealed his name to me beyond surmise;
Hence was I able thus to answer plain.
Then cried he, and at once upright did rise,
'How saidst thou—was? Breathes he not then the air?
The pleasant light no longer smites his eyes?'
When he of hesitation was aware
Displayed by me in forming my reply,
He fell supine, no more to reappear.
But the magnanimous, at whose bidding
I Had halted there, the same expression wore,
Nor budged a jot, nor turned his neck awry.
'And if'—resumed he where he paused before—
'They be indeed but slow that art to learn,
Than this my bed, to hear it pains me more.
But ere the fiftieth time anew shall burn
The lady's[364] face who reigneth here below,
Of that sore art thou shalt experience earn.
And as to the sweet world again thou'dst go
,Tell me, why is that people so without
Ruth for my race,[365] as all their statutes show?'

And I to him: 'The slaughter and the rout
Which made the Arbia[366] to run with red,
Cause in our fane[367] such prayers to be poured out.'
Whereon he heaved a sigh and shook his head:'
There I was not alone, nor to embrace
That cause was I, without good reason, led.
But there I was alone, when from her place
All granted Florence should be swept away. '
Twas I[368] defended her with open face.'
'So may your seed find peace some better day,'
I urged him, 'as this knot you shall untie
In which my judgment doth entangled stay
.If I hear rightly, ye, it seems, descry
Beforehand what time brings, and yet ye seem '
Neath other laws[369] as touching what is nigh.'
'Like those who see best what is far from them,
We see things,' said he, 'which afar remain;
Thus much enlightened by the Guide Supreme
.To know them present or approaching, vain
Are all our powers; and save what they relate
Who hither come, of earth no news we gain.
Hence mayst thou gather in how dead a state
Shall all our knowledge from that time be thrown
When of the future shall be closed the gate.'
Then, for my fault as if repentant grown, I said:
'Report to him who fell supine,
That still among the living breathes his son.
And if I, dumb, seemed answer to decline,
Tell him it was that I upon the knot

Was pondering then, you helped me to untwine.'
Me now my Master called, whence I besought
With more than former sharpness of the shade,
To tell me what companions he had got.
He answered me: 'Some thousand here are laid
With me; 'mong these the Second Frederick,[370]
The Cardinal[371] too; of others nought be said.'
Then was he hid; and towards the Bard antique
I turned my steps, revolving in my brain
The ominous words[372] which I had heard him speak
.He moved, and as we onward went again
Demanded of me: 'Wherefore thus amazed?'
And to his question I made answer plain. '
Within thy mind let there be surely placed,'
The Sage bade, 'what 'gainst thee thou heardest say.
Now mark me well' (his finger here he raised),
'When thou shalt stand within her gentle ray
Whose beauteous eye sees all, she will make known
The stages[373] of thy journey on life's way.'
Turning his feet, he to the left moved on;
Leaving the wall, we to the middle[374] went
Upon a path that to a vale strikes down,
Which even to us above its foulness sent.

FOOTNOTES:

352. Virtue: Virgil is here addressed by a new title, which, with the words of deep respect that follow, marks the full restoration of Dante's confidence in him as his guide.

353. Nor is there, etc.: The gate was found to be strictly guarded, but not so are the tombs.

354. Jehoshaphat: 'I will also gather all nations, and will bring them down into the valley of Jehoshaphat' (Joel iii. 2).

355. Epicurus: The unbelief in a future life, or rather the indifference to everything but the calls of ambition and worldly pleasure, common among the nobles of Dante'sage and that preceding it, went by the name of Epicureanism. It is the most radical of heresies, because adverse to the first principles of all religions. Dante, in his treatmentof heresy, dwells more on what affects conduct as does the denial of the Divine government—than on intellectual divergence from orthodox belief.

356. As well as, etc.: The question is: 'May they be seen?' The wish is a desire to speak with them.

357. Nor only now, etc.: Virgil has on previous occasions imposed silence on Dante,as, for instance, at Inf. iii. 51.

358. Be pleased, etc.: From one of the sepulchres, to be imagined as a huge sarcophagus, come words similar to the Siste Viator! common on Roman tombs.

359. Farinata: Of the great Florentine family of the Uberti, and, in the generation before Dante, leader of the Ghibeline or Imperialist party in Florence. His memory long survived among his fellow-townsmen as that of the typical noble, rough-mannered, unscrupulous, and arrogant; but yet, for one good action that he did, he at the same timeranked in the popular estimation as a patriot and a hero. Boccaccio, misled perhaps bythe mention of Epicurus, says that he loved rich and delicate fare. It is because all his thoughts were worldly that he is condemned to the city of unbelief. Dante has already (Inf. vi. 79) inquired regarding his fate. He died in 1264.

360. His brows: When Dante tells he is of the Alighieri, a Guelf family, Farinata shows some slight displeasure. Or, as a modern Florentine critic interprets the gesture, he has to think a moment before he can remember on which side the Alighieri ranged themselves—they being of the small gentry, while he was a great noble, But this glossrequires Dante to have been more free from pride of family than he really was.

361. Twice disperse: The Alighieri shared in the exile of the Guelfs in 1248 and 1260.

362. You: See also line 95. Dante never uses the plural form to a single person except when desirous of showing social as distinguished from, or over and above, moral respect.

363. Guido: Farinata's companion in the tomb is Cavalcante Cavalcanti, who, although a Guelf, was tainted with the more specially Ghibeline error of

Epicureanism.When in order to allay party rancour some of the Guelf and Ghibeline families were forced to intermarry, his son Guido took a daughter of Farinata's to wife. This wasin 1267, so that Guido was much older than Dante. Yet they were very intimate, and, intellectually, had much in common. With him Dante exchanged poems of occasion, and he terms him more than once in the Vita Nuova his chief friend. The disdain of Virgil need not mean more than is on the surface. Guido died in 1301. He is the hero of the Decameron, vi. 9.

364. The Lady: Proserpine; i.e. the moon. Ere fifty months from March 1300 were past, Dante was to see the failure of more than one attempt made by the exiles, of whom he was one, to gain entrance to Florence. The great attempt was in the beginningof 1304.

365. Ruth for my race: When the Ghibeline power was finally broken in Florence the Uberti were always specially excluded from any amnesty. There is mention ofthe political execution of at least one descendant of Farinata's. His son when being led to the scaffold said, 'So we pay our fathers' debts!'—It has been so long commonto describe Dante as a Ghibeline, though no careful writer does it now, that it may be worth while here to remark that Ghibelinism, as Farinata understood it, was practically extinct in Florence ere Dante entered political life.

366. The Arbia: At Montaperti, on the Arbia, a few miles from Siena, was fought in 1260 a great battle between the Guelf Florence and her allies on the one hand, and on the other the Ghibelines of Florence, then in exile, under Farinata; the Sienese and Tuscan Ghibelines in general; and some hundreds of men-at-arms lent by Manfred. Notwithstanding the gallant behaviour of the Florentine burghers, the Guelf defeat was overwhelming, and not only did the Arbia run red with Florentine blood—in a figure—but the battle of Montaperti ruined for a time the cause of popular liberty and general improvement in Florence.

367. Our fane: The Parliament of the people used to meet in Santa Reparata, the cathedral; and it is possible that the maintenance of the Uberti disabilities was there more than once confirmed by the general body of the citizens. The use of the word is in any case accounted for by the frequency of political conferences in churches. And the temple having been introduced, edicts are converted into 'prayers.'

368. 'Twas I, etc.: Some little time after the victory of Montaperti there was a great Ghibeline gathering from various cities at Empoli, when it was proposed, with general approval, to level Florence with the ground in revenge for the obstinate Guelfism of thepopulation. Farinata roughly declared that as long as he lived and had a sword he woulddefend his native place, and in the face of this protest the resolution was departed from.It is difficult to understand how of all the Florentine nobles, whose wealth consisted largely in house property, Farinata should have stood alone in protesting against the ruin of the city. But so it seems to have been; and in this great passage Farinata is repaid for his service, in despite of Inferno.

369. Other laws: Ciacco, in Canto vi., prophesied what was to happen in Florence, and Farinata has just told him that four years later than now he will have failed in an attempt to return from exile: yet Farinata does not know if his family is still beingpersecuted, and Cavalcanti fears that his son Guido is already numbered with the dead.Farinata replies that like the longsighted the shades can only see what is some distance off, and are ignorant of what is going on, or about to happen; which seems to imply that they forget what they once foresaw. Guido was to die within a few months, and theevent was too close at hand to come within the range of his father's vision.

370. The Second Frederick: The Emperor of that name who reigned from 1220to 1250, and waged a life-long war with the Popes for supremacy in Italy. It is not however for his enmity with Rome that he is placed in the Sixth Circle, but for his Epicureanism—as Dante understood it. From his Sicilian court a spirit of free inquiry spread through the Peninsula. With men of the stamp of Farinata it would be convertedinto a crude materialism.

371. The Cardinal: Ottaviano, of the powerful Tuscan family of the Ubaldini, a man of great political activity, and known in Tuscany as 'The Cardinal.' His sympathies were not with the Roman Court. The news of Montaperti filled him with delight, and later, when the Tuscan Ghibelines refused him money he had asked for, he burst out with 'And yet I have lost my soul for the Ghibelines—if I have a soul.' He died not earlier than 1273. After these illustrious names Farinata scorns to mention meaner ones.

372. Ominous words: Those in which Farinata foretold Dante's exile.

373. The stages, etc.: It is Cacciaguida, his ancestor, who in Paradise instructs Dantein what his future life is to be—one of poverty and exile (Parad. xvii.). This is, however,done at the request of Beatrice.

374. To the middle: Turning to the left they cut across the circle till they reach the inner boundary of the city of tombs. Here there is no wall.

CANTO XI.

We at the margin of a lofty steep
Made of great shattered stones in circle bent,
Arrived where worser torments crowd the deep
.So horrible a stench and violent
Was upward wafted from the vast abyss,[375]
Behind the cover we for shelter went
Of a great tomb where I saw written this:
'Pope Anastasius[376] is within me thrust,
Whom the straight way Photinus made to miss.'
'Now on our course a while we linger must,'
The Master said, 'be but our sense resigned
A little to it, and the filthy gust
We shall not heed.' Then I: 'Do thou but find
Some compensation lest our time should run Wasted.'
And he: 'Behold, 'twas in my mind.
Girt by the rocks before us, O my son,
Lie three small circles,'[377] he began to tell,
'Graded like those with which thou now hast done,
All of them filled with spirits miserable.
That sight[378] of them may thee henceforth suffice.
Hear how and wherefore in these groups they dwell.
Whate'er in Heaven's abhorred as wickedness
Has injury[379] for its end; in others' bane
By fraud resulting or in violent wise.
Since fraud to man alone[380] doth appertain,
God hates it most; and hence the fraudulent band

,Set lowest down, endure a fiercer pain.
Of the violent is the circle next at hand
To us; and since three ways is violence shown, '
Tis in three several circuits built and planned.
To God, ourselves, or neighbours may be done
Violence, or on the things by them possessed;
As reasoning clear shall unto thee make known.
Our neighbour may by violence be distressed
With grievous wounds, or slain; his goods and lands
By havoc, fire, and plunder be oppressed.
Hence those who wound and slay with violent hands,
Robbers, and spoilers, in the nearest round
Are all tormented in their various bands.
Violent against himself may man be found,
And 'gainst his goods; therefore without avail
They in the next are in repentance drowned
Who on themselves loss of your world entail,
Who gamble[381] and their substance madly spend,
And who when called to joy lament and wail.
And even to God may violence extend
By heart denial and by blasphemy,
Scorning what nature doth in bounty lend.
Sodom and Cahors[382] hence are doomed to lie
Within the narrowest circlet surely sealed;
And such as God within their hearts defy.
Fraud,[383] 'gainst whose bite no conscience findeth shield,
A man may use with one who in him lays
Trust, or with those who no such credence yield.
Beneath this latter kind of it decays

The bond of love which out of nature grew;
Hence, in the second circle[384] herd the race
To feigning given and flattery, who pursue
Magic, false coining, theft, and simony,
Pimps, barrators, and suchlike residue.
The other form of fraud makes nullity
Of natural bonds; and, what is more than those,
The special trust whence men on men rely.
Hence in the place whereon all things repose,
The narrowest circle and the seat of Dis,[385]
Each traitor's gulfed in everlasting woes.'
'Thy explanation, Master, as to this
Is clear,' I said, 'and thou hast plainly told
Who are the people stowed in the abyss.
But tell why those the muddy marshes hold,
The tempest-driven, those beaten by the rain,
And such as, meeting, virulently scold,
Are not within the crimson city ta'en
For punishment, if hateful unto God;
And, if not hateful, wherefore doomed to pain?'
And he to me: 'Why wander thus abroad,
More than is wont, thy wits? or how engrossed
Is now thy mind, and on what things bestowed?
Hast thou the memory of the passage lost
In which thy Ethics[386] for their subject treat
Of the three moods by Heaven abhorred the most—
Malice and bestiality complete;
And how, compared with these, incontinence Offends
God less, and lesser blame doth meet?

If of this doctrine thou extract the sense,
And call to memory what people are
Above, outside, in endless penitence,
Why from these guilty they are sundered far
Thou shalt discern, and why on them alight
The strokes of justice in less angry war.'
'O Sun that clearest every troubled sight,
So charmed am I by thy resolving speech,
Doubt yields me joy no less than knowing right.
Therefore, I pray, a little backward reach,'
I asked, 'to where thou say'st that usury
Sins 'gainst God's bounty; and this mystery teach.'
He said: 'Who gives ear to Philosophy
Is taught by her, nor in one place alone,
What nature in her course is governed by,
Even Mind Divine, and art which thence hath grown;
And if thy Physics[387] thou wilt search within,
Thou'lt find ere many leaves are open thrown,
This art by yours, far as your art can win,
Is followed close—the teacher by the taught;
As grandchild then to God your art is kin.
And from these two—do thou recall to thought
How Genesis[388] begins—should come supplie
sOf food for man, and other wealth be sought.
And, since another plan the usurer plies,
Nature and nature's child have his disdain;[389]
Because on other ground his hope relies.
But come,[390] for to advance I now am fain:
The Fishes[391] over the horizon line Quiver;

o'er Caurus now stands all the Wain;

And further yonder does the cliff decline.'

FOOTNOTES:

375. Vast abyss: They are now at the inner side of the Sixth Circle, and upon the verge of the rocky steep which slopes down from it into the Seventh. All the lower Hell lies beneath them, and it is from that rather than from the next circle in particularthat the stench arises, symbolical of the foulness of the sins which are punished there.The noisome smells which make part of the horror of Inferno are after this sometimesmentioned, but never dwelt upon (Inf. xviii. 106, and xxix. 50).

376. Pope Anastasius: The second of the name, elected Pope in 496. Photinus, bishopof Sirenium, was infected with the Sabellian heresy, but he was deposed more than a century before the time of Anastasius. Dante follows some obscure legend in charging Anastasius with heresy. The important point is that the one heretic, in the sense usuallyattached to the term, named as being in the city of unbelief, is a Pope.

377. Three small circles: The Seventh, Eighth, and Ninth; small in circumference compared with those above. The pilgrims are now deep in the hollow cone.

378. That sight, etc.: After hearing the following explanation Dante no longer asks to what classes the sinners met with belong, but only as to the guilt of individual shades.

379. Injury: They have left above them the circles of those whose sin consists in the exaggeration or misdirection of a wholesome natural instinct. Below them lie the circles filled with such as have been guilty of malicious wickedness. This manifests itself in two ways: by violence or by fraud. After first mentioning in a general way that the fraudulent are set lowest in Inferno, Virgil proceeds to define violence, andto tell how the violent occupy the circle immediately beneath them—the Seventh. Fordivision of the maliciously wicked into two classes Dante is supposed to be indebted to Cicero: 'Injury may be wrought by force or by fraud. Both are unnatural for man, but fraud is the more hateful.'—De Officiis, i. 13. It is remarkable that Virgil says nothing of those in the Sixth Circle in this account of the classes of sinners.

380. To man alone, etc.: Fraud involves the corrupt use of the powers that distinguishus from the brutes.

381. Who gamble, etc.: A different sin from the lavish spending punished in the Fourth Circle (Inf. vii.). The distinction is that between thriftlessness and the prodigality which, stripping a man of the means of living, disgusts him with life, as described in the following line. It is from among prodigals that the ranks of suicides are greatly filled, and here they are appropriately placed together. It may seem strange that in hisclassification of guilt Dante should rank violence to one's self as a more heinous sin than that committed against one's neighbour. He may have in view the fact that none harm their neighbours so much as they who are oblivious of their own true interest.

382. Sodom and Cahors: Sins against nature are reckoned sins against God, as explained lower down in this Canto. Cahors in Languedoc had in the Middle Ages the reputationof being a nest of usurers. These in old English Chronicles are termed Caorsins. Withthe sins of Sodom and Cahors are ranked the denial of God and blasphemy against Him—deeper sins than the erroneous conceptions of the Divine nature and government punished in the Sixth Circle. The three concentric rings composing the Seventh Circleare all on the same level, as we shall find.

383. Fraud, etc.: Fraud is of such a nature that conscience never fails to give due warning against the sin. This is an aggravation of the guilt of it.

384. The second circle: The second now beneath them; that is, the Eighth.

385. Seat of Dis: The Ninth and last Circle.

386. Thy Ethics: The Ethics of Aristotle, in which it is said: 'With regard to manners, these three things are to be eschewed: incontinence, vice, and bestiality.' Aristotle holds incontinence to consist in the immoderate indulgence of propensities whichunder right guidance are adapted to promote lawful pleasure. It is, generally speaking,the sin of which those about whom Dante has inquired were guilty.—It has been ingeniously sought by Philalethes (Gött. Com.) to show that Virgil's disquisition is founded on this threefold classification of Aristotle's—violence being taken to be the same as bestiality, and malice as vice. But the reference to Aristotle is made with the limited purpose of justifying the lenient treatment of incontinence; in the same way as a few lines further on Genesis is referred to in support of the harsh treatment of usury.

387. Physics: The Physics of Aristotle, in which it is said: 'Art imitates nature.' Art includes handicrafts.

388. Genesis: 'And the Lord God took the man, and put him into the garden to dress it and to keep it.' 'In the sweat of thy face shalt thou eat bread.'

389. His disdain: The usurer seeks to get wealth independently of honest labour or reliance on the processes of nature. This far-fetched argument against usury closes oneof the most arid passages of the Comedy. The shortness of the Canto almost suggests that Dante had himself got weary of it.

390. But come, etc.: They have been all this time resting behind the lid of the tomb.

391. The Fishes, etc.: The sun being now in Aries the stars of Pisces begin to rise about a couple of hours before sunrise. The Great Bear lies above Caurus, the quarter of the N.N.W. wind. It seems impossible to harmonise the astronomical indications scattered throughout the Comedy, there being traces of Dante's having sometimes used details belonging rather to the day on which Good Friday fell in 1300, the 8th of April, than to the (supposed) true anniversary of the crucifixion. That this, the 25th of March, is the day he intended to conform to appears from Inf. xxi. 112.—The time is now near dawn on the Saturday morning. It is almost needless to say that Virgil speaks of the stars as he knows they are placed, but without seeing them. By what light they see in Inferno is nowhere explained. We have been told that it was dark as night (Inf. iv. 10, v. 28).

CANTO XII.

The place of our descent[392] before us lay
Precipitous, and there was something more
From sight of which all eyes had turned away.
As at the ruin which upon the shore
Of Adige[393] fell upon this side of Trent—
Through earthquake or by slip of what before
Upheld it—from the summit whence it went
Far as the plain, the shattered rocks supply
Some sort of foothold to who makes descent;
Such was the passage down the precipice high.
And on the riven gully's very brow
Lay spread at large the Cretan Infamy[394]
Which was conceived in the pretended cow.
Us when he saw, he bit himself for rage
Like one whose anger gnaws him through and through.
'Perhaps thou deemest,' called to him the Sage,
'This is the Duke of Athens[395] drawing nigh,
Who war to the death with thee on earth did wage.
Begone, thou brute, for this one passing by
Untutored by thy sister has thee found,
And only comes thy sufferings to spy,'
And as the bull which snaps what held it bound
On being smitten by the fatal blow,
Halts in its course, and reels upon the ground,
The Minotaur I saw reel to and fro;
And he, the alert, cried: 'To the passage haste;

While yet he chafes 'twere well thou down shouldst go.'
So we descended by the slippery waste[396]
Of shivered stones which many a time gave way
'Neath the new weight[397] my feet upon them placed.
I musing went; and he began to say: '
Perchance this ruined slope thou thinkest on,
Watched by the brute rage I did now allay.
But I would have thee know, when I came down
The former time[398] into this lower Hell,
The cliff had not this ruin undergone.
It was not long, if I distinguish well,
Ere He appeared who wrenched great prey from
Dis[399]From out the upmost circle. Trembling fell
Through all its parts the nauseous abyss
With such a violence, the world, I thought,
Was stirred by love; for, as they say, by this
She back to Chaos[400] has been often brought.
And then it was this ancient rampart strong
Was shattered here and at another spot.[401]
But toward the valley look. We come ere long
Down to the river of blood[402] where boiling lie
All who by violence work others wrong.'
O insane rage! O blind cupidity!
By which in our brief life we are so spurred,
Ere downward plunged in evil case for aye!
An ample ditch I now beheld engird
And sweep in circle all around the plain,
As from my Escort I had lately heard.
Between this and the rock in single train

Centaurs[403] were running who were armed with bows,
As if they hunted on the earth again.
Observing us descend they all stood close,
Save three of them who parted from the band
With bow, and arrows they in coming chose.
'What torment,' from afar one made demand,
'Come ye to share, who now descend the hill?
I shoot unless ye answer whence ye stand.'
My Master said: 'We yield no answer till
We come to Chiron[404] standing at thy side;
But thy quick temper always served thee ill.'
Then touching me: ''Tis Nessus;[405] he who died
With love for beauteous Dejanire possessed,
And who himself his own vendetta plied.
He in the middle, staring on his breast,
Is mighty Chiron, who Achilles bred;
And next the wrathful Pholus. They invest
The fosse and in their thousands round it tread,
Shooting whoever from the blood shall lift,
More than his crime allows, his guilty head.'
As we moved nearer to those creatures swift
Chiron drew forth a shaft and dressed his beard
Back on his jaws, using the arrow's cleft.
And when his ample mouth of hair was cleared,
He said to his companions: 'Have ye seen
The things the second touches straight are stirred,
As they by feet of shades could ne'er have been?'
And my good Guide, who to his breast had gone—
The part where join the natures,[406] 'Well I ween

He lives,' made answer; 'and if, thus alone,
He seeks the valley dim 'neath my control,
Necessity, not pleasure, leads him on.
One came from where the alleluiahs roll,
Who charged me with this office strange and new:
No robber he, nor mine a felon soul.
But, by that Power which makes me to pursue
The rugged journey whereupon I fare,
Accord us one of thine to keep in view,
That he may show where lies the ford, and bear
This other on his back to yonder strand;
No spirit he, that he should cleave the air.'
Wheeled to the right then Chiron gave command
To Nessus: 'Turn, and lead them, and take tent
They be not touched by any other band.'[407]
We with our trusty Escort forward went,
Threading the margin of the boiling blood
Where they who seethed were raising loud lament.
People I saw up to the chin imbrued,
'These all are tyrants,' the great Centaur said,
'Who blood and plunder for their trade pursued.
Here for their pitiless deeds tears now are shed
By Alexander,[408] and Dionysius fell,
Through whom in Sicily dolorous years were led.
The forehead with black hair so terrible
Is Ezzelino;[409] that one blond of hue,
Obizzo[410] d'Este, whom, as rumours tell,
His stepson murdered, and report speaks true.'
I to the Poet turned, who gave command:

'Regard thou chiefly him. I follow you.'
Ere long the Centaur halted on the strand,
Close to a people who, far as the throat,
Forth of that bulicamë[411] seemed to stand.
Thence a lone shade to us he pointed out
Saying: 'In God's house[412] ran he weapon through
The heart which still on Thames wins cult devout.'
Then I saw people, some with heads in view,
And some their chests above the river bore;
And many of them I, beholding, knew.
And thus the blood went dwindling more and more,
Until at last it covered but the feet:
Here took we passage[413] to the other shore.'
As on this hand thou seest still abate
In depth the volume of the boiling stream,'
The Centaur said, 'so grows its depth more great,
Believe me, towards the opposite extreme,
Until again its circling course attains
The place where tyrants must lament.
SupremeJustice upon that side involves in pains,
With Attila,[414] once of the world the pest,
Pyrrhus[415] and Sextus: and for ever drains
Tears out of Rinier of Corneto[416] pressed
And Rinier Pazzo[417] in that boiling mass,
Whose brigandage did so the roads infest.'
Then turned he back alone, the ford to pass.

FOOTNOTES:

392. Our descent: To the Seventh Circle.

393. Adige: Different localities in the valley of the Adige have been fixed on as the scene of this landslip. The Lavini di Marco, about twenty miles south of Trent, seem best to answer to the description. They 'consist of black blocks of stone and fragmentsof a landslip which, according to the Chronicle of Fulda, fell in the year 883 and overwhelmed the valley for four Italian miles' (Gsell-Fels, Ober. Ital. i. 35).

394. The Cretan Infamy: The Minotaur, the offspring of Pasiphaë; a half-bovine monster who inhabited the Cretan labyrinth, and to whom a human victim was offered once a year. He lies as guard upon the Seventh Circle—that of the violent (Inf. xi. 23,note)—and is set at the top of the rugged slope, itself the scene of a violent convulsion.

395. Duke of Athens: Theseus, instructed by Ariadne, daughter of Pasiphaë and Minos, how to outwit the Minotaur, entered the labyrinth in the character of a victim, slew the monster, and then made his way out, guided by a thread he had unwound ashe went in.

396. The slippery waste: The word used here, scarco, means in modern Tuscan a place where earth or stones have been carelessly shot into a heap.

397. The new weight: The slope had never before been trodden by mortal foot.

398. The former time: When Virgil descended to evoke a shade from the Ninth Circle(Inf. ix. 22).

399. Prey from Dis: The shades delivered from Limbo by Christ (Inf. iv. 53). The expression in the text is probably suggested by the words of the hymn Vexilla: Prædamque tulit Tartaris.

400. To Chaos: The reference is to the theory of Empedocles, known to Dante throughthe refutation of it by Aristotle. The theory was one of periods of unity and division innature, according as love or hatred prevailed.

401. Another spot: See Inf. xxi. 112. The earthquake at the Crucifixion shook even Inferno to its base.

402. The river of blood: Phlegethon, the 'boiling river.' Styx and Acheron have been already passed. Lethe, the fourth infernal river, is placed by Dante in Purgatory. The first round or circlet of the Seventh Circle is filled by Phlegethon.

403. Centaurs: As this round is the abode of such as are guilty of violence against their neighbours, it is guarded by these brutal monsters, half-man and half-horse.

404. Chiron: Called the most just of the Centaurs.

405. Nessus: Slain by Hercules with a poisoned arrow. When dying he gave Dejanirahis blood-stained shirt, telling her it would insure the faithfulness to her of any whom she loved. Hercules wore it and died of the venom; and thus Nessus avenged himself.

406. The natures: The part of the Centaur where the equine body is joined on to the human neck and head.

407. Other band: Of Centaurs.

408. Alexander: It is not known whether Alexander the Great or a petty Thessalian tyrant is here meant. Dionysius: The cruel tyrant of Syracuse.

409. Ezzelino: Or Azzolino of Romano, the greatest Lombard Ghibeline of his time. He was son-in-law of Frederick II., and was Imperial Vicar of the Trevisian Mark. Towards the close of Fredrick's life, and for some years after, he exercised almost independent power in Vicenza, Padua, and Verona. Cruelty, erected into a system, was his chief instrument of government, and 'in his dungeons men found something worse than death.' For Italians, says Burckhardt, he was the most impressive political personage of the thirteenth century; and around his memory, as around Frederick's, there gathered strange legends. He died in 1259, of a wound received in battle. When urged to confess his sins by the monk who came to shrive him, he declared that the only sin on his conscience was negligence in revenge. But this may be mythical, as may also be the long black hair between his eyebrows, which rose up stiff and terribleas his anger waxed.

410. Obizzo: The second Marquis of Este of that name. He was lord of Ferrara. There seems little, if any, evidence extant of his being specially cruel. As a strong Guelf he took sides with Charles of Anjou against Manfred. He died in 1293, smothered, it was believed, by a son, here called a stepson for his unnatural conduct. But though Dante vouches for the truth of the rumour it seems to have been an invention.

411. That bulicamë: The stream of boiling blood is probably named from the bulicamë, or hot spring, best known to Dante—that near Viterbo (see Inf. xiv. 79). And it may bethat the mention of the bulicamë suggests the reference at line 119.

412. In God's house: Literally, 'In the bosom of God.' The shade is that of Guy, sonof Simon of Montfort and Vicar in Tuscany of Charles of Anjou. In 1271 he stabbed, in the Cathedral of Viterbo, Henry, son of Richard of Cornwall and cousin of Edward I. of England. The motive of the murder was to revenge the death of his father, Simon, at Evesham. The body of the young prince was conveyed to England, and the heart was placed in a vase upon the tomb of the Confessor. The shade of Guy stands up to the chin in blood among the worst of the tyrants, and alone, because of the enormity of his crime.

413. Here took we passage: Dante on Nessus' back. Virgil has fallen behind to allow the Centaur to act as guide; and how he crosses the stream Dante does not see.

414. Attila: King of the Huns, who invaded part of Italy in the fifth century; and who, according to the mistaken belief of Dante's age, was the devastator of Florence.

415. Pyrrhus: King of Epirus. Sextus: Son of Pompey; a great sea-captain who fought against the Triumvirs. The crime of the first, in Dante's eyes, is that he fought with Rome; of the second, that he opposed Augustus.

416. Rinier of Corneto: Who in Dante's time disturbed the coast of the States of the Church by his robberies and violence.

417. Rinier Pazzo: Of the great family of the Pazzi of Val d'Arno, was excommunicated in 1269 for robbing ecclesiastics.

CANTO XIII.

Ere Nessus landed on the other shore
We for our part within a forest[418] drew,
Which of no pathway any traces bore.
Not green the foliage, but of dusky hue;
Not smooth the boughs, but gnarled and twisted round;
For apples, poisonous thorns upon them grew.
No rougher brakes or matted worse are found
Where savage beasts betwixt Corneto[419] roam
And Cecina,[419] abhorring cultured ground.
The loathsome Harpies[420] nestle here at home,
Who from the Strophades the Trojans chased
With dire predictions of a woe to come.
Great winged are they, but human necked and faced,
With feathered belly, and with claw for toe;
They shriek upon the bushes wild and waste.
'Ere passing further, I would have thee know,'
The worthy Master thus began to say,
'Thou'rt in the second round, nor hence shalt go
Till by the horrid sand thy footsteps stay.
Give then good heed, and things thou'lt recognise
That of my words will prove[421] the verity.'
Wailings on every side I heard arise:
Of who might raise them I distinguished nought;
Whereon I halted, smitten with surprise.
I think he thought that haply 'twas my thought
The voices came from people 'mong the trees,

Who, to escape us, hiding-places sought;
Wherefore the Master said: 'From one of these
Snap thou a twig, and thou shalt understand
How little with thy thought the fact agrees.'
Thereon a little I stretched forth my hand
And plucked a tiny branch from a great thorn.
'Why dost thou tear me?' made the trunk demand.
When dark with blood it had begun to turn,
It cried a second time: 'Why wound me thus?
Doth not a spark of pity in thee burn?
Though trees we be, once men were all of us;
Yet had our souls the souls of serpents been
Thy hand might well have proved more piteous.'
As when the fire hath seized a fagot green
At one extremity, the other sighs,
And wind, escaping, hisses; so was seen,
At where the branch was broken, blood to rise
And words were mixed with it. I dropped the spray
And stood like one whom terror doth surprise.
The Sage replied: 'Soul vexed with injury,
Had he been only able to give trust
To what he read narrated in my lay,[422]
His hand toward thee would never have been thrust.
'Tis hard for faith; and I, to make it plain,
Urged him to trial, mourn it though I must.
But tell him who thou wast; so shall remain
This for amends to thee, thy fame shall blow
Afresh on earth, where he returns again.'
And then the trunk: 'Thy sweet words charm me so,

I cannot dumb remain; nor count it hard
If I some pains upon my speech bestow.
For I am he[423] who held both keys in ward
Of Frederick's heart, and turned them how I would,
And softly oped it, and as softly barred,
Till scarce another in his counsel stood.
To my high office I such loyalty bore,
It cost me sleep and haleness of my blood.
The harlot[424] who removeth nevermore
From Cæsar's house eyes ignorant of shame—
A common curse, of courts the special sore—
Set against me the minds of all aflame,
And these in turn Augustus set on fire,
Till my glad honours bitter woes became.
My soul, filled full with a disdainful ire,
Thinking by means of death disdain to flee,'
Gainst my just self unjustly did conspire.
I swear even by the new roots of this tree
My fealty to my lord I never broke,
For worthy of all honour sure was he.
If one of you return 'mong living folk,
Let him restore my memory, overthrown
And suffering yet because of envy's stroke.'
Still for a while the poet listened on,
Then said: 'Now he is dumb, lose not the hour,
But make request if more thou'dst have made known.'
And I replied: 'Do thou inquire once more
Of what thou thinkest[425] I would gladly know;
I cannot ask; ruth wrings me to the core.'

On this he spake: 'Even as the man shall do,
And liberally, what thou of him hast prayed,
Imprisoned spirit, do thou further show
How with these knots the spirits have been made
Incorporate; and, if thou canst, declare
If from such members e'er is loosed a shade.'
Then from the trunk came vehement puffs of air;
Next, to these words converted was the wind:
'My answer to you shall be short and clear.
When the fierce soul no longer is confined
In flesh, torn thence by action of its own,
To the Seventh Depth by Minos 'tis consigned.
No choice is made of where it shall be thrown
Within the wood; but where by chance 'tis flung
It germinates like seed of spelt that's sown.
A forest tree it grows from sapling young;
Eating its leaves, the Harpies cause it pain,
And open loopholes whence its sighs are wrung.
We for our vestments shall return again
Like others, but in them shall ne'er be clad:[426]
Men justly lose what from themselves they've ta'en.
Dragged hither by us, all throughout the sad
Forest our bodies shall be hung on high;
Each on the thorn of its destructive shade.'
While to the trunk we listening lingered nigh,
Thinking he might proceed to tell us more,
A sudden uproar we were startled by
Like him who, that the huntsman and the boar
To where he stands are sweeping in the chase,

Knows by the crashing trees and brutish roar.
Upon our left we saw a couple race
Naked[427] and scratched; and they so quickly fled
The forest barriers burst before their face.
'Speed to my rescue, death!' the foremost pled.
The next, as wishing he could use more haste;
'Not thus, O Lano,[428] thee thy legs bested
When one at Toppo's tournament thou wast.'
Then, haply wanting breath, aside he stepped,
Merged with a bush on which himself he cast.
Behind them through the forest onward swept
A pack of dogs, black, ravenous, and fleet,
Like greyhounds from their leashes newly slipped.
In him who crouched they made their teeth to meet,
And, having piecemeal all his members rent,
Haled them away enduring anguish great.
Grasping my hand, my Escort forward went
And led me to the bush which, all in vain,
Through its ensanguined openings made lament.
'James of St. Andrews,'[429] it we heard complain;
'What profit hadst thou making me thy shield?
For thy bad life doth blame to me pertain?'
Then, halting there, this speech my Master held:
'Who wast thou that through many wounds dost sigh,
Mingled with blood, words big with sorrow swelled?'
'O souls that hither come,' was his reply,
'To witness shameful outrage by me borne,
Whence all my leaves torn off around me lie,
Gather them to the root of this drear thorn.

My city[430] for the Baptist changed of yore

Her former patron; wherefore, in return,

He with his art will make her aye deplore;

And were it not some image doth remain

Of him where Arno's crossed from shore to shore,

Those citizens who founded her again

On ashes left by Attila,[431] had spent

Their labour of a surety all in vain.

In my own house[432] I up a gibbet went.'

FOOTNOTES:

418. A forest: The second round of the Seventh Circle consists of a belt of tangled forest, enclosed by the river of blood, and devoted to suicides and prodigals.

419. Corneto and Cecina: Corncto is a town on the coast of what used to be the States of the Church; Cecina a stream not far south of Leghorn. Between them lies theMaremma, a district of great natural fertility, now being restored again to cultivation,but for ages a neglected and poisonous wilderness.

420. Harpies: Monsters with the bodies of birds and the heads of women. In the Æneid iii., they are described as defiling the feast of which the Trojans were aboutto partake on one of the Strophades—islands of the Ægean; and on that occasion the prophecy was made that Æneas and his followers should be reduced to eat their tablesere they acquired a settlement in Italy. Here the Harpies symbolise shameful waste anddisgust with life.

421. Will prove, etc.: The things seen by Dante are to make credible what Virgil tells(Æn. iii.) of the blood and piteous voice that issued from the torn bushes on the tomb of Polydorus.

422. My lay: See previous note. Dante thus indirectly acknowledges his debt to Virgil;and, perhaps, at the same time puts in his claim to an imaginative licence equal to thattaken by his master. On a modern reader the effect of the reference is to weaken the verisimilitude of the incident.

423. For I am he, etc.: The speaker is Pier delle Vigne, who from being a begging student of Bologna rose to be the Chancellor of the Emperor Frederick II., the chief councillor of that monarch, and one of the brightest ornaments of his intellectual court. Peter was perhaps the more endeared to his master because, like him, he was a poet ofno mean order. There are two accounts of what caused his disgrace. According to one of these he was found to have betrayed Frederick's interests in favour of the Pope's; and according to the other he tried to poison him. Neither is it known whether he committed suicide; though he is said to have done so after being disgraced, by dashinghis brains out against a church wall in Pisa. Dante clearly follows this legend. The whole episode is eloquent of the esteem in which Peter's memory was held by Dante.His name is not mentioned in Inferno, but yet the promise is amply kept that it shall flourish on earth again, freed from unmerited disgrace. He died about 1249.

424. The harlot: Envy.

425. Of what thou thinkest, etc.: Virgil never asks a question for his own satisfaction.He knows who the spirits are, what brought them there, and which of them will speakhonestly out on the promise of having his fame refreshed in the world. It should be noted how, by a hint, he has made Peter aware of who he is (line 48); a delicate attention yielded to no other shade in the Inferno, except Ulysses (Inf. xxvi. 79), and, perhaps, Brunetto Latini (Inf. xv. 99).

426. In them shall ne'er be clad: Boccaccio is herc at great pains to save Dante froma charge of contradicting the tenet of the resurrection of the flesh.

427. Naked: These are the prodigals; their nakedness representing the state to whichin life they had reduced themselves.

428. Lano: Who made one of a club of prodigals in Siena (Inf. xxix. 130) and soon ran through his fortune. Joining in a Florentine expedition in 1288 against Arezzo, herefused to escape from a defeat encountered by his side at Pieve del Toppo, preferring,as was supposed, to end his life at once rather than drag it out in poverty.

429. James of St. Andrews: Jacopo da Sant' Andrea, a Paduan who inherited enormouswealth which did not last him for long. He literally threw money away, and would burna house for the sake of the blaze. His death has been placed in 1239.

430. My city, etc.: According to tradition the original patron of Florence was Mars. InDante's time an ancient statue, supposed to be of that god, stood upon the Old Bridgeof Florence. It is referred to in Parad. xvi. 47 and 145. Benvenuto says that he had heard from Boccaccio, who had frequently heard it from old people, that the statue was regarded with great awe. If a boy flung stones or mud at it, the bystanders wouldsay of him that he would make a bad end. It was lost in the great flood of 1333. Here the Florentine shade represents Mars as troubling Florence with wars in revenge for being cast off as a patron.

431. Attila: A confusion with Totila. Attila was never so far south as Tuscany. Neitheris there reason to believe that when Totila took the city he destroyed it. But the legendwas that it was rebuilt in the time of Charles the Great.

432. My own house, etc.: It is not settled who this was who hanged himself from thebeams of his own roof. One of the Agli, say some; others, one of the Mozzi. Boccaccioand Peter Dante remark that suicide by hanging was common in Florence. ButDante's text seems pretty often to have suggested the invention of details in support or illustration of it.

CANTO XIV.

Me of my native place the dear constraint[433]
Led to restore the leaves which round were strewn,
To him whose voice by this time was grown faint.
Thence came we where the second round joins on
Unto the third, wherein how terrible
The art of justice can be, is well shown.
But, clearly of these wondrous things to tell,
I say we entered on a plain of sand
Which from its bed doth every plant repel.
The dolorous wood lies round it like a band,
As that by the drear fosse is circled round.
Upon its very edge we came to a stand.
And there was nothing within all that bound
But burnt and heavy sand; like that once trod
Beneath the feet of Cato[434] was the ground.
Ah, what a terror, O revenge of God!
Shouldst thou awake in any that may read
Of what before mine eyes was spread abroad.
I of great herds of naked souls took heed.
Most piteously was weeping every one;
And different fortunes seemed to them decreed.
For some of them[435] upon the ground lay prone,
And some were sitting huddled up and bent,
While others, restless, wandered up and down.
More numerous were they that roaming went
Than they that were tormented lying low;

But these had tongues more loosened to lament.
O'er all the sand, deliberate and slow,
Broad open flakes of fire were downward rained,
As 'mong the Alps[436] in calm descends the snow.
Such Alexander[437] saw when he attained
The hottest India; on his host they fell
And all unbroken on the earth remained;
Wherefore he bade his phalanxes tread well
The ground, because when taken one by one
The burning flakes they could the better quell.
So here eternal fire[438] was pouring down;
As tinder 'neath the steel, so here the sands
Kindled, whence pain more vehement was known.
And, dancing up and down, the wretched hands[439]
Beat here and there for ever without rest;
Brushing away from them the falling brands.
And I: 'O Master, by all things confessed
Victor, except by obdurate evil powers
Who at the gate[440] to stop our passage pressed,
Who is the enormous one who noway cowers
Beneath the fire; with fierce disdainful air
Lying as if untortured by the showers?'
And that same shade, because he was aware
That touching him I of my Guide was fain
To learn, cried: 'As in life, myself I bear
In death. Though Jupiter should tire again
His smith, from whom he snatched in angry bout
The bolt by which I at the last was slain;[441]
Though one by one he tire the others out

At the black forge in Mongibello[442] placed,
While "Ho, good Vulcan, help me!" he shall shout—
The cry he once at Phlegra's[443] battle raised;
Though hurled with all his might at me shall fly
His bolts, yet sweet revenge he shall not taste.'
Then spake my Guide, and in a voice so high
Never till then heard I from him such tone:
'O Capaneus, because unquenchably
Thy pride doth burn, worse pain by thee is known.
Into no torture save thy madness wild
Fit for thy fury couldest thou be thrown.'
Then, to me turning with a face more mild,
He said: 'Of the Seven Kings was he of old,
Who leaguered Thebes, and as he God reviled
Him in small reverence still he seems to hold;
But for his bosom his own insolence
Supplies fit ornament,[444] as now I told.
Now follow; but take heed lest passing hence
Thy feet upon the burning sand should tread;
But keep them firm where runs the forest fence.'[445]
We reached a place—nor any word we said—
Where issues from the wood a streamlet small;
I shake but to recall its colour red.
Like that which does from Bulicamë[446] fall,
And losel women later 'mong them share;
So through the sand this brooklet's waters crawl.
Its bottom and its banks I was aware
Were stone, and stone the rims on either side.
From this I knew the passage[447] must be there.

‘Of all that I have shown thee as thy guide
Since when we by the gateway[448] entered in,
Whose threshold unto no one is denied,
Nothing by thee has yet encountered been
So worthy as this brook to cause surprise,
O’er which the falling fire-flakes quenched are seen.’
These were my Leader’s words. For full supplies
I prayed him of the food of which to taste
Keen appetite he made within me rise.
‘In middle sea there lies a country waste,
Known by the name of Crete,’ I then was told,
‘Under whose king[449] the world of yore was chaste.
There stands a mountain, once the joyous hold
Of woods and streams; as Ida ’twas renowned,
Now ’tis deserted like a thing grown old.
For a safe cradle ’twas by Rhea found.
To nurse her child[450] in; and his infant cry,
Lest it betrayed him, she with clamours drowned.
Within the mount an old man towereth high.
Towards Damietta are his shoulders thrown;
On Rome, as on his mirror, rests his eye.
His head is fashioned of pure gold alone;
Of purest silver are his arms and chest;
’Tis brass to where his legs divide; then down
From that is all of iron of the best,
Save the right foot, which is of baken clay;
And upon this foot doth he chiefly rest.
Save what is gold, doth every part display
A fissure dripping tears; these, gathering all

Together, through the grotto pierce a way.
From rock to rock into this deep they fall,
Feed Acheron[451] and Styx and Phlegethon,
Then downward travelling by this strait canal,
Far as the place where further slope is none,
Cocytus form; and what that pool may be
I say not now. Thou'lt see it further on.'
'If this brook rises,' he was asked by me,
'Within our world, how comes it that no trace
We saw of it till on this boundary?'
And he replied: 'Thou knowest that the place
Is round, and far as thou hast moved thy feet,
Still to the left hand[452] sinking to the base,
Nath'less thy circuit is not yet complete.
Therefore if something new we chance to spy,
Amazement needs not on thy face have seat.'
I then: 'But, Master, where doth Lethe lie,
And Phlegethon? Of that thou sayest nought;
Of this thou say'st, those tears its flood supply.'
'It likes me well to be by thee besought;
But by the boiling red wave,' I was told,
'To half thy question was an answer brought.
Lethe,[453] not in this pit, shalt thou behold.
Thither to wash themselves the spirits go,
When penitence has made them spotless souled.'
Then said he: 'From the wood 'tis fitting now
That we depart; behind me press thou nigh.
Keep we the margins, for they do not glow,
And over them, ere fallen, the fire-flakes die.'

FOOTNOTES:

433. Dear constraint: The mention of Florence has awakened Dante to pity, and he willingly complies with the request of the unnamed suicide (Inf. xiii. 142). As a rule, the only service he consents to yield the souls with whom he converses in Inferno is torestore their memory upon earth; a favour he does not feign to be asked for in this case,out of consideration, it may be, for the family of the sinner.

434. Cato: Cato of Utica, who, after the defeat of Pompey at Pharsalia, led his brokenarmy across the Libyan desert to join King Juba.

435. Some of them, etc.: In this the third round of the Seventh Circle are punished thoseguilty of sins of violence against God, against nature, and against the arts by which alone a livelihood can honestly be won. Those guilty as against God, the blasphemers,lie prone like Capaneus (line 46), and are subject to the fiercest pain. Those guilty of unnatural vice are stimulated into ceaseless motion, as described in Cantos XV. And XVI. The usurers, those who despise honest industry and the humanising arts of life, are found crouching on the ground (Inf. xvii. 43).

436. The Alps: Used here for mountains in general.

437. Such Alexander, etc.: The reference is to a pretended letter of Alexander to Aristotle, in which he tells of the various hindrances met with by his army from snowand rain and showers of fire. But in that narrative it is the snow that is trampled down, while the flakes of fire are caught by the soldiers upon their outspread cloaks. The storyof the shower of fire may have been suggested by Plutarch's mention of the mineral oil in the province of Babylon, a strange thing to the Greeks; and of how they were entertained by seeing the ground, which had been sprinkled with it, burst into flame.

438. Eternal fire: As always, the character of the place and of the punishment bears arelation to the crimes of the inhabitants. They sinned against nature in a special sense, and now they are confined to the sterile sand where the only showers that fall are showers of fire.

439. The wretched hands: The dance, named in the original the tresca, was one in which the performers followed a leader and imitated him in all his gestures, waving their hands as he did, up and down, and from side to side. The simile is caught straightfrom common life.

440. At the gate: Of the city of Dis (Inf. viii. 82).

441. Was slain, etc.: Capaneus, one of the Seven Kings, as told below, when storming the walls of Thebes, taunted the other gods with impunity, but his blasphemy against Jupiter was answered by a fatal bolt.

442. Mongibello: A popular name of Etna, under which mountain was situated the smithy of Vulcan and the Cyclopes.

443. Phlegra: Where the giants fought with the gods.

444. Fit ornament, etc.: Even if untouched by the pain he affects to despise, he would yet suffer enough from the mad hatred of God that rages in his breast. Capaneus is thenearest approach to the Satan of Milton found in the Inferno. From the need of gettinglaw enough by which to try the heathen Dante is led into some inconsistency. After condemning the virtuous heathen to Limbo for their ignorance of the one true God, he now condemns the wicked heathen to this circle for despising false gods. Jupiter herestands for, as need scarcely be said, the Supreme Ruler; and in that sense he is termedGod (line 69). But it remains remarkable that the one instance of blasphemous defiance of God should be taken from classical fable.

445. The forest fence: They do not trust themselves so much as to step upon the sand,but look out on it from the verge of the forest which encircles it, and which as they travel they have on the left hand.

446. Bulicamë: A hot sulphur spring a couple of miles from Viterbo, greatly frequented for baths in the Middle Ages; and, it is said, especially by light women. The water boils up into a large pool, whence it flows by narrow channels; sometimes by one and sometimes by another, as the purposes of the neighbouring peasants require. Sulphurous fumes rise from the water as it runs. The incrustation of the bottom, sides,and edges of those channels gives them the air of being solidly built.

447. The passage: On each edge of the canal there is a flat pathway of solid stone; and Dante sees that only by following one of these can a passage be gained across thedesert, for to set foot on the sand is impossible for him owing to the falling flakes of fire. There may be found in his description of the solid and flawless masonry of the canal a trace of the pleasure taken in good building by the contemporaries of Arnolfo. Nor is it without meaning that the sterile sands, the abode of such as despised honest labour, is crossed by a perfect work of art which they are forbidden ever to set foot upon.

448. The gateway: At the entrance to Inferno.

449. Whose king: Saturn, who ruled the world in the Golden Age. He, as the devourerof his own offspring, is the symbol of Time; and the image of Time is therefore set byDante in the island where he reigned.

450. Her child: Jupiter, hidden in the mountain from his father Saturn.

451. Feed Acheron, etc.: The idea of this image is taken from the figure in Nebuchadnezzar's dream in Daniel ii. But here, instead of the Four Empires, the materials of the statue represent the Four Ages of the world; the foot of clay on which itstands being the present time, which is so bad that even iron were too good to representit. Time turns his back to the outworn civilisations of the East, and his face to Rome, which, as the seat of the Empire and the Church, holds the secret of the future. The tearsof time shed by every Age save that of Gold feed the four infernal streams and pools of Acheron, Styx, Phlegethon, and Cocytus. Line 117 indicates that these are all fed by the same water; are in fact different names for the same flood of tears. The reason why Dante has not hitherto observed the connection between them is that he has not made a complete circuit of each or indeed of any circle, as Virgil reminds him at line 124, etc. The rivulet by which they stand drains the boiling Phlegethon—where the water is all changed to blood, because in it the murderers are punished—and flowing through the forest of the suicides and the desert of the blasphemers, etc., tumbles intothe Eighth Circle as described in Canto xvi. 103. Cocytus they are afterward to reach. An objection to this account of the infernal rivers as being all fed by the same waters may be found in the difference of volume of the great river of Acheron (Inf. iii. 71) andof this brooklet. But this difference is perhaps to be explained by the evaporation from the boiling waters of Phlegethon and of this stream which drains it. Dante is almost theonly poet applied to whom such criticism would not be trifling. Another difficult point is how Cocytus should not in time have filled, and more than filled, the Ninth Circle.

452. To the left hand: Twice only as they descend they turn their course to the right hand (Inf. ix. 132, and xvii. 31). The circuit of the Inferno they do not complete till they reach the very base.

453. Lethe: Found in the Earthly Paradise, as described in Purgatorio xxviii. 130.

CANTO XV.

Now lies[454] our way along one of the margins hard;
Steam rising from the rivulet forms a cloud,
Which 'gainst the fire doth brook and borders guard.
Like walls the Flemings, timorous of the flood
Which towards them pours betwixt Bruges and Cadsand,[455]
Have made, that ocean's charge may be withstood;
Or what the Paduans on the Brenta's strand
To guard their castles and their homesteads rear,
Ere Chiarentana[456] feel the spring-tide bland;
Of the same fashion did those dikes appear,
Though not so high[457] he made them, nor so vast,
Whoe'er the builder was that piled them here.
We, from the wood when we so far had passed
I should not have distinguished where it lay
Though I to see it backward glance had cast,
A group of souls encountered on the way,
Whose line of march was to the margin nigh.
Each looked at us—as by the new moon's ray
Men peer at others 'neath the darkening sky—
Sharpening his brows on us and only us,
Like an old tailor on his needle's eye.
And while that crowd was staring at me thus,
One of them knew me, caught me by the gown,
And cried aloud: 'Lo, this is marvellous!'[458]
And straightway, while he thus to me held on,
I fixed mine eyes upon his fire-baked face,

And, spite of scorching, seemed his features known,
And whose they were my memory well could trace;
And I, with hand[459] stretched toward his face below,
Asked: 'Ser Brunetto![460] and is this your place?'
'O son,' he answered, 'no displeasure show,
If now Brunetto Latini shall some way
Step back with thee, and leave his troop to go.'
I said: 'With all my heart for this I pray,
And, if you choose, I by your side will sit;
If he, for I go with him, grant delay.'
'Son,' said he, 'who of us shall intermit
Motion a moment, for an age must lie
Nor fan himself when flames are round him lit.
On, therefore! At thy skirts I follow nigh
Then shall I overtake my band again,
Who mourn a loss large as eternity.'
I dared not from the path step to the plain
To walk with him, but low I bent my head,[461]
Like one whose steps are all with reverence ta'en.
'What fortune or what destiny,' he said,
'Hath brought thee here or e'er thou death hast seen;
And who is this by whom thou'rt onward led?'
'Up yonder,' said I, 'in the life serene,
I in a valley wandered all forlorn
Before my years had full accomplished been.
I turned my back on it but yestermorn;[462] Again
I sought it when he came in sight
Guided by whom[463] I homeward thus return.'
And he to me: 'Following thy planet's light[464]

Thou of a glorious haven canst not fail,
If in the blithesome life I marked aright.
And had my years known more abundant tale,
Seeing the heavens so held thee in their grace
I, heartening thee, had helped thee to prevail.
But that ungrateful and malignant race
Which down from Fiesole[465] came long ago,
And still its rocky origin betrays,
Will for thy worthiness become thy foe;
And with good reason, for 'mong crab-trees wild
It ill befits the mellow fig to grow.
By widespread ancient rumour are they styled
A people blind, rapacious, envious, vain:
See by their manners thou be not defiled.
Fortune reserves such honour for thee, fain
Both sides[466] will be to enlist thee in their need;
But from the beak the herb shall far remain.
Let beasts of Fiesole go on to tread
Themselves to litter, nor the plants molest,
If any such now spring on their rank bed,
In whom there flourishes indeed the blest
Seed of the Romans who still lingered there
When of such wickedness 'twas made the nest.'
'Had I obtained full answer to my prayer,
You had not yet been doomed,' I then did say,
'This exile from humanity to bear.
For deep within my heart and memory
Lives the paternal image good and dear
Of you, as in the world, from day to day,

How men escape oblivion you made clear;
My thankfulness for which shall in my speech
While I have life, as it behoves, appear.
I note what of my future course you teach.
Stored with another text[467] it will be glozed
By one expert, should I that Lady reach.
Yet would I have this much to you disclosed:
If but my conscience no reproaches yield,
To all my fortune is my soul composed.
Not new to me the hint by you revealed;
Therefore let Fortune turn her wheel apace,
Even as she will; the clown[468] his mattock wield.'
Thereon my Master right about[469] did face,
And uttered this, with glance upon me thrown:
'He hears[470] to purpose who doth mark the place.'
And none the less I, speaking, still go on
With Ser Brunetto; asking him to tell
Who of his band[471] are greatest and best known.
And he to me: 'To hear of some is well,
But of the rest 'tis fitting to be dumb,
And time is lacking all their names to spell.
That all of them were clerks, know thou in sum,
All men of letters, famous and of might;
Stained with one sin[472] all from the world are come.
Priscian[473] goes with that crowd of evil plight,
Francis d'Accorso[474] too; and hadst thou mind
For suchlike trash thou mightest have had sight
Of him the Slave[475] of Slaves to change assigned
From Arno's banks to Bacchiglione, where

His nerves fatigued with vice he left behind.

More would I say, but neither must I fare

Nor talk at further length, for from the sand

I see new dust-clouds[476] rising in the air,

I may not keep with such as are at hand.

Care for my Treasure;[477] for I still survive

In that my work. I nothing else demand.'

Then turned he back, and ran like those who strive

For the Green Cloth[478] upon Verona's plain;

And seemed like him that shall the first arrive,

And not like him that labours all in vain.

FOOTNOTES:

454. *Now lies, etc.:* The stream on issuing from the wood flows right across the wasteof sand which that encompasses. To follow it they must turn to the right, as always when, their general course being to the left, they have to cross a Circle. But such a veering to the right is a consequence of their leftward course, and not an exception to it.

455. *Cadsand:* An island opposite to the mouth of the great canal of Bruges.

456. *Chiarentana:* What district or mountain is here meant has been much disputed. It can be taken for Carinthia only on the supposition that Dante was ignorant of wherethe Brenta rises. At the source of that river stands the Monte Chiarentana, but it may be a question how old that name is. The district name of it is Canzana, or Carenzana.

457. *Not so high, etc.:* This limitation is very characteristic of Dante's style of thought, which compels him to a precision that will produce the utmost possible effectof verisimilitude in his description. Most poets would have made the walls far higher and more vast, by way of lending grandeur to the conception.

458. *Marvellous:* To find Dante, whom he knew, still living, and passing through the Circle.

459. *With hand, etc.:* 'With my face bent to his' is another reading, but there seems to be most authority for that in the text.—The fiery shower forbids Dante to stoop overthe edge of the causeway. To Brunetto, who is some feet below

him, he throws out hisopen hand, a gesture of astonishment mingled with pity.

460. Ser Brunetto: Brunetto Latini, a Florentine, was born in 1220. As a notary he was entitled to be called Ser, or Messer. As appears from the context, Dante was under great intellectual obligations to him, not, we may suppose, as to a tutor so much as to an active-minded and scholarly friend of mature age, and possessed of a ripe experience of affairs. The social respect that Dante owed him is indicated by the use of the plural form of address. See note, Inf. x. 51. Brunetto held high appointments in the Republic. Perhaps with some exaggeration, Villani says of him that he was the first to refine the Florentines, teaching them to speak correctly, and to administer State affairs on fixed principles of politics (Cronica, viii. 10). A Guelf in politics, he shared in the exile of his party after the Ghibeline victory of Montaperti in 1260, and for some years resided in Paris. There is reason to suppose that he returned to Florence in 1269,and that he acted as prothonotary of the court of Charles of Valois' vicar-general in Tuscany. His signature as secretary to the Council of Florence is found under the dateof 1273. He died in 1294, when Dante was twenty-nine, and was buried in the cloisterof Santa Maria Maggiore, where his tombstone may still be seen. (Not in Santa MariaNovella.) Villani mentions him in his Chronicle with some reluctance, seeing he was a'worldly man.' His life must indeed have been vicious to the last, before Dante could have had the heart to fix him in such company. Brunetto's chief works are the Tesoroand Tesoretto. For the Tesoro, see note at line 119. The Tesoretto, or Little Treasure, is an allegorical poem in Italian rhymed couplets. In it he imagines himself, as he is on his return from an embassy to Alphonso of Castile, meeting a scholar of Bologna of whom he asks 'in smooth sweet words for news of Tuscany.' Having been toldof the catastrophe of Montaperti he wanders out of the beaten way into the Forestof Roncesvalles, where he meets with various experiences; he is helped by Ovid, is instructed by Ptolemy, and grows penitent for his sins. In this, it will be seen, there is a general resemblance to the action of the Comedy. There are even turns of expression that recall Dante (e.g. beginning of Cap. iv.); but all together amounts to little.

461. Low I bent my head: But not projecting it beyond the line of safety, strictly defined by the edge of the causeway. We are to imagine to ourselves the fire of Sodomfalling on Brunetto's upturned face, and missing Dante's head only by an inch.

462. Yestermorn: This is still the Saturday. It was Friday when Dante met Virgil.

463. Guided by whom: Brunetto has asked who the guide is, and Dante does not tell him. A reason for the refusal has been ingeniously found in the fact that among the numerous citations of the Treasure Brunetto seldom quotes Virgil. See also the charge brought against Guido Cavalcanti (Inf. x. 63), of holding Virgil in disdain. But it is explanation enough of Dante's omission to name his guide that he is passing through Inferno to gain experience for himself, and not to satisfy the curiosity of the shades hemeets. See note on line 99.

464. Thy planet's light: Some think that Brunetto had cast Dante's horoscope. In a remarkable passage (Parad. xxii. 112) Dante attributes any genius he may have to the influence of the Twins, which constellation was in the ascendant when he was born. See also Inf. xxvi. 23. But here it is more likely that Brunetto refers to his observationof Dante's good qualities, from which he gathered that he was well starred.

465. Fiesole: The mother city of Florence, to which also most of the Fiesolans were believed to have migrated at the beginning of the eleventh century. But all the Florentines did their best to establish a Roman descent for themselves; and Dante among them. His fellow-citizens he held to be for the most part of the boorish Fiesolanbreed, rude and stony-hearted as the mountain in whose cleft the cradle of their race was seen from Florence.

466. Both sides: This passage was most likely written not long after Dante had ceased to entertain any hope of winning his way back to Florence in the company of the Whites, whose exile he shared, and when he was already standing in proud isolation from Black and White, from Guelf and Ghibeline. There is nothing to show that his expectation of being courted by both sides ever came true. Never a strong partisan,he had, to use his own words, at last to make a party by himself, and stood out an Imperialist with his heart set on the triumph of an Empire far nobler than that the Ghibeline desired. Dante may have hoped to hold a place of honour some day in the council of a righteous Emperor; and this may be the glorious haven with the dream ofwhich he was consoled in the wanderings of his exile.

467. Another text: Ciacco and Farinata have already hinted at the troubles that lie ahead of him (Inf. vi. 65, and x. 79).

468. The clown, etc.: The honest performance of duty is the best defence against adverse fortune.

469. Right about: In traversing the sands they keep upon the right-hand margin of theembanked stream, Virgil leading the way, with Dante behind him on the right so that Brunetto may see and hear him well.

470. He hears, etc.: Of all the interpretations of this somewhat obscure sentence thatseems the best which applies it to Virgil's Quicquid erit, superanda omnis fortuna ferendo est—'Whatever shall happen, every fate is to be vanquished by endurance' (Æn. v. 710). Taking this way of it, we have in the form of Dante's profession of indifference to all the adverse fortune that may be in store for him a refined compliment to his Guide; and in Virgil's gesture and words an equally delicate revelation of himself to Brunetto, in which is conveyed an answer to the question at line 48, 'Who is this that shows the way?'—Otherwise, the words convey Virgil's approbation of Dante's having so well attended to his advice to store Farinata's prophecy in his memory (Inf.x.127).

471. His band: That is, the company to which Brunetto specially belongs, and from which for the time he has separated himself.

472. Stained with one sin: Dante will not make Brunetto individually confess his sin.

473. Priscian: The great grammarian of the sixth century; placed here without any reason, except that he is a representative teacher of youth.

474. Francis d'Accorso: Died about 1294. The son of a great civil lawyer, he was himself professor of the civil law at Bologna, where his services were so highly prizedthat the Bolognese forbade him, on pain of the confiscation of his goods, to accept aninvitation from Edward I. to go to Oxford.

475. Of him the Slave, etc.: One of the Pope's titles is Servus Servorum Domini. The application of it to Boniface, so hated by Dante, may be ironical: 'Fit servant of such a slave to vice!' The priest referred to so contemptuously is Andrea, of the greatFlorentine family of the Mozzi, who was much engaged in the political affairs of his time, and became Bishop of Florence in 1286. About ten years later he was translated to Vicenza, which stands on the Bacchiglione; and he died shortly afterwards. According to Benvenuto he was a ridiculous preacher and a man of dissolute manners. What is now most interesting about him is that he was Dante's chief pastor during his early manhood, and is consigned by him to the same disgraceful circle of Inferno as his beloved master Brunetto Latini—a terrible evidence of the corruption of life among the churchmen as well as the scholars of the thirteenth century.

476. New dust-clouds: Raised by a band by whom they are about to be met.

477. My Treasure: The Trésor, or Tesoro, Brunetto's principal work, was written byhim in French as being 'the pleasantest language, and the most widely spread.' In it hetreats of things in general in the encyclopedic fashion set him by Alphonso of Castile. The first half consists of a summary of civil and natural history. The second is devotedto ethics, rhetoric, and politics. To a great extent it is a compilation, containing, for instance, a translation, nearly complete, of the Ethics of Aristotle—not, of course, direct from the Greek. It is written in a plodding style, and speaks to more industry than genius. To it Dante is indebted for some facts and fables.

478. The Green Cloth: To commemorate a victory won by the Veronese there was instituted a race to be run on the first Sunday of Lent. The prize was a piece of green cloth. The competitors ran naked.—Brunetto does not disappear into the gloom without a parting word of applause from his old pupil. Dante's rigorous sentence on his beloved master is pronounced as softly as it can be. We must still wonder that he has the heart to bring him to such an awful judgment.

CANTO XVI.

Now could I hear the water as it fell
To the next circle[479] with a murmuring sound
Like what is heard from swarming hives to swell;
When three shades all together with a bound
Burst from a troop met by us pressing on
'Neath rain of that sharp torment. O'er the ground
Toward us approaching, they exclaimed each one:
'Halt thou, whom from thy garb[480] we judge to be
A citizen of our corrupted town.'
Alas, what scars I on their limbs did see,
Both old and recent, which the flames had made:
Even now my ruth is fed by memory.
My Teacher halted at their cry, and said:
'Await a while:' and looked me in the face;
'Some courtesy to these were well displayed
.And but that fire—the manner of the place—
Descends for ever, fitting 'twere to find
Rather than them, thee quickening thy pace.'
When we had halted, they again combined
In their old song; and, reaching where we stood,
Into a wheel all three were intertwined.
And as the athletes used, well oiled and nude,
To feel their grip and, wary, watch their chance,
Ere they to purpose strike and wrestle could;
So each of them kept fixed on me his glance
As he wheeled round,[481] and in opposing ways

His neck and feet seemed ever to advance.
'Ah, if the misery of this sand-strewn place
Bring us and our petitions in despite,'
One then began, 'and flayed and grimy face;
Let at the least our fame goodwill incite
To tell us who thou art, whose living feet
Thus through Inferno wander without fright.
For he whose footprints, as thou see'st, I beat,
Though now he goes with body peeled and nude,
More than thou thinkest, in the world was great.
The grandson was he of Gualdrada good;
He, Guidoguerra,[482] with his armèd hand
Did mighty things, and by his counsel shrewd.
The other who behind me treads the sand
Is one whose name should on the earth be dear;
For he is Tegghiaio[483] Aldobrand.
And I, who am tormented with them here,
James Rusticucci[484] was; my fierce and proud
Wife of my ruin was chief minister.'
If from the fire there had been any shroud
I should have leaped down 'mong them, nor have earned
Blame, for my Teacher sure had this allowed.
But since I should have been all baked and burned,
Terror prevailed the goodwill to restrain
With which to clasp them in my arms I yearned.
Then I began: ''Twas not contempt but pain
Which your condition in my breast awoke,
Where deeply rooted it will long remain,
When this my Master words unto me spoke,

By which expectancy was in me stirred
That ye who came were honourable folk.
I of your city[485] am, and with my word
Your deeds and honoured names oft to recall
Delighted, and with joy of them I heard.
To the sweet fruits I go, and leave the gall,
As promised to me by my Escort true;
But first I to the centre down must fall.'
'So may thy soul thy members long endue
With vital power,' the other made reply,
'And after thee thy fame[486] its light renew;
As thou shalt tell if worth and courtesy
Within our city as of yore remain,
Or from it have been wholly forced to fly.
For William Borsier,[487] one of yonder train,
And but of late joined with us in this woe,
Causeth us with his words exceeding pain.'
'Upstarts, and fortunes suddenly that grow,
Have bred in thee pride and extravagance,[488]
Whence tears, O Florence! thou art shedding now.'
Thus cried I with uplifted countenance.
The three, accepting it for a reply,
Glanced each at each as hearing truth men glance.
And all: 'If others thou shalt satisfy
As well at other times[489] at no more cost,
Happy thus at thine ease the truth to cry!
Therefore if thou escap'st these regions lost,
Returning to behold the starlight fair,
Then when "There was I,"[490] thou shalt make thy boast,

Something of us do thou 'mong men declare.'
Then broken was the wheel, and as they fled
Their nimble legs like pinions beat the air.
So much as one Amen! had scarce been said
Quicker than what they vanished from our view.
On this once more the way my Master led.
I followed, and ere long so near we drew
To where the water fell, that for its roar
Speech scarcely had been heard between us two.
And as the stream which of all those which pour
East (from Mount Viso counting) by its own
Course falls the first from Apennine to shore—
As Acquacheta[491] in the uplands known
By name, ere plunging to its bed profound;
Name lost ere by Forlì its waters run—
Above St. Benedict with one long bound,
Where for a thousand[492] would be ample room,
Falls from the mountain to the lower ground;
Down the steep cliff that water dyed in gloom
We found to fall echoing from side to side,
Stunning the ear with its tremendous boom.
There was a cord about my middle tied,
With which I once had thought that I might hold
Secure the leopard with the painted hide.
When this from round me I had quite unrolled
To him I handed it, all coiled and tight;
As by my Leader I had first been told.
Himself then bending somewhat toward the right,[493]
He just beyond the edge of the abyss

Threw down the cord,[494] which disappeared from sight.
'That some strange thing will follow upon this
Unwonted signal which my Master's eye
Thus follows,' so I thought, 'can hardly miss.'
Ah, what great caution need we standing by
Those who behold not only what is done,
But who have wit our hidden thoughts to spy!
He said to me: 'There shall emerge, and soon,
What I await; and quickly to thy view
That which thou dream'st of shall be clearly known.'[495]
From utterance of truth which seems untrue
A man, whene'er he can, should guard his tongue;
Lest he win blame to no transgression due.
Yet now I must speak out, and by the song
Of this my Comedy, Reader, I swear—
So in good liking may it last full long!—
I saw a shape swim upward through that air.
All indistinct with gross obscurity,
Enough to fill the stoutest heart with fear:
Like one who rises having dived to free
An anchor grappled on a jagged stone,
Or something else deep hidden in the sea;
With feet drawn in and arms all open thrown.

FOOTNOTES:

479. *The next circle:* The Eighth.

480. *Thy garb:* 'Almost every city,' says Boccaccio, 'had in those times its peculiar ashion of dress distinct from that of neighboring cities.'

481. As he wheeled round: Virgil and Dante have come to a halt upon the embankment. The three shades, to whom it is forbidden to be at rest for a moment, clasping one another as in a dance, keep wheeling round in circle upon the sand.

482. Guidoguerra: A descendant of the Counts Guidi of Modigliana. Gualdrada was the daughter of Bellincion Berti de' Ravignani, praised for his simple habits in the Paradiso, xv. 112. Guidoguerra was a Guelf leader, and after the defeat of Montaperti acted as Captain of his party, in this capacity lending valuable aid to Charles of Anjou at the battle of Benevento, 1266, when Manfred was overthrown. He had no children, and left the Commonwealth of Florence his heir.

483. Tegghiaio: Son of Aldobrando of the Adimari. His name should be dear in Florence, because he did all he could to dissuade the citizens from the campaign which ended so disastrously at Montaperti.

484. James Rusticucci: An accomplished cavalier of humble birth, said to have been a retainer of Dante's friends the Cavalcanti. The commentators have little to tell of him except that he made an unhappy marriage, which is evident from the text. Of the sins of him and his companions there is nothing known beyond what is to be inferred from the poet's words, and nothing to say, except that when Dante consigned men of their stamp, frank and amiable, to the Infernal Circles, we may be sure that he only executed a verdict already accepted as just by the whole of Florence. And when we find him impartially damning Guelf and Ghibeline we may be equally sure that he looked for the aid of neither party, and of no family however powerful in the State, to bring his banishment to a close. He would even seem to be careful to stop any hole by which he might creep back to Florence. When he did return, it was to be in the train of the Emperor, so he hoped, and as one who gives rather than seeks forgiveness.

485. Of your city, etc.: At line 32 Rusticucci begs Dante to tell who he is. He tells that he is of their city, which they have already gathered from his berretta and the fashion of his gown; but he tells nothing, almost, of himself. Unless to Farinata, indeed, he never makes an open breast to any one met in Inferno. But here he does all that courtesy requires.

486. Thy fame: Dante has implied in his answer that he is gifted with oratorical powers and is the object of a special Divine care; and the illustrious Florentine, frankly acknowledging the claim he makes, adjures him by the fame which is his in store to appease an eager curiosity about the Florence which even in Inferno is the first thought of every not ignoble Florentine.

487. William Borsiere: A Florentine, witty and well bred, according to Boccaccio. Being once at Genoa he was shown a fine new palace by its miserly owner, and was asked to suggest a subject for a painting with which to adorn the hall. The subject was to be something that nobody had ever seen. Borsiere proposed liberality as something that the miser at any rate had never yet got a good sight of; an answer of which it is not easy to detect either the wit or the courtesy, but which is said to have converted the churl to liberal ways (Decam. i. 8). He is here introduced as an authority on the noble style of manners.

488. Pride and extravagance: In place of the nobility of mind that leads to great actions, and the gentle manners that prevail in a society where there is a due subordination of rank to rank and well-defined duties for every man. This, the aristocratic in a noble sense, was Dante's ideal of a social state; for all his instincts were those of a Florentine aristocrat, corrected though they were by his good sense and his thirst for a reign of perfect justice. During his own time he had seen Florence grow more and more democratic; and he was irritated—unreasonably, considering that it was only a sign of the general prosperity—at the spectacle of the amazing growth of wealth in the hands of low-born traders, who every year were coming more to the front and monopolising influence at home and abroad at the cost of their neighbours and rivals with longer pedigrees and shorter purses. In Paradiso xvi. Dante dwells at length on the degeneracy of the Florentines.

489. At other times: It is hinted that his outspokenness will not in the future always give equal satisfaction to those who hear.

490. There was I, etc.: Forsan et hæc olim meminisse juvabit.—Æn. i. 203.

491. Acquacheta: The fall of the water of the brook over the lofty cliff that sinks from the Seventh to the Eighth Circle is compared to the waterfall upon the Montone at the monastery of St. Benedict, in the mountains above Forlì. The Po rises in Monte Viso. Dante here travels in imagination from Monte Viso down through Italy, and finds that all the rivers which rise on the left hand, that is, on the north-east of the Apennine, fall into the Po, till the Montone is reached, that river falling into the Adriatic by a course of its own. Above Forlì it was called Acquacheta. The Lamone, north of the Montone, now follows an independent course to the sea, having cut a new bed for itself since Dante's time.

492. Where for a thousand, etc.: In the monastery there was room for many more monks, say most of the commentators; or something to the like effect. Mr. Longfellow's interpretation seems better: Where the height of the fall is so great that it would divide into a thousand falls.

493. Toward the right: The attitude of one about to throw.

494. The cord: The services of Geryon are wanted to convey them down the next reach of the pit; and as no voice could be heard for the noise of the waterfall, and no signal be made to catch the eye amid the gloom, Virgil is obliged to call the attention of the monster by casting some object into the depth where he lies concealed. But, since they are surrounded by solid masonry and slack sand, one or other of them must supply something fit to throw down; and the cord worn by Dante is fixed on as what can bestbe done without. There may be a reference to the cord of Saint Francis, which Dante, according to one of his commentators, wore when he was a young man, following in this a fashion common enough among pious laymen who had no thought of ever becoming friars. But the simile of the cord, as representing sobriety and virtuous purpose, is notstrange to Dante. In Purg. vii. 114 he describes Pedro of Arragon as being girt with the cord of every virtue; and Pedro was no Franciscan. Dante's cord may therefore betaken as standing for vigilance or self-control. With it he had hoped to get the better ofthe leopard (Inf. i. 32), and may have trusted in it for support as against the terrors of Inferno. But although he has been girt with it ever since he entered by the gate, it has not saved him from a single fear, far less from a single danger; and now it is cast away as useless. Henceforth, more than ever, he is to confide wholly in Virgil and have no confidence in himself. Nor is he to be girt again till he reaches the coast of Purgatory, and then it is to be with a reed, the emblem of humility.—But, however explained, theincident will always be somewhat of a puzzle.

495. Dante attributes to Virgil full knowledge of all that is in his own mind. He thus heightens our conception of his dependence on his guide, with whose will his will is blent, and whose thoughts are always found to be anticipating his own. Few readers will care to be constantly recalling to mind that Virgil represents enlightened human reason. But even if we confine ourselves to the easiest sense of the narrative, the studyof the relations between him and Dante will be found one of the most interesting suggested by the poem—perhaps only less so than that of Dante's moods of wonder, anger, and pity.

CANTO XVII.

'Behold the monster[496] with the pointed tail,
Who passes mountains[497] and can entrance make
Through arms and walls! who makes the whole world ail,
Corrupted by him!' Thus my Leader spake,
And beckoned him that he should land hard by,
Where short the pathways built of marble break.
And that foul image of dishonesty
Moving approached us with his head and chest,
But to the bank[498] drew not his tail on high.
His face a human righteousness expressed,
'Twas so benignant to the outward view;
A serpent was he as to all the rest.
On both his arms hair to the arm-pits grew:
On back and chest and either flank were knot[499]
And rounded shield portrayed in various hue;
No Turk or Tartar weaver ever brought
To ground or pattern a more varied dye;[500]
Nor by Arachne[501] was such broidery wrought.
As sometimes by the shore the barges lie
Partly in water, partly on dry land;
And as afar in gluttonous Germany,[502]
Watching their prey, alert the beavers stand;
So did this worst of brutes his foreparts fling
Upon the stony rim which hems the sand.
All of his tail in space was quivering,
Its poisoned fork erecting in the air,

Which scorpion-like was armèd with a sting.
My Leader said: 'Now we aside must fare
A little distance, so shall we attain
Unto the beast malignant crouching there.'
So we stepped down upon the right,[503] and then
A half score steps[504] to the outer edge did pace,
Thus clearing well the sand and fiery rain.
And when we were hard by him I could trace
Upon the sand a little further on
Some people sitting near to the abyss.
'That what this belt containeth may be known
Completely by thee,' then the Master said;
'To see their case do thou advance alone.
Let thy inquiries be succinctly made.
While thou art absent I will ask of him,
With his strong shoulders to afford us aid.'
Then, all alone, I on the outmost rim
Of that Seventh Circle still advancing trod,
Where sat a woful folk.[505] Full to the brim
Their eyes with anguish were, and overflowed;
Their hands moved here and there to win some ease,
Now from the flames, now from the soil which glowed.
No otherwise in summer-time one sees,
Working its muzzle and its paws, the hound
When bit by gnats or plagued with flies or fleas.
And I, on scanning some who sat around
Of those on whom the dolorous flames alight,
Could recognise[506] not one. I only found
A purse hung from the throat of every wight,

Each with its emblem and its special hue;
And every eye seemed feasting on the sight.
As I, beholding them, among them drew,
I saw what seemed a lion's face and mien
Upon a yellow purse designed in blue.
Still moving on mine eyes athwart the scene
I saw another scrip, blood-red, display
A goose more white than butter could have been.
And one, on whose white wallet blazoned lay
A pregnant sow[507] in azure, to me said:
'What dost thou in this pit? Do thou straightway
Begone; and, seeing thou art not yet dead,
Know that Vitalian,[508] neighbour once of mine,
Shall on my left flank one day find his bed.
A Paduan I: all these are Florentine;
And oft they stun me, bellowing in my ear:
"Come, Pink of Chivalry,[509] for whom we pine,
Whose is the purse on which three beaks appear:"'
Then he from mouth awry his tongue thrust out[510]
Like ox that licks its nose; and I, in fear
Lest more delay should stir in him some doubt
Who gave command I should not linger long,
Me from those wearied spirits turned about.
I found my Guide, who had already sprung
Upon the back of that fierce animal:
He said to me: 'Now be thou brave and strong.
By stairs like this[511] we henceforth down must fall.
Mount thou in front, for I between would sit
So thee the tail shall harm not nor appal.'

Like one so close upon the shivering fit
Of quartan ague that his nails grow blue,
And seeing shade he trembles every whit,
I at the hearing of that order grew;
But his threats shamed me, as before the face
Of a brave lord his man grows valorous too.
On the great shoulders then I took my place,
And wished to say, but could not move my tongue
As I expected: ‘Do thou me embrace!’
But he, who other times had helped me ’mong
My other perils, when ascent I made
Sustained me, and strong arms around me flung,
And, ‘Geryon, set thee now in motion!’ said;
‘Wheel widely; let thy downward flight be slow;
Think of the novel burden on thee laid.’
As from the shore a boat begins to go
Backward at first, so now he backward pressed,
And when he found that all was clear below,
He turned his tail where earlier was his breast;
And, stretching it, he moved it like an eel,
While with his paws he drew air toward his chest.
More terror Phaëthon could hardly feel
What time he let the reins abandoned fall,
Whence Heaven was fired,[512] as still its tracts reveal;
Nor wretched Icarus, on finding all
His plumage moulting as the wax grew hot,
While, ‘The wrong road!’ his father loud did call;
Than what I felt on finding I was brought
Where nothing was but air and emptiness;

For save the brute I could distinguish nought.
He slowly, slowly swims; to the abyss
Wheeling he makes descent, as I surmise
From wind felt 'neath my feet and in my face.
Already on the right I heard arise
From out the caldron a terrific roar,[513]
Whereon I stretch my head with down-turned eyes.
Terror of falling now oppressed me sore;
Hearing laments, and seeing fires that burned,
My thighs I tightened, trembling more and more.
Earlier I had not by the eye discerned
That we swept downward; scenes of torment now
Seemed drawing nearer wheresoe'er we turned.
And as a falcon (which long time doth go
Upon the wing, not finding lure[514] or prey),
While 'Ha!' the falconer cries, 'descending so!'
Comes wearied back whence swift it soared away;
Wheeling a hundred times upon the road,
Then, from its master far, sulks angrily:
So we, by Geryon in the deep bestowed,
Were 'neath the sheer-hewn precipice set down:
He, suddenly delivered from our load,
Like arrow from the string was swiftly gone.

FOOTNOTES:

496. The monster: Geryon, a mythical king of Spain, converted here into the symbolof fraud, and set as the guardian demon of the Eighth Circle, where the fraudulentare punished. There is nothing in the mythology to justify this account of Geryon;and it seems that Dante has created a monster to serve his purpose. Boccaccio, in his Genealogy of the Gods (Lib. i.), repeats the description of Geryon given by 'Dante the Florentine, in his poem written in the Florentine tongue, one certainly of no little importance among poems;' and adds that Geryon reigned in the Balearic Isles, and was used to decoy travellers with his benignant countenance, caressing words, and every kind of friendly lure, and then to murder them when asleep.

497. Who passes mountains, etc.: Neither art nor nature affords any defence against

fraud.

498. The bank: Not that which confines the brook but the inner limit of the Seventh Circle, from which the precipice sinks sheer into the Eighth, and to which the embankment by which the travellers have crossed the sand joins itself on. Virgil has beckoned Geryon to come to that part of the bank which adjoins the end of the causeway.

499. Knot and rounded shield: Emblems of subtle devices and subterfuges.

500. Varied dye: Denoting the various colours of deceit.

501. Arachne: The Lydian weaver changed into a spider by Minerva. See Purg. xii. 43.

502. Gluttonous Germany: The habits of the German men-at-arms in Italy, odious to the temperate Italians, explains this gibe.

503. The right: This is the second and last time that, in their course through Inferno, they turn to the right. See Inf. ix. 132. The action may possibly have a symbolical meaning, and refer to the protection against fraud which is obtained by keeping to a righteous course. But here, in fact, they have no choice, for, traversing the Inferno as they do to the left hand, they came to the right bank of the stream which traverses the fiery sands, followed it, and now, when they would leave its edge, it is from the right embankment that they have to step down, and necessarily to the right hand.

504. A half score steps, etc.: Traversing the stone-built border which lies between the sand and the precipice. Had the brook flowed to the very edge of the Seventh Circle before tumbling down the rocky wall it is clear that they might have kept to the embankment until they were clear beyond the edge of the sand. We are therefore to figure to ourselves the water as plunging down at a point some yards, perhaps the width of the border, short of the true limit of the circle; and this is a touch of local truth, since waterfalls in time always wear out a funnel for themselves by eating back the precipice down which they tumble. It was into this funnel that Virgil flung the cord, and up it that Geryon was seen to ascend, as if by following up the course of the water he would find out who had made the signal. To keep to the narrow causeway where itran on by the edge of this gulf would seem too full of risk.

505. *Woful folk:* Usurers; those guilty of the unnatural sin of contemning the legitimatemodes of human industry. They sit huddled up on the sand, close to its bound of solidmasonry, from which Dante looks down on them. But that the usurers are not found only at the edge of the plain is evident from Inf. xiv. 19.

506. *Could recognise, etc.:* Though most of the group prove to be from Florence Dante recognises none of them; and this denotes that nothing so surely creates a secondnature in a man, in a bad sense, as setting the heart on money. So in the Fourth Circlethose who, being unable to spend moderately, are always thinking of how to keep or get money are represented as 'obscured from any recognition' (Inf. vii. 44).

507. *A pregnant sow*: The azure lion on a golden field was the arms of the Gianfigliazzi, eminent usurers of Florence; the white goose on a red ground was the arms of the Ubriachi of Florence; the azure sow, of the Scrovegni of Padua.

508. *Vitalian:* A rich Paduan noble, whose palace was near that of the Scrovegni.

509. *Pink of Chivalry*: 'Sovereign Cavalier;' identified by his arms as Ser Giovanni Buiamonte, still alive in Florence in 1301, and if we are to judge from the text, the greatest usurer of all. A northern poet of the time would have sought his usurers inthe Jewry of some town he knew, but Dante finds his among the nobles of Padua and Florence. He ironically represents them as wearing purses ornamented with their coats of arms, perhaps to hint that they pursued their dishonourable trade under shelter of their noble names—their shop signs, as it were. The whole passage may havebeen planned by Dante so as to afford him the opportunity of damning the still living Buiamonte without mentioning his name.

510. *His tongue thrust out:* As if to say: We know well what sort of fine gentleman Buiamonte is.

511. *By stairs like this:* The descent from one circle to another grows more difficult the further down they come. They appear to have found no special obstacle in the nature of the ground till they reached the bank sloping down to the Fifth Circle, the pathway down which is described as terrible (Inf. vii. 105). The descent into the Seventh Circleis made practicable, and nothing more (Inf. xii. I).

512. *Heaven was fired*: As still appears in the Milky Way. In the Convito, ii. 15, Dante discusses the various explanations of what causes the brightness of that part of the heavens.

513. *A terrific roar:* Of the water falling to the ground. On beginning the descent theyhad left the waterfall on the left hand, but Geryon, after fetching one or

more great circles, passes in front of it, and then they have it on the right. There is no further mention of the waters of Phlegethon till they are found frozen in Cocytus (Inf. xxxii. 23). Philalethes suggests that they flow under the Eighth Circle.

514. Lure: An imitation bird used in training falcons. Dante describes the sulky, slowdescent of a falcon which has either lost sight of its prey, or has failed to discover where the falconer has thrown the lure. Geryon has descended thus deliberately owingto the command of Virgil.

CANTO XVIII.

Of iron colour, and composed of stone,
A place called Malebolge[515] is in Hell,
Girt by a cliff of substance like its own.
In that malignant region yawns a well[516]
Right in the centre, ample and profound;
Of which I duly will the structure tell.
The zone[517] that lies between them, then, is round—
Between the well and precipice hard and high;
Into ten vales divided is the ground.
As is the figure offered to the eye,
Where numerous moats a castle's towers enclose
That they the walls may better fortify;
A like appearance was made here by those.
And as, again, from threshold of such place
Many a drawbridge to the outworks goes;
So ridges from the precipice's base
Cutting athwart the moats and barriers run,
Till at the well join the extremities.[518]
From Geryon's back when we were shaken down'
Twas here we stood, until the Poet's feet
Moved to the left, and I, behind, came on.
New torments on the right mine eyes did meet
With new tormentors, novel woe on woe;
With which the nearer Bolgia was replete.
Sinners, all naked, in the gulf below,
This side the middle met us; while they strode

On that side with us, but more swift did go.[519]
Even so the Romans, that the mighty crowd
Across the bridge, the year of Jubilee,
Might pass with ease, ordained a rule of road[520]—
Facing the Castle, on that side should be
The multitude which to St. Peter's hied;
So to the Mount on this was passage free.
On the grim rocky ground, on either side,
I saw horned devils[521] armed with heavy whip
Which on the sinners from behind they plied.
Ah, how they made the wretches nimbly skip
At the first lashes; no one ever yet
But sought from the second and the third to slip.
And as I onward went, mine eyes were set
On one of them; whereon I called in haste:
'This one already I have surely met!'
Therefore to know him, fixedly I gazed;
And my kind Leader willingly delayed,
While for a little I my course retraced.
On this the scourged one, thinking to evade
My search, his visage bent without avail,
For: 'Thou that gazest on the ground,' I said,
'If these thy features tell trustworthy tale,
Venedico Caccianimico[522] thou!
But what has brought thee to such sharp regale?'[523]
And he, 'I tell it 'gainst my will, I trow,
But thy clear accents[524] to the old world bear
My memory, and make me all avow.
I was the man who Ghisola the fair

To serve the Marquis' evil will led on,
Whatever[525] the uncomely tale declare.
Of Bolognese here weeping not alone
Am I; so full the place of them, to-day
'Tween Reno and Savena[526] are not known
So many tongues that Sipa deftly say:
And if of this thou'dst know the reason why,
Think but how greedy were our hearts alway.'
To him thus speaking did a demon cry:
'Pander, begone!' and smote him with his thong;
'Here are no women for thy coin to buy.'
Then, with my Escort joined, I moved along.
Few steps we made until we there had come,
Where from the bank a rib of rock was flung.
With ease enough up to its top we clomb,
And, turning on the ridge, bore to the right;[527]
And those eternal circles[528] parted from.
When we had reached where underneath the height
A passage opes, yielding the scourged a way,
My Guide bade: 'Tarry, so to hold in sight
Those other spirits born in evil day,
Whose faces until now from thee have been
Concealed, because with ours their progress lay.'
Then from the ancient bridge by us were seen
The troop which toward us on that circuit sped,
Chased onward, likewise, by the scourges keen.
And my good Master, ere I asked him, said:
'That lordly one now coming hither, see,
By whom, despite of pain, no tears are shed

.What mien he still retains of majesty!
'Tis Jason, who by courage and by guile
The Colchians of the ram deprived. '
Twas he Who on his passage by the Lemnian isle,
Where all of womankind with daring hand
Upon their males had wrought a murder vile,
With loving pledges and with speeches bland
The tender-yeared Hypsipyle betrayed,
Who had herself a fraud on others planned.
Forlorn he left her then, when pregnant made.
That is the crime condemns him to this pain;
And for Medea[529] too is vengeance paid.
Who in his manner cheat compose his train.
Of the first moat sufficient now is known,
And those who in its jaws engulfed remain.'
Already had we by the strait path gone
To where 'tis with the second bank dovetailed—
The buttress whence a second arch is thrown.
Here heard we who in the next Bolgia wailed[530]
And puffed for breath; reverberations told
They with their open palms themselves assailed.
he sides were crusted over with a mould
Plastered upon them by foul mists that rise,
And both with eyes and nose a contest hold.
The bottom is so deep, in vain our eyes
Searched it till further up the bridge we went,
To where the arch o'erhangs what under lies.
Ascended there, our eyes we downward bent,
And I saw people in such ordure drowned,

A very cesspool 'twas of excrement.
And while I from above am searching round,
One with a head so filth-smeared I picked out,
I knew not if 'twas lay, or tonsure-crowned.
'Why then so eager,' asked he with a shout,
'To stare at me of all the filthy crew?'
And I to him: 'Because I scarce can doubt
That formerly thee dry of hair I knew,
Alessio Interminei[531] the Lucchese;
And therefore thee I chiefly hold in view.'
Smiting his head-piece, then, his words were these:'
'Twas flattery steeped me here; for, using such,
My tongue itself enough could never please.'
'Now stretch thou somewhat forward, but not much,'
Thereon my Leader bade me, 'and thine eyes
Slowly advance till they her features touch
And the dishevelled baggage recognise,
Clawing her yonder with her nails unclean,
Now standing up, now squatting on her thighs.
'Tis harlot Thais,[532] who, when she had been
Asked by her lover, "Am I generous
And worthy thanks?" said, "Greatly so, I ween."
Enough[533] of this place has been seen by us.'

FOOTNOTES:

515. Malebolge: Or Evil Pits; literally, Evil Pockets.

516. A well: The Ninth and lowest Circle, to be described in Canto xxxii., etc.

517. The zone: The Eighth Circle, in which the fraudulent of all species are punished, lies between the precipice and the Ninth Circle. A vivid picture of the enormous heightof the enclosing wall has been presented to us at the close of the preceding Canto. As in the description of the Second Circle the atmosphere is represented as malignant, being murky and disturbed with tempest; so the Malebolge is called malignant too, being allof barren iron-coloured rock. In both cases the surroundings of the sinners may well bespoken of as malign, adverse to any thought of goodwill and joy.

518. The extremities: The Malebolge consists of ten circular pits or fosses, one insideof another. The outermost lies under the precipice which falls sheer from the SeventhCircle; the innermost, and of course the smallest, runs immediately outside of the 'Well,' which is the Ninth Circle. The Bolgias or valleys are divided from each other by rocky banks; and, each Bolgia being at a lower level than the one that encloses it, theinside of each bank is necessarily deeper than the outside. Ribs or ridges of rock—like spokes of a wheel to the axle-tree—run from the foot of the precipice to the outer rimof the 'Well,' vaulting the moats at right angles with the course of them. Thus each ribtakes the form of a ten-arched bridge. By one or other of these Virgil and Dante now travel towards the centre and the base of Inferno; their general course being downward,though varied by the ascent in turn of the hog-backed arches over the moats.

519. More swift: The sinners in the First Bolgia are divided into two gangs, moving in opposite directions, the course of those on the outside being to the right, as looked at by Dante. These are the shades of panders; those in the inner current are such as seduced on their own account. Here a list of the various classes of sinners contained inthe Bolgias of the Eighth Circle may be given:—

1st	Bolgia—	Seducers,	CANTO	XVIII.
2d	"	Flatterers,	"	"
3d	"	Simoniacs,	"	XIX.
4th	"	Soothsayers,	"	XX.
5th	"	Barrators,	"	XXI. XXII.
6th	"	Hypocrites,	"	XXIII.
7th	"	Thieves,	"	XXIV. XXV.
8th	"	Evil Counsellors,	"	XXVI. XXVII.
9th	"	Scandal and Heresy Mongers,	"	XXVIII. XXIX.
10th	"	Falsifiers,	"	XXIX. XXX.

520. A rule of road: In the year 1300 a Jubilee was held in Rome with Plenary Indulgence for all pilgrims. Villani says that while it lasted the number of strangers inRome was never less than two hundred thousand. The bridge and castle spoken of in the text are those of St. Angelo. The Mount is probably the Janiculum.

521. Horned devils: Here the demons are horned—terrible remembrancers to the sinner of the injured husband.

522. Venedico Caccianimico: A Bolognese noble, brother of Ghisola, whom he inveigled into yielding herself to the Marquis of Este, lord of Ferrara. Venedico died between 1290 and 1300.

523. Such sharp regale: 'Such pungent sauces.' There is here a play of words on the Salse, the name of a wild ravine outside the walls of Bologna, where the bodies of felons were thrown. Benvenuto says it used to be a taunt among boys at Bologna: Yourfather was pitched into the Salse.

524. Thy clear accents: Not broken with sobs like his own and those of his companions.

525. Whatever, etc.: Different accounts seem to have been current about the affair of Ghisola.

526. 'Tween Reno, etc.: The Reno and Savena are streams that flow past Bologna. Sipa is Bolognese for Maybe, or for Yes. So Dante describes Tuscany as the country where Si is heard (Inf. xxxiii. 80). With regard to the vices of the Bolognese, Benvenutosays: 'Dante had studied in Bologna, and had seen and observed all these things.'

527. To the right: This is only an apparent departure from their leftward course. Moving as they were to the left along the edge of the Bolgia, they required to turn to the right to cross the bridge that spanned it.

528. Those eternal circles: The meaning is not clear; perhaps it only is that they have now done with the outer stream of sinners in this Bolgia, left by them engaged in endless procession round and round.

529. Medea: When the Argonauts landed on Lemnos, they found it without any males, the women, incited by Venus, having put them all to death, with the exception of Thoas, saved by his daughter Hypsipyle. When Jason deserted her he sailed for Colchis, and with the assistance of Medea won the Golden Fleece. Medea, who accompanied him from Colchis, was in turn deserted by him.

530. Who in the next Bolgia wailed: The flatterers in the Second Bolgia.

531. Alessio Interminei: Of the Great Lucchese family of the Interminelli, to which the famous Castruccio Castrucani belonged. Alessio is know to have been living in 1295. Dante may have known him personally. Benvenuto says he was so liberal of his flattery that he spent it even on menial servants.

532. Thais: In the Eunuch of Terence, Thraso, the lover of that courtesan, asks Gnatho, their go-between, if she really sent him many thanks for the present of a slave-girl he had sent her. 'Enormous!' says Gnatho. It proves what great store Dante set on ancient instances when he thought this worth citing.

533. Enough, etc.: Most readers will agree with Virgil.

CANTO XIX.

O Simon Magus![534] ye his wretched crew!
The gifts of God, ordained to be the bride
Of righteousness, ye prostitute that you
With gold and silver may be satisfied;
Therefore for you let now the trumpet[535] blow,
Seeing that ye in the Third Bolgia 'bide.
Arrived at the next tomb,[536] we to the brow
Of rock ere this had finished our ascent,
Which hangs true plumb above the pit below.
What perfect art, O Thou Omniscient,
Is Thine in Heaven and earth and the bad world found!
How justly does Thy power its dooms invent!
The livid stone, on both banks and the ground,
I saw was full of holes on every side,
All of one size, and each of them was round.
No larger seemed they to me nor less wide
Than those within my beautiful St. John[537]
For the baptizers' standing-place supplied;
And one of which, not many years agone,
I broke to save one drowning; and I would
Have this for seal to undeceive men known.
Out of the mouth of each were seen protrude
A sinner's feet, and of the legs the small
Far as the calves; the rest enveloped stood
.And set on fire were both the soles of all,
Which made their ankles wriggle with such throes

As had made ropes and withes asunder fall.
And as flame fed by unctuous matter goes
Over the outer surface only spread;
So from their heels it flickered to the toes.
'Master, who is he, tortured more,' I said,
'Than are his neighbours, writhing in such woe;
And licked by flames of deeper-hearted red?'
And he: 'If thou desirest that below
I bear thee by that bank[538] which lowest lies,
Thou from himself his sins and name shalt know.'
And I: 'Thy wishes still for me suffice:
Thou art my Lord, and knowest I obey
Thy will; and dost my hidden thoughts surprise.'
To the fourth barrier then we made our way,
And, to the left hand turning, downward went
Into the narrow hole-pierced cavity;
Nor the good Master caused me make descent
From off his haunch till we his hole were nigh
Who with his shanks was making such lament.
'Whoe'er thou art, soul full of misery,
Set like a stake with lower end upcast,'
I said to him, 'Make, if thou canst, reply.'
I like a friar[539] stood who gives the last
Shrift to a vile assassin, to his side
Called back to win delay for him fixed fast.'
Art thou arrived already?' then he cried,
'Art thou arrived already, Boniface?
By several years the prophecy[540] has lied.
Art so soon wearied of the wealthy place,

For which thou didst not fear to take with guile,
Then ruin the fair Lady?'[541] Now my case
Was like to theirs who linger on, the while
They cannot comprehend what they are told,
And as befooled[542] from further speech resile.
But Virgil bade me: 'Speak out loud and bold,
"I am not he thou thinkest, no, not he!"'
And I made answer as by him controlled.
The spirit's feet then twisted violently,
And, sighing in a voice of deep distress,
He asked: 'What then requirest thou of me?
If me to know thou hast such eagerness,
That thou the cliff hast therefore ventured down,
Know, the Great Mantle sometime was my dress.
I of the Bear, in sooth, was worthy son:
As once, the Cubs to help, my purse with gain
I stuffed, myself I in this purse have stown.
Stretched out at length beneath my head remain
All the simoniacs[543] that before me went,
And flattened lie throughout the rocky vein.
I in my turn shall also make descent,
Soon as he comes who I believed thou wast,
When I asked quickly what for him was meant.
O'er me with blazing feet more time has past,
While upside down I fill the topmost room,
Than he his crimsoned feet shall upward cast;
For after him one viler still shall come,
A Pastor from the West,[544] lawless of deed
:To cover both of us his worthy doom.

A modern Jason[545] he, of whom we read
In Maccabees, whose King denied him nought:
With the French King so shall this man succeed.'
Perchance I ventured further than I ought,
But I spake to him in this measure free:
'Ah, tell me now what money was there sought
Of Peter by our Lord, when either key
He gave him in his guardianship to hold?
Sure He demanded nought save: "Follow me!"
Nor Peter, nor the others, asked for gold
Or silver when upon Matthias fell
The lot instead of him, the traitor-souled.
Keep then thy place, for thou art punished well,[546]
And clutch the pelf, dishonourably gained,
Which against Charles[547] made thee so proudly swell.
And, were it not that I am still restrained
By reverence[548] for those tremendous keys,
Borne by thee while the glad world thee contained,
I would use words even heavier than these;
Seeing your avarice makes the world deplore,
Crushing the good, filling the bad with ease.
'Twas you, O Pastors, the Evangelist bore
In mind what time he saw her on the flood
Of waters set, who played with kings the whore;
Who with seven heads was born; and as she would
By the ten horns to her was service done,
Long as her spouse[549] rejoiced in what was good.
Now gold and silver are your god alone:
What difference 'twixt the idolater and you,

Save that ye pray a hundred for his one?
Ah, Constantine,[550] how many evils grew—
Not from thy change of faith, but from the gift
Wherewith thou didst the first rich Pope endue!'
While I my voice continued to uplift
To such a tune, by rage or conscience stirred
Both of his soles he made to twist and shift.
My Guide, I well believe, with pleasure heard;
Listening he stood with lips so well content
To me propounding truthful word on word.
Then round my body both his arms he bent,
And, having raised me well upon his breast,
Climbed up the path by which he made descent.
Nor was he by his burden so oppressed
But that he bore me to the bridge's crown,
Which with the fourth joins the fifth rampart's crest.
And lightly here he set his burden down,
Found light by him upon the precipice,
Up which a goat uneasily had gone.
And thence another valley met mine eyes.

FOOTNOTES:

534. Simon Magus: The sin of simony consists in setting a price on the exercise of a spiritual grace or the acquisition of a spiritual office. Dante assails it at headquarters, that is, as it was practised by the Popes; and in their case it took, among other forms, that of ecclesiastical nepotism.

535. The trumpet: Blown at the punishment of criminals, to call attention to their sentence.

536. The next tomb: The Third Bolgia, appropriately termed a tomb, because its manner of punishment is that of a burial, as will be seen.

537. St. John: The church of St. John's, in Dante's time, as now, the Baptistery of Florence. In Parad. xxv. he anticipates the day, if it should ever come, when he shall return to Florence, and in the church where he was baptized a Christian be crowned as a Poet. Down to the middle of the sixteenth century all baptisms, except in cases of urgent necessity, were celebrated in St. John's; and, even there, only on the eves of Easter and Pentecost. For protection against the crowd, the officiating priests were provided with standing-places, circular cavities disposed around the great font. To these Dante compares the holes of this Bolgia, for the sake of introducing a defence of himself from a charge of sacrilege. Benvenuto tells that once when some boys were playing about the church one of them, to hide himself from his companions, squeezed himself into a baptizer's standing-place, and made so tight a fit of it that he could not be rescued till Dante with his own hands plied a hammer upon the marble, and so saved the child from drowning. The presence of water in the cavity may be explained by the fact of the church's being at that time lighted by an unglazed opening in the roof; and as baptisms were so infrequent the standing-places, situated as they were in the centre of the floor, may often have been partially flooded. It is easy to understand how bitterly Dante would resent a charge of irreverence connected with his 'beautiful St. John's;' 'that fair sheep-fold' (Parad. xxv. 5).

538. That bank, etc.: Of each Bolgia the inner bank is lower than the outer; the whole of Malebolge sloping towards the centre of the Inferno.

539. Like a friar, etc.: In those times the punishment of an assassin was to be stuck head downward in a pit, and then to have earth slowly shovelled in till he was suffocated. Dante bends down, the better to hear what the sinner has to say, like a friar recalled by the felon on the pretence that he has something to add to his confession.

540. The prophecy: 'The writing.' The speaker is Nicholas III., of the great Roman family of the Orsini, and Pope from 1277 to 1280; a man of remarkable bodily beauty and grace of manner, as well as of great force of character. Like many other Holy Fathers he was either a great hypocrite while on his promotion, or else he degenerated very quickly after getting himself well settled on the Papal Chair. He is said to have been the first Pope who practised simony with no attempt at concealment. Boniface VIII., whom he is waiting for to relieve him, became Pope in 1294, and died in 1303. None of the four Popes between 1280 and 1294 were simoniacs; so that Nicholas was uppermost in the hole for twenty-three years. Although ignorant of what is now passing on the earth, he can refer back to his foreknowledge of some years earlier (see Inf. x. 99) as if to a prophetic writing, and finds that according to this it is still three years too soon, it being now only 1300, for the arrival of Boniface. This is the usual explanation of the passage. To it lies the objection that foreknowledge of the present that can be referred back to is the same thing as knowledge of it, and with this the spirits in Inferno are not endowed. But Dante elsewhere shows that he finds it hard to observe the limitation. The alternative explanation, supported by the use of scritto (writing) in the text, is that Nicholas refers to some prophecy once current about his successors in Rome.

541. The fair Lady: The Church. The guile is that shown by Boniface in getting his predecessor Celestine v. to abdicate (Inf. iii. 60).

542. As befooled: Dante does not yet suspect that it is with a Pope he is speaking. Heis dumbfounded at being addressed as Boniface.

543. All the simoniacs: All the Popes that had been guilty of the sin.

544. A Pastor from the West: Boniface died in 1303, and was succeeded by BenedictXI., who in his turn was succeeded by Clement V., the Pastor from the West. Benedict was not stained with simony, and so it is Clement that is to relieve Boniface; and he is to come from the West, that is, from Avignon, to which the Holy See was removedby him. Or the reference may simply be to the country of his birth. Elsewhere he is spoken of as 'the Gascon who shall cheat the noble Henry' of Luxemburg (Parad. xvii.82).—This passage has been read as throwing light on the question of when the Infernowas written. Nicholas says that from the time Boniface arrives till Clement relieves him will be a shorter period than that during which hc has himself been in Inferno, that is to say, a shorter time than twenty years. Clement died in 1314; and so, it is held,we find a date before which the Inferno was, at least, not published. But Clement was known for years before his death to be ill of a disease usually soon fatal. He became Pope in 1305, and the wonder was that he survived so long as nine years. Dante keeps his prophecy safe—if it is a prophecy; and there does seem internal evidence to provethe publication of the Inferno to have taken place long before 1314.—It is needless topoint out how the censure of Clement gains in force if read as having been published before his death.

545. Jason: Or Joshua, who purchased the office of High Priest from Antiochus Epiphanes, and innovated the customs of the Jews (2 Maccab. iv. 7).

546. Punished well: At line 12 Dante has admired the propriety of the Divine distribution of penalties. He appears to regard with a special complacency that which he invents for the simoniacs. They were industrious in multiplying benefices for their kindred; Boniface, for example, besides Cardinals, appointed about twenty Archbishops and Bishops from among his own relatives. Here all the simoniacal Popes have to be contented with one place among them. They paid no regard to whether a post was well filled or not: here they are set upside down.

547. Charles: Nicholas was accused of taking a bribe to assist Peter of Arragon

in ousting Charles of Anjou from the kingdom of Sicily.

548. By reverence, etc.: Dante distinguishes between the office and the unworthy holder of it. So in Purgatory he prostrates himself before a Pope (Purg. xix. 131).

549. Her spouse: In the preceding lines the vision of the Woman in the Apocalypse isapplied to the corruption of the Church, represented under the figure of the seven-hilled Rome seated in honour among the nations and receiving observance from the kings of the earth till her spouse, the Pope, began to prostitute her by making merchandise of her spiritual gifts. Of the Beast there is no mention here, his qualities being attributedto the Woman.

550. Ah, Constantine, etc.: In Dante's time, and for some centuries later, it was believed that Constantine, on transferring the seat of empire to Byzantium, had made a gift to the Pope of rights and privileges almost equal to those of the Emperor. Romewas to be the Pope's; and from his court in the Lateran he was to exercise supremacy over all the West. The Donation of Constantine, that is, the instrument conveying theserights, was a forgery of the Middle Ages.

CANTO XX.

Now of new torment must my verses tell,
And matter for the Twentieth Canto win
Of Lay the First,[551] which treats of souls in Hell.
Already was I eager to begin
To peer into the visible profound,[552]
Which tears of agony was bathèd in:
And I saw people in the valley round;
Like that of penitents on earth the pace
At which they weeping came, nor uttering[553] sound.
When I beheld them with more downcast gaze,[554]
That each was strangely screwed about I learned,
Where chest is joined to chin. And thus the face
Of every one round to his loins was turned;
And stepping backward[555] all were forced to go,
For nought in front could be by them discerned.
Smitten by palsy although one might show
Perhaps a shape thus twisted all awry,
I never saw, and am to think it slow.
As, Reader,[556] God may grant thou profit by
Thy reading, for thyself consider well
If I could then preserve my visage dry
When close at hand to me was visible
Our human form so wrenched that tears, rained down
Out of the eyes, between the buttocks fell.
In very sooth I wept, leaning upon
A boss of the hard cliff, till on this wise

My Escort asked: 'Of the other fools[557] art one?
Here piety revives as pity dies;
For who more irreligious is than he
In whom God's judgments to regret give rise?
Lift up, lift up thy head, and thou shalt see
Him for whom earth yawned as the Thebans saw,
All shouting meanwhile: "Whither dost thou flee,Amphiaraüs?[558]
Wherefore thus withdraw From battle?"
But he sinking found no rest
Till Minos clutched him with all-grasping claw.
Lo, how his shoulders serve him for a breast!
Because he wished to see too far before
Backward he looks, to backward course addressed.
Behold Tiresias,[559] who was changed all o'er,
Till for a man a woman met the sight,
And not a limb its former semblance bore;
And he behoved a second time to smite
The same two twisted serpents with his wand,
Ere he again in manly plumes was dight.
With back to him, see Aruns next at hand,
Who up among the hills of Luni, where
Peasants of near Carrara till the land,
Among the dazzling marbles[560] held his lair
Within a cavern, whence could be descried
The sea and stars of all obstruction bare.
The other one, whose flowing tresses hide
Her bosom, of the which thou seest nought,
And all whose hair falls on the further side,
Was Manto;[561] who through many regions sought:

Where I was born, at last her foot she stayed.
It likes me well thou shouldst of this be taught.
When from this life her father exit made,
And Bacchus' city had become enthralled,
She for long time through many countries strayed.
'Neath mountains by which Germany is walled
And bounded at Tirol, a lake there lies
High in fair Italy, Benacus[562] called.
The waters of a thousand springs that rise'
Twixt Val Camonica and Garda flow
Down Pennine; and their flood this lake supplies.
And from a spot midway, if they should go
Thither, the Pastors[563] of Verona, Trent,
And Brescia might their blessings all bestow.
Peschiera,[564] with its strength for ornament,
Facing the Brescians and the Bergamese
Lies where the bank to lower curve is bent.
And there the waters, seeking more of ease,
For in Benacus is not room for all,
Forming a river, lapse by green degrees.
The river, from its very source, men call
No more Benacus—'tis as Mincio known,
Which into Po does at Governo fall.
A flat it reaches ere it far has run,
Spreading o'er which it feeds a marshy fen,
Whence oft in summer pestilence has grown.
Wayfaring here the cruel virgin, when
She found land girdled by the marshy flood,
Untilled and uninhabited of men,

That she might 'scape all human neighbourhood
Stayed on it with her slaves, her arts to ply;
And there her empty body was bestowed.
On this the people from the country nigh
Into that place came crowding, for the spot,
Girt by the swamp, could all attack defy,
And for the town built o'er her body sought
A name from her who made it first her seat,
Calling it Mantua, without casting lot.[565]
The dwellers in it were in number great,
Till stupid Casalodi[566] was befooled
And victimised by Pinamonte's cheat.
Hence, shouldst thou ever hear (now be thou schooled!)
Another story to my town assigned,
Let by no fraud the truth be overruled.'
And I: 'Thy reasonings, Master, to my mind
So cogent are, and win my faith so well,
What others say I shall black embers find.
But of this people passing onward tell,
If thou, of any, something canst declare,
For all my thoughts[567] on that intently dwell.'
And then he said: 'The one whose bearded hair
Falls from his cheeks upon his shoulders dun,
Was, when the land of Greece[568] of males so bare
Was grown the very cradles scarce held one,
An augur;[569] he with Calchas gave the sign
In Aulis through the first rope knife to run.
Eurypylus was he called, and in some line
Of my high Tragedy[570] is sung the same,

As thou know'st well, who mad'st it wholly thine
.That other, thin of flank, was known to fame
As Michael Scott;[571] and of a verity
He knew right well the black art's inmost game.
Guido Bonatti,[572] and Asdente see
Who mourns he ever should have parted from
His thread and leather; but too late mourns he.
Lo the unhappy women who left loom,
Spindle, and needle that they might divine;
With herb and image[573] hastening men's doom.
But come; for where the hemispheres confine
Cain and the Thorns[574] is falling, to alight
Underneath Seville on the ocean line.
The moon was full already yesternight;
Which to recall thou shouldst be well content,
For in the wood she somewhat helped thy plight.'
Thus spake he to me while we forward went.

FOOTNOTES:

551. Lay the First: The Inferno.

552. The visible profound: The Fourth Bolgia, where soothsayers of every kind are punished. Their sin is that of seeking to find out what God has made secret. That suchdiscoveries of the future could be made by men, Dante seems to have had no doubt; but he regards the exercise of the power as a fraud on Providence, and also credits the adepts in the black art with ruining others by their spells (line 123).

553. Nor uttering, etc.: They who on earth told too much are now condemned to be forever dumb. It will be noticed that with none of them does Dante converse.

554. More downcast gaze: Standing as he does on the crown of the arch, the nearer they come to him the more he has to decline his eyes.

555. Stepping backward: Once they peered far into the future; now they cannot see astep before them.

556. *As, Reader, etc.:* Some light may be thrown on this unusual, and, at first sight, inexplicable display of pity, by the comment of Benvenuto da Imola:—'It is the wisest and most virtuous of men that are most subject to this mania of divination; and of this Dante is himself an instance, as is well proved by this book of his.' Dante reminds thereader how often since the journey began he has sought to have the veil of the future lifted; and would have it understood that he was seized by a sudden misgiving as to whether he too had not overstepped the bounds of what, in that respect, is allowed andright.

557. *Of the other fools:* Dante, weeping like the sinners in the Bolgia, is asked by Virgil: 'What, art thou then one of them?' He had been suffered, without reproof, to show pity for Francesca and Ciacco. The terrors of the Lord grow more cogent as theydescend, and even pity is now forbidden.

558. *Amphiaraüs*: One of the Seven Kings who besieged Thebes. He foresaw his owndeath, and sought by hiding to evade it; but his wife revealed his hiding-place, and hewas forced to join in the siege. As he fought, a thunderbolt opened a chasm in the earth,into which he fell.

559. *Tiresias*: A Theban soothsayer whose change of sex is described by Ovid (Metam. iii.).

560. *The dazzling marbles:* Aruns, a Tuscan diviner, is introduced by Lucan as prophesying great events to come to pass in Rome—the Civil War and the victoriesof Cæsar. His haunt was the deserted city of Luna, situated on the Gulf of Spezia, andunder the Carrara mountains (Phars. i. 586).

561. *Manto:* A prophetess, a native of Thebes the city of Bacchus, and daughter of Tiresias.—Here begins a digression on the early history of Mantua, the native cityof Virgil. In his account of the foundation of it Dante does not agree with Virgil, attributing to a Greek Manto what his master attributes to an Italian one (Æn. x. 199).

562. *Benacus:* The ancient Benacus, now known as the Lake of Garda.

563. *The Pastors, etc.:* About half-way down the western side of the lake a stream falls into it, one of whose banks, at its mouth, is in the diocese of Trent, and the otherin that of Brescia, while the waters of the lake are in that of Verona. The three Bishops, standing together, could give a blessing each to his own diocese.

564. *Peschiera*: Where the lake drains into the Mincio. It is still a great fortress.

565. *Without casting lot*; Without consulting the omens, as was usual when a city wasto be named.

566. *Casalodi:* Some time in the second half of the thirteenth century Alberto

Casalodi was befooled out of the lordship of Mantua by Pinamonte Buonacolsi. Benvenuto tells the tale as follows:—Pinamonte was a bold, ambitious man, with a great troop of armed followers; and, the nobility being at that time in bad odour with the people at large, he persuaded the Count Albert that it would be a popular measure to banish thesuspected nobles for a time. Hardly was this done when he usurped the lordship; and by expelling some of the citizens and putting others of them to death he greatly thinnedthe population of the city.

567. All my thoughts, etc.: The reader's patience is certainly abused by this digressionof Virgil's, and Dante himself seems conscious that it is somewhat ill-timed.

568. The land of Greece, etc.: All the Greeks able to bear arms being engaged in theTrojan expedition.

569. An augur: Eurypylus, mentioned in the Second Æneid as being employed by the Greeks to consult the oracle of Apollo regarding their return to Greece. From the auspices Calchas had found at what hour they should set sail for Troy. Eurypylus canbe said only figuratively to have had to do with cutting the cable.

570. Tragedy: The Æneid. Dante defines Comedy as being written in a style inferiorto that of Tragedy, and as having a sad beginning and a happy ending (Epistle to Can Grande, 10). Elsewhere he allows the comic poet great licence in the use of common language (Vulg. El. ii. 4). By calling his own poem a Comedy he, as it were, disarms criticism.

571.Michael Scott: Of Balwearie in Scotland, familiar to English readers through the Lay of the Last Minstrel. He flourished in the course of the thirteenth century, and made contributions to the sciences, as they were then deemed, of astrology, alchemy, and physiognomy. He acted for some time as astrologer to the Emperor Frederick II., and the tradition of his accomplishments powerfully affected the Italian imagination for a century after his death. It was remembered that the terrible Frederick, after being warned by him to beware of Florence, had died at a place called Firenzuola; and more than one Italian city preserved with fear and trembling his dark sayings regarding theirfate. Villani frequently quotes his prophecies; and Boccaccio speaks of him as a great necromancer who had been in Florence. A commentary of his on Aristotle was printedat Venice in 1496. The thinness of his flanks may refer to a belief that he could make himself invisible at will.

572. Guido Bonatti: Was a Florentine, a tiler by trade, and was living in 1282. Whenbanished from his own city he took refuge at Forlì and became astrologer to Guido ofMontefeltro (Inf. xxvii.), and was credited with helping his master to a great victory.—Asdente: A cobbler of Parma, whose prophecies were long renowned, lived in the twelfth century. He is given in the Convito (iv. 16) as an instance that a man may be very notorious without being truly noble.

573. Herb and image: Part of the witch's stock in trade. All that was done to a waxenimage of him was suffered by the witch's victim.

574. Cain and the Thorns: The moon. The belief that the spots in the moon are causedby Cain standing in it with a bundle of thorns is referred to at Parad. ii. 51. Although itis now the morning of the Saturday, the 'yesternight' refers to the night of Thursday, when Dante found some use of the moon in the Forest. The moon is now setting on the line dividing the hemisphere of Jerusalem, in which they are, from that of the Mount of Purgatory. According to Dante's scheme of the world, Purgatory is the true opposite of Jerusalem; and Seville is ninety degrees from Jerusalem. As it was full moon the night before last, and the moon is now setting, it is now fully an hour after sunrise. But, as has already been said, it is not possible to reconcile the astronomical indications thoroughly with one another.—Virgil serves as clock to Dante, for they can see nothing of the skies.

CANTO XXI.

Conversing still from bridge to bridge[575] we went;
But what our words I in my Comedy
Care not to tell. The top of the ascent
Holding, we halted the next pit to spy Of
Malebolge, with plaints bootless all:
There, darkness[576] full of wonder met the eye.
As the Venetians[577] in their Arsenal
Boil the tenacious pitch at winter-tide,
To caulk the ships with for repairs that call;
For then they cannot sail; and so, instead,
One builds his bark afresh, one stops with tow
His vessel's ribs, by many a voyage tried;
One hammers at the poop, one at the prow;
Some fashion oars, and others cables twine,
And others at the jib and main sails sew:
So, not by fire, but by an art Divine,
Pitch of thick substance boiled in that low Hell,
And all the banks did as with plaster line.
I saw it, but distinguished nothing well
Except the bubbles by the boiling raised,
Now swelling up and ceasing now to swell.
While down upon it fixedly I gazed,
'Beware, beware!' my Leader to me said,
And drew me thence close to him. I, amazed,
Turned sharply round, like him who has delayed,
Fain to behold the thing he ought to flee,

Then, losing nerve, grows suddenly afraid,
Nor lingers longer what there is to see;
For a black devil I beheld advance
Over the cliff behind us rapidly.
Ah me, how fierce was he of countenance!
What bitterness he in his gesture put,
As with spread wings he o'er the ground did dance!
Upon his shoulders, prominent and acute,
Was perched a sinner[578] fast by either hip;
And him he held by tendon of the foot.
He from our bridge: 'Ho, Malebranche![579] Grip
An Elder brought from Santa Zita's town:[580]
Stuff him below; myself once more I slip
Back to the place where lack of such is none.
There, save Bonturo, barrates[581] every man,
And No grows Yes that money may be won.'
He shot him down, and o'er the cliff began
To run; nor unchained mastiff o'er the ground,
Chasing a robber, swifter ever ran.
The other sank, then rose with back bent round;
But from beneath the bridge the devils cried:
'Not here the Sacred Countenance[582] is found,
One swims not here as on the Serchio's[583] tide;
So if thou wouldst not with our grapplers deal
Do not on surface of the pitch abide.'
Then he a hundred hooks[584] was made to feel.
'Best dance down there,' they said the while to him,
'Where, if thou canst, thou on the sly mayst steal.'
So scullions by the cooks are set to trim

The caldrons and with forks the pieces steep
Down in the water, that they may not swim.
And the good Master said to me:
'Now creepBehind a rocky splinter for a screen;
So from their knowledge thou thyself shalt keep
And fear not thou although with outrage keen
I be opposed, for I am well prepared,
And formerly[585] have in like contest been.'
Then passing from the bridge's crown he fared
To the sixth bank,[586] and when thereon he stood
He needed courage doing what he dared.
In the same furious and tempestuous mood
In which the dogs upon the beggar leap,
Who, halting suddenly, seeks alms or food,
They issued forth from underneath the deep
Vault of the bridge, with grapplers 'gainst him stretched;
But he exclaimed: 'Aloof, and harmless keep!
Ere I by any of your hooks be touched,
Come one of you and to my words give ear;
And then advise you if I should be clutched.'
All cried: 'Let Malacoda then go near;'
On which one moved, the others standing still.
He coming said: 'What will this[587] help him here?'
'O Malacoda, is it credible
That I am come,' my Master then replied,
'Secure your opposition to repel,
Without Heaven's will, and fate, upon my side?
Let me advance, for 'tis by Heaven's behest
That I on this rough road another guide.'

Then was his haughty spirit so depressed,
He let his hook drop sudden to his feet,
And, 'Strike him not!' commanded all the rest
My Leader charged me thus: 'Thou, from thy seat
Where 'mid the bridge's ribs thou crouchest low,
Rejoin me now in confidence complete.'
Whereon I to rejoin him was not slow;
And then the devils, crowding, came so near,
I feared they to their paction false might show.
So at Caprona[588] saw I footmen fear,
Spite of their treaty, when a multitude
Of foes received them, crowding front and rear.
With all my body braced I closer stood
To him, my Leader, and intently eyed
The aspect of them, which was far from good.
Lowering their grapplers, 'mong themselves they cried:
'Shall I now tickle him upon the thigh?'
'Yea, see thou clip him deftly,' one replied.
The demon who in parley had drawn nigh
Unto my Leader, upon this turned round;
'Scarmiglione, lay thy weapon by!'
He said; and then to us: 'No way is found
Further along this cliff, because, undone,
All the sixth arch lies ruined on the ground.
But if it please you further to pass on,
Over this rocky ridge advancing climb
To the next rib,[589] where passage may be won.
Yestreen,[590] but five hours later than this time,
Twelve hundred sixty-six years reached an end,

Since the way lost the wholeness of its prime.
Thither I some of mine will straightway send
To see that none peer forth to breathe the air:
Go on with them; you they will not offend. You,
Alichin[591] and Calcabrin, prepare
To move,' he bade; 'Cagnazzo, thou as well;
Guiding the ten, thou, Barbariccia, fare.
With Draghignazzo, Libicocco fell,
Fanged Ciriatto, Graffiacane too,
Set on, mad Rubicant and Farfarel:
Search on all quarters round the boiling glue.
Let these go safe, till at the bridge they be,
Which doth unbroken[592] o'er the caverns go.'
'Alas, my Master, what is this I see?'
Said I, 'Unguided, let us forward set,
If thou know'st how. I wish no company.
If former caution thou dost not forget,
Dost thou not mark how each his teeth doth grind,
The while toward us their brows are full of threat?'
And he: 'I would not fear should fill thy mind;
Let them grin all they will, and all they can;
'Tis at the wretches in the pitch confined.'
They wheeled and down the left hand bank began
To march, but first each bit his tongue,[593] and passed
The signal on to him who led the van.
He answered grossly as with trumpet blast.

FOOTNOTES:

575. From bridge to bridge: They cross the barrier separating the Fourth from the FifthBolgia, and follow the bridge which spans the Fifth until they have reached the crownof it. We may infer that the conversation of Virgil and Dante turned on foreknowledgeof the future.

576. Darkness, etc.: The pitch with which the trench of the Bolgia is filled absorbs most of the scanty light accorded to Malebolge.

577. The Venetians: But for this picturesque description of the old Arsenal, and a passing mention of the Rialto in one passage of the Paradiso, and of the Venetian coinage in another, it could not be gathered from the Comedy, with all its wealth of historical and geographical references, that there was such a place as Venice in the Italy of Dante. Unlike the statue of Time (Inf. xiv.), the Queen of the Adriatic had her face set eastwards. Her back was turned and her ears closed as in a proud indifferenceto the noise of party conflicts which filled the rest of Italy.

578. A sinner: This is the only instance in the Inferno of the arrival of a sinner at hisspecial place of punishment. See Inf. v. 15, note.

579. Malebranche: Evil Claws, the name of the devils who have the sinners of this Bolgia in charge.

580. Santa Zita's town: Zita was a holy serving-woman of Lucca, who died some time between 1270 and 1280, and whose miracle-working body is still preserved in the church of San Frediano. Most probably, although venerated as a saint, she was not yet canonized at the time Dante writes of, and there may be a Florentine sneer hiddenin the description of Lucca as her town. Even in Lucca there was some differenceof opinion as to her merits, and a certain unlucky Ciappaconi was pitched into the Serchio for making fun of the popular enthusiasm about her. See Philalethes, Gött. Com. In Lucca the officials that were called Priors in Florence, were named Elders. The commentators give a name to this sinner, but it is only guesswork.

581. Save Bonturo, barrates, etc.: It is the barrators, those who trafficked in offices and sold justice, that are punished in this Bolgia. The greatest barrator of all in Lucca,say the commentators, was this Bonturo; but there seems no proof of it, though there isof his arrogance. He was still living in 1314.

582. The Sacred Countenance: An image in cedar wood, of Byzantine workmanship,still preserved and venerated in the cathedral of Lucca. According to the legend, it wascarved from memory by Nicodemus, and after being a long time lost was found againin the eighth century by an Italian bishop travelling in Palestine. He brought it to the coast at Joppa, where it was received by a vessel without sail or oar, which, with its sacred freight, floated westwards and was next seen at the port of Luna. All efforts toapproach the bark were vain, till the Bishop of Lucca descended to the seashore, and to him the vessel resigned itself and suffered him to take the image into his keeping. 'Believe what you like of all this,' says Benvenuto; 'it is no article of faith.'—The sinner has come to the surface, bent as if in an attitude of prayer, when he is met by this taunt.

583. The Serchio: The stream which flows past Lucca.

584. A hundred hooks: So many devils with their pronged hooks were waiting to receive the victim. The punishment of the barrators bears a relation to their sins. Theywrought their evil deeds under all kinds of veils and excuses, and are now themselveseffectually buried out of sight. The pitch sticks as close to them as bribes ever did to their fingers. They misused wards and all subject to them, and in their turn are clawedand torn by their devilish guardians.

585. Formerly, etc.: On the occasion of his previous descent (Inf. ix. 22).

586. The sixth bank: Dante remains on the crown of the arch overhanging the pitch- filled moat. Virgil descends from the bridge by the left hand to the bank on the inner side of the Fifth Bolgia.

587. What will this, etc.: As if he said: What good will this delay do him in the long-run?

588. At Caprona: Dante was one of the mounted militia sent by Florence in 1289 to help the Lucchese against the Pisans, and was present at the surrender by the Pisan garrison of the Castle of Caprona. Some make the reference to be to a siege of the same stronghold by the Pisans in the following year, when the Lucchese garrison, having surrendered on condition of having their lives spared, were met as they issuedforth with cries of 'Hang them! Hang them!' But of this second siege it is only a Pisancommentator that speaks.

589. The next rib: Malacoda informs them that the arch of rock across the Sixth Bolgia in continuation of that by which they have crossed the Fifth is in ruins, but thatthey will find a whole bridge if they keep to the left hand along the rocky bank on theinner edge of the pitch-filled moat. But, as appears further on, he is misleading them. It will be remembered that from the precipice enclosing the Malebolge there run morethan one series of bridges or ribs into the central well of Inferno.

590. Yestreen, etc.: This is the principal passage in the Comedy for fixing the dateof the journey. It is now, according to the text, twelve hundred and sixty-six yearsand a day since the crucifixion. Turning to the Convito, iv. 23, we find Dante giving his reasons for believing that Jesus, at His death, had just completed His thirty-fourthyear. This brings us to the date of 1300 A.D. But according to Church tradition the crucifixion happened on the 25th March, and to get thirty-four years His life must be counted from the incarnation, which was held to have taken place on the same date, namely the 25th March. It was in

Dante's time optional to reckon from the incarnation or the birth of Christ. The journey must therefore be taken to have begun on Friday the 25th March, a fortnight before the Good Friday of 1300; and, counting strictly from the incarnation, on the first day of 1301—the first day of the new century. So we find Boccaccio in his unfinished commentary saying in Inf. iii. that it will appear from Canto xxi. that Dante began his journey in MCCCI.—The hour is now five hours before that at which the earthquake happened which took place at the death of Jesus. This is held by Dante (Convito iv. 23), who professes to follow the account by Saint Luke, to have been at the sixth hour, that is, at noon; thus the time is now seven in the morning.

591. Alichino, etc.: The names of the devils are all descriptive: Alichino, for instance, is the Swooper; but in this and the next Canto we have enough of the horrid crew without considering too closely how they are called.

592. Unbroken: Malacoda repeats his lie.

593. Each bit his tongue, etc.: The demons, aware of the cheat played by Malacoda, show their devilish humour by making game of Virgil and Dante.—Benvenuto is amazed that a man so involved in his own thoughts as Dante was, should have been such a close observer of low life as this passage shows him. He is sure that he laughed to himself as he wrote the Canto.

CANTO XXII.

Horsemen I've seen in march across the field,
Hastening to charge, or, answering muster, stand,
And sometimes too when forced their ground to yield;
I have seen skirmishers upon your land,
O Aretines![594] and those on foray sent;
With trumpet and with bell[595] to sound command
Have seen jousts run and well-fought tournament,
With drum, and signal from the castle shown,
And foreign music with familiar blent;
But ne'er by blast on such a trumpet blown
Beheld I horse or foot to motion brought,
Nor ship by star or landmark guided on.
With the ten demons moved we from the spot;
Ah, cruel company! but 'with the good
In church, and in the tavern with the sot.'
Still to the pitch was my attention glued
Fully to see what in the Bolgia lay,
And who were in its burning mass imbrued.
As when the dolphins vaulted backs display,
Warning to mariners they should prepare
To trim their vessel ere the storm makes way;
So, to assuage the pain he had to bear,
Some wretch would show his back above the tide,
Then swifter plunge than lightnings cleave the air.
And as the frogs close to the marsh's side
With muzzles thrust out of the water stand,

While feet and bodies carefully they hide;
So stood the sinners upon every hand.
But on beholding Barbariccia nigh
Beneath the bubbles[596] disappeared the band.
I saw what still my heart is shaken by:
One waiting, as it sometimes comes to pass
That one frog plunges, one at rest doth lie;
And Graffiacan, who nearest to him was,
Him upward drew, clutching his pitchy hair:
To me he bore the look an otter has.
I of their names[597] ere this was well aware,
For I gave heed unto the names of all
When they at first were chosen. 'Now prepare,
And, Rubicante, with thy talons fall
Upon him and flay well,' with many cries
And one consent the accursed ones did call
.I said: 'O Master, if in any wise
Thou canst, find out who is the wretched wight
Thus at the mercy of his enemies.'
Whereon my Guide drew full within his sight
Asking him whence he came, and he replied:
'In kingdom of Navarre[598] I first saw light.
Me servant to a lord my mother tied;
Through her I from a scoundrel sire did spring,
Waster of goods and of himself beside.
As servant next to Thiebault,[599] righteous king,
I set myself to ply barratorship;
And in this heat discharge my reckoning.'
And Ciriatto, close upon whose lip

On either side a boar-like tusk did stand,
Made him to feel how one of them could rip.
The mouse had stumbled on the wild cat band;
But Barbariccia locked him in embrace,
And, 'Off while I shall hug him!' gave command.
Round to my Master then he turned his face:
'Ask more of him if more thou wouldest know,
While he against their fury yet finds grace.'
My Leader asked: 'Declare now if below
The pitch 'mong all the guilty there lies here
A Latian?'[600] He replied: 'Short while ago
From one[601] I parted who to them lived near;
And would that I might use him still for shield,
Then hook or claw I should no longer fear,'
Said Libicocco: 'Too much grace we yield.'
And in the sinner's arm he fixed his hook,
And from it clean a fleshy fragment peeled.
But seeing Draghignazzo also took
Aim at his legs, the leader of the Ten
Turned swiftly round on them with angry look.
On this they were a little quieted; then
Of him who still gazed on his wound my Guide
Without delay demanded thus again:
'Who was it whom, in coming to the side,
Thou say'st thou didst do ill to leave behind?'
'Gomita of Gallura,'[602] he replied,
'A vessel full of fraud of every kind,
Who, holding in his power his master's foes,
So used them him they bear in thankful mind;

For, taking bribes, he let slip all of those,
He says; and he in other posts did worse,
And as a chieftain 'mong barrators rose.
Don Michael Zanche[603] doth with him converse,
From Logodoro, and with endless din
They gossip[604] of Sardinian characters.
But look, ah me! how yonder one doth grin.
More would I say, but that I am afraid
He is about to claw me on the skin.'
To Farfarel the captain turned his head,
For, as about to swoop, he rolled his eye,
And, 'Cursed hawk, preserve thy distance!' said.
'If ye would talk with, or would closer spy,'
The frighted wretch began once more to say,
'Tuscans or Lombards, I will bring them nigh.
But let the Malebranche first give way,
That of their vengeance they may not have fear,
And I to this same place where now I stay
For me, who am but one, will bring seven near
When I shall whistle as we use to do
Whenever on the surface we appear.'
On this Cagnazzo up his muzzle threw,
Shaking his head and saying: 'Hear the cheat
He has contrived, to throw himself below.'
Then he who in devices was complete:
'Far too malicious, in good sooth,' replied,'
When for my friends I plan a sorer fate.'
This, Alichin withstood not but denied
The others' counsel,[605] saying: 'If thou fling

Thyself hence, thee I strive not to outstride.
But o'er the pitch I'll dart upon the wing.
Leave we the ridge,[606] and be the bank a shield;
And see if thou canst all of us outspring.'
O Reader, hear a novel trick revealed.
All to the other side turned round their eyes,
He first[607] who slowest was the boon to yield.
In choice of time the Navarrese was wise;
Taking firm stand, himself he forward flung,
Eluding thus their hostile purposes.
Then with compunction each of them was stung,
But he the most[608] whose slackness made them fail;
Therefore he started, 'Caught!' upon his tongue.
But little it bested, nor could prevail
His wings 'gainst fear. Below the other went,
While he with upturned breast aloft did sail.
And as the falcon, when, on its descent,
The wild duck suddenly dives out of sight,
Returns outwitted back, and malcontent;
To be befooled filled Calcabrin with spite.
Hovering he followed, wishing in his mind
The wretch escaping should leave cause for fight.
When the barrator vanished, from behind
He on his comrade with his talons fell
And clawed him, 'bove the moat with him entwined.
The other was a spar-hawk terrible
To claw in turn; together then the two
Plunged in the boiling pool. The heat full well
How to unlock their fierce embraces knew;

But yet they had no power[609] to rise again,

So were their wings all plastered o'er with glue.

Then Barbariccia, mourning with his train,

Caused four to fly forth to the other side

With all their grapplers. Swift their flight was ta'en

.Down to the place from either hand they glide,

Reaching their hooks to those who were limed fast,

And now beneath the scum were being fried.

And from them thus engaged we onward passed.

FOOTNOTES:

594. O Aretines: Dante is mentioned as having taken part in the campaign of 1289 against Arezzo, in the course of which the battle of Campaldino was fought. But the text can hardly refer to what he witnessed in that campaign, as the field of it was almostconfined to the Casentino, and little more than a formal entrance was made on the true Aretine territory; while the chronicles make no mention of jousts and forays. There is, however, no reason to think but that Dante was engaged in the attack made by Florence on the Ghibeline Arezzo in the early summer of the preceding year. In a few days the Florentines and their allies had taken above forty castles and strongholds, and devastated the enemy's country far and near; and, though unable to take the capital, they held all kinds of warlike games in front of it. Dante was then twenty-three years of age, and according to the Florentine constitution of that period would, in a full musterof the militia, be required to serve as a cavalier without pay, and providing his own horse and arms.

595. Bell: The use of the bell for martial music was common in the Italy of the thirteenth century. The great war-bell of the Florentines was carried with them into the field.

596. Beneath the bubbles, etc.: As the barrators took toll of the administration of justice and appointment to offices, something always sticking to their palms, so now they are plunged in the pitch; and as they denied to others what should be the common blessing of justice, now they cannot so much as breathe the air without paying dearly for it to the demons.

597. Their names: The names of all the demons. All of them urge Rubicante, the 'madred devil,' to flay the victim, shining and sleek with the hot pitch, who is held fast by Graffiacane.

598. In kingdom of Navarre, etc.: The commentators give the name of John Paul to this shade, but all that is known of him is found in the text.

599. *Thiebault:* King of Navarre and second of that name. He accompanied his father-in-law, Saint Louis, to Tunis, and died on his way back, in 1270.

600. *A Latian*: An Italian.

601. *From one, etc.:* A Sardinian. The barrator prolongs his answer so as to procure arespite from the fangs of his tormentors.

602. *Gomita of Gallura*: 'Friar Gomita' was high in favour with Nino Visconti (Purg.viii. 53), the lord of Gallura, one of the provinces into which Sardinia was divided under the Pisans. At last, after bearing long with him, the 'gentle Judge Nino' hangedGomita for setting prisoners free for bribes.

603. *Don Michael Zanche*: Enzo, King of Sardinia, married Adelasia, the lady of Logodoro, one of the four Sardinian judgedoms or provinces. Of this province Zanche,seneschal to Enzo, acquired the government during the long imprisonment of his master, or upon his death in 1273. Zanche's daughter was married to Branca d'Oria, by whom Zanche was treacherously slain in 1275 (Inf. xxxiii. 137). There seems to benothing extant to support the accusation implied in the text.

604. *They gossip, etc.:* Zanche's experience of Sardinia was of an earlier date than Gomita's. It has been claimed for, or charged against, the Sardinians, that more than other men they delight in gossip touching their native country. These two, if it can besupposed that, plunged among and choked with pitch, they still cared for Sardinian talk,would find material enough in the troubled history of their land. In 1300 it belonged partly to Genoa and partly to Pisa.

605. *The others' counsel*: Alichino, confident in his own powers, is willing to risk an experiment with the sinner. The other devils count a bird in the hand worth two in thebush.

606. *The ridge:* Not the crown of the great rocky barrier between the Fifth and the Sixth Bolgias, for it is not on that the devils are standing; neither are they allowedto pass over it (Inf. xxiii. 55). We are to figure them to ourselves as standing on a ledge running between the fosse and the foot of the enclosing rocky steep—a pathwaycontinued under the bridges and all round the Bolgia for their convenience as guardiansof it. The bank adjoining the pitch will serve as a screen for the sinner if the demons retire to the other side of this ledge.

607. *He first, etc.*: Cagnazzo. See line 106.

608. *He the most, etc.:* Alichino, whose confidence in his agility had led to the outwitting of the band.

609. *No power:* The foolish ineptitude of the devils for anything beyond their special function of hooking up and flaying those who appear on the surface of the pitch, and their irrational fierce playfulness as of tiger cubs, convey a vivid impression of the limits set to their diabolical power, and at the same time heighten the sense of what Dante's feeling of insecurity must have been while in such inhuman companionship.

CANTO XXIII.

Silent, alone, not now with company
We onward went, one first and one behind,
As Minor Friars[610] use to make their way.
On Æsop's fable[611] wholly was my mind
Intent, by reason of that contest new—
The fable where the frog and mouse we find;
For Mo and Issa[612] are not more of hue
Than like the fable shall the fact appear,
If but considered with attention due.
And as from one thought springs the next, so here
Out of my first arose another thought,
Until within me doubled was my fear.
For thus I judged: Seeing through us[613] were brought
Contempt upon them, hurt, and sore despite,
They needs must be to deep vexation wrought
.If anger to malevolence unite,
Then will they us more cruelly pursue
Than dog the hare which almost feels its bite.
All my hair bristled, I already knew,
With terror when I spake: 'O Master, try
To hide us quick' (and back I turned to view
What lay behind), 'for me they terrify,
These Malebranche following us; from dread
I almost fancy I can feel them nigh.'
And he: 'Were I a mirror backed with lead
I should no truer glass that form of thine,

Than all thy thought by mine is answered.
For even now thy thoughts accord with mine,
Alike in drift and featured with one face;
And to suggest one counsel they combine.
If the right bank slope downward at this place,
To the next Bolgia[614] offering us a way,
Swiftly shall we evade the imagined chase.'
Ere he completely could his purpose say,
I saw them with their wings extended wide,
Close on us; as of us to make their prey.
Then quickly was I snatched up by my
Guide:Even as a mother when, awaked by cries,
She sees the flames are kindling at her side,
Delaying not, seizes her child and flies;
Careful for him her proper danger mocks,
Nor even with one poor shift herself supplies.
And he, stretched out upon the flinty rocks,
Himself unto the precipice resigned
Which one side of the other Bolgia blocks.
A swifter course ne'er held a stream confined,
That it may turn a mill, within its race,
Where near the buckets 'tis the most declined
Than was my Master's down that rock's sheer face;
Nor seemed I then his comrade, as we sped,
But like a son locked in a sire's embrace.
And barely had his feet struck on the bed
Of the low ground, when they were seen to stand
Upon the crest, no more a cause of dread.[615]
For Providence supreme, who so had planned

In the Fifth Bolgia they should minister,
Them wholly from departure thence had banned.
'Neath us we saw a painted people fare,
Weeping as on their way they circled slow,
Crushed by fatigue to look at, and despair.
Cloaks had they on with hoods pulled down full low
Upon their eyes, and fashioned, as it seemed,
Like those which at Cologne[616] for monks they sew.
The outer face was gilt so that it gleamed;
Inside was all of lead, of such a weight
Frederick's[617] to these had been but straw esteemed.
O weary robes for an eternal state!
With them we turned to the left hand once more,
Intent upon their tears disconsolate.
But those folk, wearied with the loads they bore,
So slowly crept that still new company
Was ours at every footfall on the floor.
Whence to my Guide I said: 'Do thou now try
To find some one by name or action known,
And as we go on all sides turn thine eye.'
And one, who recognised the Tuscan tone,
Called from behind us: 'Halt, I you entreat
Who through the air obscure are hastening on;
Haply in me thou what thou seek'st shalt meet.'
Whereon my Guide turned round and said:
'Await,And keep thou time with pacing of his feet.'
I stood, and saw two manifesting great
Desire to join me, by their countenance;
But their loads hampered them and passage strait.[618]

And, when arrived, me with an eye askance[619]
They gazed on long time, but no word they spoke;
Then, to each other turned, held thus parlance:
'His heaving throat[620] proves him of living folk.
If they are of the dead, how could they gain
To walk uncovered by the heavy cloak?'
Then to me: 'Tuscan, who dost now attain
To the college of the hypocrites forlorn,
To tell us who thou art show no disdain.'
And I to them: 'I was both bred and born
In the great city by fair Arno's stream,
And wear the body I have always worn.
But who are ye, whose suffering supreme
Makes tears, as I behold, to flood the cheek;
And what your mode of pain that thus doth gleam?' '
Ah me, the yellow mantles,' one to speak
Began, 'are all of lead so thick, its weight
Maketh the scales after this manner creak.
We, Merry Friars[621] of Bologna's state,
I Catalano, Loderingo he,
Were by thy town together designate,
As for the most part one is used to be,
To keep the peace within it; and around
Gardingo,[622] what we were men still may see.
'I made beginning: 'Friars, your profound—'
But said no more, on suddenly seeing there
One crucified by three stakes to the ground,
Who, when he saw me, writhed as in despair,
Breathing into his beard with heavy sigh.

And Friar Catalan, of this aware,
Said: 'He thus fixed, on whom thou turn'st thine eye,
Counselled the Pharisees that it behoved
One man as victim[623] for the folk should die.
Naked, thou seest, he lies, and ne'er removed
From where, set 'cross the path, by him the weight
Of every one that passes by is proved.
And his wife's father shares an equal fate,
With others of the Council, in this fosse;
For to the Jews they proved seed reprobate.'
Meanwhile at him thus stretched upon the crossVirgil,[624]
I saw, displayed astonishment—
At his mean exile and eternal loss.
And then this question to the Friars he sent:
'Be not displeased, but, if ye may, avow
If on the right[625] hand there lies any vent
By which we, both of us,[626] from hence may go,
Nor need the black angelic company
To come to help us from this valley low.'
'Nearer than what thou think'st,' he made reply,
'A rib there runs from the encircling wall,[627]
The cruel vales in turn o'erarching high;
Save that at this 'tis rent and ruined all.
Ye can climb upward o'er the shattered heap
Where down the side the piled-up fragments fall.'
His head bent down a while my Guide did keep,
Then said: 'He warned us[628] in imperfect wise,
Who sinners with his hook doth clutch and steep.'
The Friar: 'At Bologna[629] many a vice

I heard the Devil charged with, and among
The rest that, false, he father is of lies.'
Then onward moved my Guide with paces long,
And some slight shade of anger on his face.
I with him parted from the burdened throng,
Stepping where those dear feet had left their trace.

FOOTNOTES:

610. Minor Friars: In the early years of their Order the Franciscans went in couplesupon their journeys, not abreast but one behind the other.

611. Æsop's fable: This fable, mistakenly attributed to Æsop, tells of how a frog enticed a mouse into a pond, and how they were then both devoured by a kite. To discover the aptness of the simile would scarcely be reward enough for the continuedmental effort Dante enjoins. So much was everything Greek or Roman then held in reverence, that the mention even of Æsop is held to give dignity to the page.

612. Mo and Issa: Two words for now.

613. Through us: The quarrel among the fiends arose from Dante's insatiable desire to confer with 'Tuscan or Lombard.'

614. To the next Bolgia: The Sixth. They are now on the top of the circular ridge that divides it from the Fifth. From the construction of Malebolge the ridge is deeper on theinner side than on that up which they have travelled from the pitch.

615. No more a cause of dread: There seems some incongruity between Virgil's dreadof these smaller devils and the ease with which he cowed Minos, Charon, and Pluto. But his character gains in human interest the more he is represented as sympathising with Dante in his terrors; and in this particular case the confession of fellow-feeling prepares the way for the beautiful passage which follows it (line 38, etc.), one full of an almost modern tenderness.

616. Cologne: Some make it Clugny, the great Benedictine monastery; but all the old commentators and most of the mss. read Cologne. All that the text necessarily carriesis that the cloaks had great hoods. If, in addition, a reproach of clumsiness is implied,it would agree well enough with the Italian estimate of German people and things.

617. Frederick's, etc.: The Emperor Frederick II.; but that he used any torture of leaden sheets seems to be a fabrication of his enemies.

618. Passage strait: Through the crowd of shades, all like themselves weighed down by the leaden cloaks. There is nothing in all literature like this picture of the heavily- burdened shades. At first sight it seems to be little of a torture compared with what we have already seen, and yet by simple touch after touch an impression is created of the intolerable weariness of the victims. As always, too, the punishment answers to the sin. The hypocrites made a fair show in the flesh, and now their mantles which look like gold are only of base lead. On earth they were of a sad countenance, trying to seem better than they were, and the load which to deceive others they voluntarily assumed in life is now replaced by a still heavier weight, and one they cannot throw off if they would. The choice of garb conveys an obvious charge of hypocrisy against the Friars, then greatly fallen away from the purity of their institution, whether Franciscans or Dominicans.

619. An eye askance: They cannot turn their heads.

620. His heaving throat: In Purgatory Dante is known for a mortal by his casting a shadow. Here he is known to be of flesh and blood by the act of respiration; yet, as appears from line 113, the shades, too, breathe as well as perform other functions of living bodies. At least they seem so to do, but this is all only in appearance. They only seem to be flesh and blood, having no weight, casting no shadow, and drawing breath in a way of their own. Dante, as has been said (Inf. vi. 36), is hard put to it to make them subject to corporal pains and yet be only shadows.

621. Merry Friars: Knights of the Order of Saint Mary, instituted by Urban IV. in 1261. Whether the name of Frati Godenti which they here bear was one of reproach or was simply descriptive of the easy rule under which they lived, is not known. Married men might, under certain conditions, enter the Order. The members were to hold themselves aloof from public office, and were to devote themselves to the defence of the weak and the promotion of justice and religion. The two monkish cavaliers of the text were in 1266 brought to Florence as Podestas, the Pope himself having urged them to go. There is much uncertainty as to the part they played in Florence, but none as to the fact of their rule having been highly distasteful to the Florentines, or as to the other fact, that in Florence they grew wealthy. The Podesta, or chief magistrate, was always a well-born foreigner. Probably some monkish rule or custom forbade either Catalano or Loderingo to leave the monastery singly.

622. Gardingo: A quarter of Florence, in which many palaces were destroyed about the time of the Podestaship of the Frati.

623. One man as victim: St. John xi. 50. Caiaphas and Annas, with the Scribes and Pharisees who persecuted Jesus to the death, are the vilest hypocrites of all. They lie naked across the path, unburdened by the leaden cloak, it is true, but only that they may feel the more keenly the weight of the punishment of all the hypocrites of the world.

624. Virgil: On Virgil's earlier journey through Inferno Caiaphas and the others were not here, and he wonders as at something out of a world to him unknown.

625. On the right: As they are moving round the Bolgia to the left, the rocky barrierbetween them and the Seventh Bolgia is on their right.

626. We, both of us: Dante, still in the body, as well as Virgil, the shade.[627]

627. The encircling wall: That which encloses all the Malebolge.

628. He warned us: Malacoda (Inf. xxi. 109) had assured him that the next rib of rock ran unbroken across all the Bolgias, but it too, like all the other bridges, proves to have been, at the time of the earthquake, shattered where it crossed this gulf of the hypocrites. The earthquake told most on this Bolgia, because the death of Christ and the attendant earthquake were, in a sense, caused by the hypocrisy of Caiaphas and the rest.

629. At Bologna: Even in Inferno the Merry Friar must have his joke. He is a gentleman, but a bit of a scholar too; and the University of Bologna is to him what Marischal College was to Captain Dalgetty.

CANTO XXIV.

In season of the new year, when the sun
Beneath Aquarius[630] warms again his hair,
And somewhat on the nights the days have won;
When on the ground the hoar-frost painteth fair
A mimic image of her sister white—
But soon her brush of colour is all bare—
The clown, whose fodder is consumed outright,
Rises and looks abroad, and, all the plain
Beholding glisten, on his thigh doth smite.
Returned indoors, like wretch that seeks in vain
What he should do, restless he mourns his case;
But hope revives when, looking forth again,
He sees the earth anew has changed its face.
Then with his crook he doth himself provide,
And straightway doth his sheep to pasture chase:
So at my Master was I terrified,
His brows beholding troubled; nor more slow
To where I ailed[631] the plaster was applied.
For when the broken bridge[632] we stood below
My Guide turned to me with the expression sweet
Which I beneath the mountain learned to know.
His arms he opened, after counsel meet
Held with himself, and, scanning closely o'er
The fragments first, he raised me from my feet;
And like a man who, working, looks before,
With foresight still on that in front bestowed,

Me to the summit of a block he bore
And then to me another fragment showed, Saying:
'By this thou now must clamber on;
But try it first if it will bear thy load.'
The heavy cowled[633] this way could ne'er have gone,
For hardly we, I holpen, he so light,
Could clamber up from shattered stone to stone.
And but that on the inner bank the height
Of wall is not so great, I say not he,
But for myself I had been vanquished quite.
But Malebolge[634] to the cavity
Of the deep central pit is planned to fall;
Hence every Bolgia in its turn must be
High on the out, low on the inner wall;
So to the summit we attained at last,
Whence breaks away the topmost stone[635] of all
.My lungs were so with breathlessness harassed,
The summit won, I could no further go;
And, hardly there, me on the ground I cast
'Well it befits that thou shouldst from thee throw
All sloth,' the Master said; 'for stretched in down
Or under awnings none can glory know.
And he who spends his life nor wins renown
Leaves in the world no more enduring trace
Than smoke in air, or foam on water blown.
Therefore arise; o'ercome thy breathlessness
By force of will, victor in every fight
When not subservient to the body base.
Of stairs thou yet must climb a loftier flight:[636]'

Tis not enough to have ascended these.
Up then and profit if thou hear'st aright.'
Rising I feigned to breathe with greater ease
Than what I felt, and spake: 'Now forward plod,
For with my courage now my strength agrees.'
Up o'er the rocky rib we held our road;
And rough it was and difficult and strait,
And steeper far[637] than that we earlier trod.
Speaking I went, to hide my wearied state,
When from the neighbouring moat a voice we heard
Which seemed ill fitted to articulate.
Of what it said I knew not any word,
Though on the arch[638] that vaults the moat set high;
But he who spake appeared by anger stirred.
Though I bent downward yet my eager eye,
So dim the depth, explored it all in vain;
I then: 'O Master, to that bank draw nigh,
And let us by the wall descent obtain,
Because I hear and do not understand,
And looking down distinguish nothing plain.'
'My sole reply to thee,' he answered bland,
'Is to perform; for it behoves,' he said,
'With silent act to answer just demand.'
Then we descended from the bridge's head,[639]
Where with the eighth bank is its junction wrought;
And full beneath me was the Bolgia spread.
And I perceived that hideously 'twas fraught
With serpents; and such monstrous forms they bore
,Even now my blood is curdled at the thought.

Henceforth let sandy Libya boast no more!
Though she breed hydra, snake that crawls or flies,
Twy-headed, or fine-speckled, no such store
Of plagues, nor near so cruel, she supplies,
Though joined to all the land of Ethiop,
And that which by the Red Sea waters lies. '
Midst this fell throng and dismal, without hope
A naked people ran, aghast with fear—
No covert for them and no heliotrope.[640]
Their hands[641] were bound by serpents at their rear,
Which in their reins for head and tail did get
A holding-place: in front they knotted were.
And lo! to one who on our side was set
A serpent darted forward, him to bite
At where the neck is by the shoulders met.
Nor O nor I did any ever write
More quickly than he kindled, burst in flame,
And crumbled all to ashes. And when quite
He on the earth a wasted heap became,
The ashes[642] of themselves together rolled,
Resuming suddenly their former frame.
Thus, as by mighty sages we are told,
The Phœnix[643] dies, and then is born again,
When it is close upon five centuries old.
In all its life it eats not herb nor grain,
But only tears that from frankincense flow;
It, for a shroud, sweet nard and myrrh contain.
And as the man who falls and knows not how,
By force of demons stretched upon the ground,

Or by obstruction that makes life run low,
When risen up straight gazes all around
In deep confusion through the anguish keen
He suffered from, and stares with sighs profound:
So was the sinner, when arisen, seen.
Justice of God, how are thy terrors piled,
Showering in vengeance blows thus big with teen!
My Guide then asked of him how he was styled.
Whereon he said: 'From Tuscany I rained,
Not long ago, into this gullet wild.
From bestial life, not human, joy I gained,
Mule that I was; me, Vanni Fucci,[644] brute,
Pistoia, fitting den, in life contained.'
I to my Guide: 'Bid him not budge a foot,
And ask[645] what crime has plunged him here below.
In rage and blood I knew him dissolute.'
The sinner heard, nor insincere did show,
But towards me turned his face and eke his mind,
With spiteful shame his features all aglow;
Then said: 'It pains me more thou shouldst me find
And catch me steeped in all this misery,
Than when the other life I left behind.
What thou demandest I can not deny:
I'm plunged[646] thus low because the thief I played
Within the fairly furnished sacristy;
And falsely to another's charge 'twas laid.
Lest thou shouldst joy[647] such sight has met thy view
If e'er these dreary regions thou evade,
Give ear and hearken to my utterance true:

The Neri first out of Pistoia fail,

Her laws and parties Florence shapes anew;

Mars draws a vapour out of Magra's vale,

Which black and threatening clouds accompany:

Then bursting in a tempest terrible

Upon Piceno shall the war run high;

The mist by it shall suddenly be rent,

And every Bianco[648] smitten be thereby:

And I have told thee that thou mayst lament.'

FOOTNOTES:

630. Aquarius: The sun is in the constellation of Aquarius from the end of January till the end of February; and already, say in the middle of February, the day is nearly as long as the night.

631. Where I ailed, etc.: As the peasant is in despair at seeing the earth white with what he thinks is snow, so was Dante at the signs of trouble on Virgil's face. He has mistaken anger at the cheat for perplexity as to how they are to escape from the Bolgia;and his Master's smile is grateful and reassuring to him as the spectacle of the green earth to the despairing shepherd.

632. The broken bridge: They are about to escape from the bottom of the Sixth Bolgiaby climbing the wall between it and the Seventh, at the point where the confused fragments of the bridge Friar Catalano told them of (Inf. xxiii. 133) lie piled up againstthe wall, and yield something of a practicable way.

634. The heavy cowled: He finds his illustration on the spot, his mind being still full of the grievously burdened hypocrites.

635. But Malebolge, etc.: Each Bolgia in turn lies at a lower level than the one beforeit, and consequently the inner side of each dividing ridge or wall is higher than the outer; or, to put it otherwise, in each Bolgia the wall they come to last—that nearest thecentre of the Inferno, is lower than that they first reach—the one enclosing the Bolgia.

635. The topmost stone: The stone that had formed the beginning of the arch at this end of it.

636. A loftier flight: When he ascends the Mount of Purgatory.

637. Steeper far, etc.: Rougher and steeper than the rib of rock they followed till they had crossed the Fifth Bolgia. They are now travelling along a different spoke of the wheel.

638. The arch, etc.: He has gone on hiding his weariness till he is on the top of the arch that overhangs the Seventh Bolgia—that in which thieves are punished.

639. Front the bridge's head: Further on they climb up again (Inf. xxvi. 13) by the projecting stones which now supply them with the means of descent. It is a disputed point how far they do descend. Clearly it is further than merely from the bridge to the lower level of the wall dividing the Seventh from the Eighth Bolgia; but not so far as to the ground of the moat. Most likely the stones jut forth at the angle formed by the junction of the bridge and the rocky wall. On one of the lowest of these they find a standing-place whence they can see clearly what is in the Bolgia.

640. Heliotrope: A stone supposed to make the bearer of it invisible.

641.Their hands, etc.: The sinners in this Bolgia are the thieves, not the violent robbers and highwaymen but those crime involves a betrayal of trust. After all their cunning thefts they are naked now; and, though here is nothing to steal, hands are firmly bound behind them.

642. The ashes, etc.: The sufferings of the thieves, if looked closely into, will be found appropriate to their sins. They would fain but cannot steal themselves away, and in addition to the constant terror of being found out they are subject to pains the essence ofwhich consists in the deprivation—the theft from them—of their unsubstantial bodies,which are all that they now have to lose. In the case of this victim the deprivation is only temporary.

643. The Phœnix: Dante here borrows very directly from Ovid (Metam. xv.).

644. Vanni Fucci: Natural son of a Pistoiese noble and a poet of some merit, who bore a leading part in the ruthless feuds of Blacks and Whites which distracted Pistoiatowards the close of the thirteenth century.

645. And ask, etc.: Dante wishes to find out why Fucci is placed among the thieves, and not in the circle of the violent. The question is framed so as to compel confessionof a crime for which the sinner had not been condemned in life; and he flushes with rage at being found among the cowardly thieves.

646. I'm plunged, etc.: Fucci was concerned in the theft of treasure from the Cathedral Church of St. James at Pistoia. Accounts vary as to the circumstances under which thecrime was committed, and as to who suffered for it. Neither is it certainly known whenFucci died, though his recent arrival in the Bolgia agrees with the view that he was stillactive on the side of the Blacks in the last year of the century. In the fierceness of his retort to Dante we have evidence of their old acquaintance and old enmity.

647. Lest thou shouldst joy: Vanni, a Nero or Black, takes his revenge for being found here by Dante, who was, as he knew, associated with the Bianchi or Whites, byprophesying an event full of disaster to these.

648. Every Bianco, etc.: The Blacks, according to Villani (viii. 45), were driven fromPistoia in May 1301. They took refuge in Florence, where their party, in the followingNovember under the protection of Charles of Valois, finally gained the upper hand, and began to persecute and expel the Whites, among whom was Dante. Mars, the god of war, or, more probably, the planet of war, draws a vapour from the valley of the Magra, a small stream which flows into the Mediterranean on the northern confine ofTuscany. This vapour is said to signify Moroello Malaspina, a noble of that district andan active leader of the Blacks, who here figure as murky clouds. The Campo Piceno is the country west of Pistoia. There Moroello bursts on his foes like a lightning-flashout of its cloud. This seems to refer to a pitched battle that should have happened soonafter the Blacks recovered their strength; but the chroniclers tell of none such, though some of the commentators do. The fortress of Seravalle was taken from the Pistoiese, itis true, in 1302, and Moroello is said to have been the leader of the force which starvedit into submission. He was certainly present at the great siege of Pistoia in 1305, whenthe citizens suffered the last rigours of famine.—This prophecy by Fucci recalls thoseby Farinata and Ciacco.

CANTO XXV.

The robber,[649] when his words were ended so,
Made both the figs and lifted either fist, Shouting:
'There, God! for them at thee I throw.'
Then were the snakes my friends; for one 'gan twist
And coiled itself around the sinner's throat,
As if to say: 'Now would I have thee whist.'
Another seized his arms and made a knot,
Clinching itself upon them in such wise
He had no power to move them by a jot.
Pistoia![650] thou, Pistoia, shouldst devise
To burn thyself to ashes, since thou hast
Outrun thy founders in iniquities.
The blackest depths of Hell through which
I passed Showed me no soul 'gainst
God so filled with spite, No, not even he who down
Thebes' wall[651] was cast.
He spake no further word, but turned to flight;
And I beheld a Centaur raging sore
Come shouting: 'Of the ribald give me sight!'
I scarce believe Maremma[652] yieldeth more
Snakes of all kinds than what composed the load
Which on his back, far as our form, he bore.
Behind his nape, with pinions spread abroad,
A dragon couchant on his shoulders lay
To set on fire whoever bars his road.
'This one is Cacus,'[653] did my Master say,

‘Who underneath the rock of Aventine
Watered a pool with blood day after day.
Not with his brethren[654] runs he in the line,
Because of yore the treacherous theft he wrought
Upon the neighbouring wealthy herd of kine:
Whence to his crooked course an end was brought
’Neath Hercules’ club, which on him might shower down
A hundred blows; ere ten he suffered nought.’
While this he said, the other had passed on;
And under us three spirits forward pressed
Of whom my Guide and I had nothing known
But that: ‘Who are ye?’ they made loud request.
Whereon our tale[655] no further could proceed;
And toward them wholly we our wits addressed.
I recognised them not, but gave good heed;
Till, as it often haps in such a case,
To name another, one discovered need,
Saying: ‘Now where stopped Cianfa[656] in the race?’
Then, that my Guide might halt and hearken well,
On chin[657] and nose I did my finger place.
If, Reader, to believe what now I tell
Thou shouldst be slow, I wonder not, for I
Who saw it all scarce find it credible.
While I on them my brows kept lifted high
A serpent, which had six feet, suddenly flew
At one of them and held him bodily.
Its middle feet about his paunch it drew,
And with the two in front his arms clutched fast,
And bit one cheek and the other through and through.

Its hinder feet upon his thighs it cast,
Thrusting its tail between them till behind,
Distended o'er his reins, it upward passed.
The ivy to a tree could never bind
Itself so firmly as this dreadful beast
Its members with the other's intertwined.
Each lost the colour that it once possessed,
And closely they, like heated wax, unite,
The former hue of neither manifest:
Even so up o'er papyrus,[658] when alight,
Before the flame there spreads a colour dun,
Not black as yet, though from it dies the white.
The other two meanwhile were looking on,
Crying: 'Agnello, how art thou made new!
Thou art not twain, and yet no longer one.'
A single head was moulded out of two;
And on our sight a single face arose,
Which out of both lost countenances grew.
Four separate limbs did but two arms compose;
Belly with chest, and legs with thighs did grow
To members such as nought created shows.
Their former fashion was all perished now:
The perverse shape did both, yet neither seem;
And, thus transformed, departed moving slow.
And as the lizard, which at fierce extreme
Of dog-day heat another hedge would gain,
Flits 'cross the path swift as the lightning's gleam;
Right for the bellies of the other twain
A little snake[659] quivering with anger sped,

Livid and black as is a pepper grain,
And on the part by which we first are fed
Pierced one of them; and then upon the ground
It fell before him, and remained outspread.
The wounded gazed on it, but made no sound.
Rooted he stood[660] and yawning, scarce awake
,As seized by fever or by sleep profound.
It closely watched him and he watched the snake,
While from its mouth and from his wound 'gan swell
Volumes of smoke which joined one cloud to make.
Be Lucan henceforth dumb, nor longer tell
Of plagued Sabellus and Nassidius,[661]
But, hearkening to what follows, mark it well.
Silent be Ovid: of him telling us
How Cadmus[662] to a snake, and to a fount
Changed Arethuse,[663] I am not envious;
For never of two natures front to front
In metamorphosis, while mutually
The forms[664] their matter changed, he gives account.
'Twas thus that each to the other made reply:
Its tail into a fork the serpent split;
Bracing his feet the other pulled them nigh:
And then in one so thoroughly were knit
His legs and thighs, no searching could divine
At where the junction had been wrought in it.
The shape, of which the one lost every sign,
The cloven tail was taking; then the skin
Of one grew rough, the other's soft and fine.
I by the armpits saw the arms drawn in;

And now the monster's feet, which had been small,
What the other's lost in length appeared to win.
Together twisted, its hind feet did fall
And grew the member men are used to hide:
For his the wretch gained feet with which to crawl.
Dyed in the smoke they took on either side
A novel colour: hair unwonted grew
On one; the hair upon the other died.
The one fell prone, erect the other drew,
With cruel eyes continuing to glare,
'Neath which their muzzles metamorphose knew.
The erect to his brows drew his. Of stuff to spare
Of what he upward pulled, there was no lack;
So ears were formed on cheeks that erst were bare.
Of that which clung in front nor was drawn back,
Superfluous, on the face was formed a nose,
And lips absorbed the skin that still was slack.
His muzzle who lay prone now forward goes;
Backward into his head his ears he draws
Even as a snail appears its horns to lose.
The tongue, which had been whole and ready was
For speech, cleaves now; the forked tongue of the snake
Joins in the other: and the smoke has pause.[665]
The soul which thus a brutish form did take,
Along the valley, hissing, swiftly fled;
The other close behind it spluttering spake,
Then, toward it turning his new shoulders, said
Unto the third: 'Now Buoso down the way
May hasten crawling, as I earlier sped.'

Ballast which in the Seventh Bolgia lay
Thus saw I shift and change. Be my excuse
The novel theme,[666] if swerves my pen astray.
And though these things mine eyesight might confuse
A little, and my mind with fear divide,
Such secrecy they fleeing could not use
But that Puccio Sciancatto plain I spied;
And he alone of the companions three
Who came at first, was left unmodified.
For the other, tears, Gaville,[667] are shed by thee.

FOOTNOTES:

649. The robber, etc.: By means of his prophecy Fucci has, after a fashion, taken revenge on Dante for being found by him among the cheating thieves instcad of amongthe nobler sinners guilty of blood and violence. But in the rage of his wounded pride he must insult even Heaven, and this he does by using the most contemptuous gesturein an Italian's repertory. The fig is made by thrusting the thumb between the next twofingers. In the English 'A fig for him!' we have a reference to the gesture.

650. Pistoia: The Pistoiese bore the reputation of being hard and pitiless. The traditionwas that their city had been founded by such of Catiline's followers as survived his defeat on the Campo Piceno. 'It is no wonder,' says Villani (i. 32) 'that, being the descendants as they are of Catiline and his followers, the Pistoiese have always been ruthless and cruel to strangers and to one another.'

651. Who down Thebes' wall: Capaneus (Inf. xiv. 63).

652. Maremma: See note, Inf. xiii. 8.

653. Cacus: Dante makes him a Centaur, but Virgil (Æn. viii.) only describes him ashalf human. The pool was fed with the blood of his human victims. The herd was the spoil Hercules took from Geryon. In the Æneid Cacus defends himself from Herculesby vomiting a fiery smoke; and this doubtless suggested the dragon of the text.

654. His brethren: The Centaurs who guard the river of blood (Inf. xii. 56). In Fucci, as a sinner guilty of blood and violence above most of the thieves, the Centaur Cacus takes a special malign interest.

655. Our tale: Of Cacus. It is interrupted by the arrival of three sinners whom Dante does not at first recognise as he gazes down on them, but only when they begin to speak among themselves. They are three noble citizens of Florence: Agnello Brunelleschi, Buoso degli Abati, and Puccio Sciancatto de' Galigai—all said to have pilfered in private life, or to have abused their tenure of high office by plundering the Commonwealth. What is certainly known of them is that they were Florentine thievesof quality.

656. Cianfa: Another Florentine gentleman, one of the Donati. Since his companionslost sight of him he has been transformed into a six-footed serpent. Immediately appearing, he darts upon Agnello.

657. On chin, etc.: A gesture by which silence is requested. The mention of Cianfa shows Dante that he is among Florentines.

658. Papyrus: The original is papiro, the word used in Dante's time for a wick madeout of a reed like the papyrus; papér being still the name for a wick in some dialects.—(Scartazzini.) It cannot be shown that papiro was ever employed for paper in Italian. This, however, does not prove that Dante may not so use it in this instance, adopting it from the Latin papyrus. Besides, he says that the brown colour travels up over the papiro; while it goes downward on a burning wick. Nor would the simile, if drawn from a slowly burning lamp-wick, agree with the speed of the change described in the text.

659. A little snake: As transpires from the last line of the Canto, this is Francesco, ofthe Florentine family of the Cavalcanti, to which Dante's friend Guido belonged. He wounds Buoso in the navel, and then, instead of growing into one new monster as wasthe case with Cianfa and Agnello, they exchange shapes, and when the transformation is complete Buoso is the serpent and Francesco is the human shade.

660. Rooted he stood, etc.: The description agrees with the symptoms of snake-bite, one of which is extreme drowsiness.

661. Sabellus and Nassidius: Were soldiers of Cato's army whose death by snake-bitein the Libyan desert is described by Lucan, Pharsal. ix. Sabbellus was burned up by thepoison, bones and all; Nassidius swelled up and burst.

662. Cadmus: Metam. iv.

663 Arethusa: Metam. v.

664. The forms, etc.: The word form is here to be taken in its scholastic sense of virtus formativa, the inherited power of modifying matter into an organised body. 'This, united to the divinely implanted spark of reason,' says Philalethes, 'constitutes, on Dante's system, a human soul. Even after death this power continues to be an essential constituent of the soul, and constructs out of the elements what seems to be a body. Here the sinners exchange the matter they have thus made their own, each retaining, however, his proper plastic energy as part of his soul.' Dante in his Convito (iii. 2) says that 'the human soul is the noblest form of all that are made under the heavens, receiving more of the Divine nature than any other.'

665. The smoke has pause: The sinners have robbed one another of all they can lose.In the punishment is mirrored the sin that plunged them here.

666. The novel theme: He has lingered longer than usual on this Bolgia, and pleads wonder of what he saw in excuse either of his prolixity or of some of the details of hisdescription. The expression is perhaps one of feigned humility, to balance his recent boast of excelling Ovid and Lucan in inventive power.

667. Gaville: The other, and the only one of those five Florentine thieves not yet named in the text, is he who came at first in the form of a little black snake, and who has now assumed the shape of Buoso. In reality he is Francesco Cavalcanti, who was slain by the people of Gaville in the upper Valdarno. Many of them were in their turn slaughtered in revenge by the Cavalcanti and their associates. It should be remarked that some of these five Florentines were of one party, some of the other. It is also noteworthy that Dante recruits his thieves as he did his usurers from the great Florentine families.—As the 'shifting and changing' of this rubbish is apt to be found confusing, the following may be useful to some readers:—There first came on the scene Agnello, Buoso, and Puccio. Cianfa, in the shape of a six-footed serpent, comesand throws himself on Agnello, and then, grown incorporate in a new strange monster, two in one, they disappear. Buoso is next wounded by Francesco, and they exchange members and bodies. Only Puccio remains unchanged.

CANTO XXVI.

Rejoice, O Florence, in thy widening fame!
Thy wings thou beatest over land and sea,
And even through Inferno spreads thy name.
Burghers of thine, five such were found by me
Among the thieves; whence I ashamed[668] grew,
Nor shall great glory thence redound to thee.
But if 'tis toward the morning[669] dreams are true,
Thou shalt experience ere long time be gone
The doom even Prato[670] prays for as thy due.
And came it now, it would not come too soon.
Would it were come as come it must with time:
'Twill crush me more the older I am grown.
Departing thence, my Guide began to climb
The jutting rocks by which we made descent
Some while ago,[671] and pulled me after him.
And as upon our lonely way we went
'Mong splinters[672] of the cliff, the feet in vain,
Without the hand to help, had labour spent.
I sorrowed, and am sorrow-smit again,
Recalling what before mine eyes there lay,
And, more than I am wont, my genius rein
From running save where virtue leads the way;
So that if happy star[673] or holier might
Have gifted me I never mourn it may.
At time of year when he who gives earth light
His face shows to us longest visible,

When gnats replace the fly at fall of night,
Not by the peasant resting on the hill
Are seen more fire-flies in the vale below,
Where he perchance doth field and vineyard[674] till,
Than flamelets I beheld resplendent glow
Throughout the whole Eighth Bolgia, when at last
I stood whence I the bottom plain could know.
And as he whom the bears avenged, when passed
From the earth Elijah, saw the chariot rise
With horses heavenward reared and mounting fast,
And no long time had traced it with his eyes
Till but a flash of light it all became,
Which like a rack of cloud swept to the skies:
Deep in the valley's gorge, in mode the same,
These flitted; what it held by none was shown,
And yet a sinner[675] lurked in every flame.
To see them well I from the bridge peered down,
And if a jutting crag I had not caught
I must have fallen, though neither thrust nor thrown.
My Leader me beholding lost in thought:
'In all the fires are spirits,' said to me;
'His flame round each is for a garment wrought.'
'O Master!' I replied, 'by hearing thee
I grow assured, but yet I knew before
That thus indeed it was, and longed to be
Told who is in the flame which there doth soar,
Cloven, as if ascending from the pyre
Where with Eteocles[676] there burned of yore
His brother.' He: 'Ulysses in that fire

And Diomedes[677] burn; in punishment
Thus held together, as they held in ire.
And, wrapped within their flame, they now repent
The ambush of the horse, which oped the door
Through which the Romans' noble seed[678] forth went.
For guile Deïdamia[679] makes deplore
In death her lost Achilles, tears they shed,
And bear for the Palladium[680] vengeance sore.'
'Master, I pray thee fervently,' I said,
'If from those flames they still can utter speech—
Give ear as if a thousand times
I pled!Refuse not here to linger,
I beseech, Until the cloven fire shall hither gain:
Thou seest how toward it eagerly I reach.'
And he: 'Thy prayers are worthy to obtain
Exceeding praise; thou hast what thou dost seek
:But see that thou from speech thy tongue refrain.
I know what thou wouldst have;
Leave me to speak,
For they perchance would hear contemptuously
Shouldst thou address them, seeing they were Greek.'[681]
Soon as the flame toward us had come so nigh
That to my Leader time and place seemed met,
I heard him thus adjure it to reply:
'O ye who twain within one fire are set,
If what I did your guerdon meriteth,
If much or little ye are in my debt
For the great verse I built while I had breath,
By one of you be openly confessed

Where, lost to men, at last he met with death.'
Of the ancient flame the more conspicuous crest
Murmuring began to waver up and down
Like flame that flickers, by the wind distressed.
At length by it was measured motion shown,
Like tongue that moves in speech; and by the flame
Was language uttered thus: 'When I had gone
From Circe[682] who a long year kept me tame
Beside her, ere the near Gaeta had
Receivèd from Æneas that new name;
No softness for my son, nor reverence sad
For my old father, nor the love I owed
Penelope with which to make her glad,
Could quench the ardour that within me glowed
A full experience of the world to gain—
Of human vice and worth. But I abroad
Launched out upon the high and open main[683]
With but one bark and but the little band
Which ne'er deserted me.[684] As far as Spain
I saw the sea-shore upon either hand,
And as Morocco; saw Sardinia's isle,
And all of which those waters wash the strand
.I and my comrades were grown old the while
And sluggish, ere we to the narrows came
Where Hercules of old did landmarks pile
For sign to men they should no further aim;
And Seville lay behind me on the right,
As on the left lay Ceuta. Then to them
I spake: "O Brothers, who through such a fight

Of hundred thousand dangers West have won,
In this short watch that ushers in the night
Of all your senses, ere your day be done,
Refuse not to obtain experience new
Of worlds unpeopled, yonder, past the sun.
Consider whence the seed of life ye drew;
Ye were not born to live like brutish herd,
But righteousness and wisdom to ensue."
My comrades to such eagerness were stirred
By this short speech the course to enter on,
They had no longer brooked restraining word.
Turning our poop to where the morning shone
We of the oars made wings for our mad flight,
Still tending left the further we had gone.
And of the other pole I saw at night
Now all the stars; and 'neath the watery plain
Our own familiar heavens were lost to sight.
Five times afresh had kindled, and again
The moon's face earthward was illumed no more,
Since out we sailed upon the mighty main;[685]
Then we beheld a lofty mountain[686] soar,
Dim in the distance; higher, as I thought,
By far than any I had seen before.
We joyed; but with despair were soon distraught
When burst a whirlwind from the new-found world
And the forequarter of the vessel caught.
With all the waters thrice it round was swirled;
At the fourth time the poop, heaved upward, rose,
The prow, as pleased Another,[687] down was hurled;

And then above us did the ocean close.'

FOOTNOTES:

668. Whence I ashamed, etc.: There is here a sudden change from irony to earnest. 'Five members of great Florentine families, eternally engaged among themselves in their shameful metamorphoses—nay, but it is too sad!'

669. Toward the morning, etc.: There was a widespread belief in the greater truthfulness of dreams dreamed as the night wears away. See Purg. ix. 13. The dreamis Dante's foreboding of what is to happen to Florence. Of its truth he has no doubt, and the only question is how soon will it be answered by the fact. Soon, he says, if it isnear to the morning that we dream true dreams—morning being the season of wakingreality in which dreams are accomplished.

670. Even Prato: A small neighbouring city, much under the influence of Florence, and somewhat oppressed by it. The commentators reckon up the disasters that afflictedFlorence in the first years of the fourteenth century, between the date of Dante's journey and the time he wrote—fires, falls of bridges, and civil strife. But such misfortunes were too much in keeping with the usual course of Florentine history to move Dante thus deeply in the retrospect; and as he speaks here in his own person the 'soon' is more naturally counted from the time at which he writes than from the date assigned by him to his pilgrimage. He is looking forward to the period when his own return in triumph to Florence was to be prepared by grievous national reverses; and, as a patriot,he feels that he cannot be wholly reconciled by his private advantage to the public misfortune. But it was all only a dream.

671. Some while ago: See note, Inf. xxiv. 79.

672. 'Mong splinters, etc.: They cross the wall or barrier between the Seventh and Eighth Bolgias. From Inf. xxiv. 63 we have learned that the rib of rock, on the line ofwhich they are now proceeding, with its arches which overhang the various Bolgias, isrougher and worse to follow than that by which they began their passage towards the centre of Malebolge.

673. Happy star: See note, Inf. xv. 55. Dante seems to have been uncertain what credence to give to the claims of astrology. In a passage of the Purgatorio (xvi. 67)he tries to establish that whatever influence the stars may possess over us we can never, except with our own consent, be influenced by them to evil.—His sorrow here,as elsewhere, is not wholly a feeling of pity for the suffering shades, but is largely mingled with misgivings for himself. The punishment of those to whose sins he feels no inclination he always beholds with equanimity. Here, as he looks down upon the false counsellors and considers what temptations there are to misapply intellectual gifts, he is smitten with dread lest his lot should one day be cast in that dismal valley and he find cause to regret that the talent of genius was ever committed to him. The memory even of what he saw makes him recollect himself and resolve to be wary.Then, as if to justify the claim to superior powers thus clearly implied, there comes a passage which in the original is of uncommon beauty.

674. Field and vineyard: These lines, redolent of the sweet Tuscan midsummer gloaming, give us amid the horrors of Malebolge something like the breath of fresh air the peasant lingers to enjoy. It may be noted that in Italy the village is often foundperched above the more fertile land, on a site originally chosen with a view to security from attack. So that here the peasant is at home from his labour.

675. And yet a sinner, etc.: The false counsellors who for selfish ends hid their true minds and misused their intellectual light to lead others astray are for ever hidden eachin his own wandering flame.

676. Eteocles: Son of Œdipus and twin brother of Polynices. The brothers slew one another, and were placed on the same funeral pile, the flame of which clove into two as if to image the discord that had existed between them (Theb. xii.).

677. And Diomedes: The two are associated in deeds of blood and guile at the siege of Troy.

678. The Romans' noble seed: The trick of the wooden horse led to the capture of Troy, and that led Æneas to wander forth on the adventures that ended in the settlementof the Trojans in Italy.

679. Deïdamia: That Achilles might be kept from joining the Greek expeditionto Troy he was sent by his mother to the court of Lycomedes, father of Deïdamia. Ulysses lured him away from his hiding-place and from Deïdamia, whom he had madea mother.

680. The Palladium: The Trojan sacred image of Pallas, stolen by Ulysses and Diomed(Æn. ii.). Ulysses is here upon his own ground.

681.They were Greek: Some find here an allusion to Dante's ignorance of the Greeklanguage and literature. But Virgil addresses them in the Lombard dialect of Italian (Inf. xxvii. 21). He acts as spokesman because those ancient Greeks were all so haughty that to a common modern mortal they would have nothing to say. He, as the author of the Æneid, has a special claim on their good-nature. It is but seldom that theshades are told who Virgil is, and never directly. Here Ulysses may infer it from the mention of the 'lofty verse.'

682. From Circe: It is Ulysses that speaks.

683. The open main: The Mediterranean as distinguished from the Ægean.

684. Which ne'er deserted me: There seems no reason for supposing, with

Philalethes, that Ulysses is here represented as sailing on his last voyage from the island of Circe and not from Ithaca. Ulysses, on the contrary, represents himself as breaking away afresh from all the ties of home. According to Homer, Ulysses had lost all his companions ere he returned to Ithaca; and in the Odyssey Tiresias prophesies to him that his last wanderings are to be inland. But any acquaintance that Dante had with Homer can only have been vague and fragmentary. He may have founded his narrative of how Ulysses ended his days upon some floating legend; or, eager to fill up what he took to be a blank in the world of imagination, he may have drawn wholly on his own creative power. In any case it is his Ulysses who, through the version of him given by a living poet, is most familiar to the English reader.

685. The mighty main: The Atlantic Ocean. They bear to the left as they sail, till their course is due south, and crossing the Equator, they find themselves under the strange skies of the southern hemisphere. For months they have seen no land.

686. A lofty mountain: This is the Mountain of Purgatory, according to Dante's geography antipodal to Jerusalem, and the only land in the southern hemisphere.

687. As pleased Another: Ulysses is proudly resigned to the failure of his enterprise, 'for he was Greek.'

CANTO XXVII.

Now, having first erect and silent grown
(For it would say no more), from us the flame,
The Poet sweet consenting,[688] had moved on;
And then our eyes were turned to one that came[689]
Behind it on the way, by sounds that burst
Out of its crest in a confusèd stream.
As the Sicilian bull,[690] which bellowed first
With his lamenting—and it was but right—
Who had prepared it with his tools accurst,[691]
Roared with the howlings of the tortured wight,
So that although constructed all of brass
Yet seemed it pierced with anguish to the height;
So, wanting road and vent by which to pass
Up through the flame, into the flame's own speech
The woeful language all converted was.
But when the words at length contrived to reach
The top, while hither thither shook the crest
As moved the tongue[692] at utterance of each,
We heard: 'Oh thou, to whom are now addressed
My words, who spakest now in Lombard phrase:
"Depart;[693] of thee I nothing more request."
Though I be late arrived, yet of thy grace
Let it not irk thee here a while to stay:
It irks not me, yet, as thou seest, I blaze.
If lately to this world devoid of day
From that sweet Latian land thou art come down

Whence all my guilt I bring, declare and say
Has now Romagna peace? because my own
Native abode was in the mountain land
'Tween springs[694] of Tiber and Urbino town.'
While I intent and bending low did stand,
My Leader, as he touched me on the side,
'Speak thou, for he is Latian,' gave command.
Whereon without delay I thus replied—
Because already[695] was my speech prepared:
'Soul, that down there dost in concealment 'bide,
In thy Romagna[696] wars have never spared
And spare not now in tyrants' hearts to rage;
But when I left it there was none declared.
No change has fallen Ravenna[697] for an age.
There, covering Cervia too with outspread wing,
Polenta's Eagle guards his heritage.
Over the city[698] which long suffering
Endured, and Frenchmen slain on Frenchmen rolled,
The Green Paws[699] once again protection fling.
The Mastiffs of Verrucchio,[700] young and old,
Who to Montagna[701] brought such evil cheer,
Still clinch their fangs where they were wont to hold.
Cities,[702] Lamone and Santerno near,
The Lion couched in white are governed by
Which changes party with the changing year.
And that to which the Savio[703] wanders nigh
As it is set 'twixt mountain and champaign
Lives now in freedom now 'neath tyranny.
But who thou art I to be told am fain:

Be not more stubborn than we others found,
As thou on earth illustrious wouldst remain.'
When first the fire a little while had moaned
After its manner, next the pointed crest
Waved to and fro; then in this sense breathed sound:
'If I believed my answer were addressed
To one that earthward shall his course retrace,
This flame should forthwith altogether rest.
But since[704] none ever yet out of this place
Returned alive, if all be true I hear,
I yield thee answer fearless of disgrace.
I was a warrior, then a Cordelier;[705]
Thinking thus girt to purge away my stain:
And sure my hope had met with answer clear
Had not the High Priest[706]—ill with him remain!
Plunged me anew into my former sin:
And why and how, I would to thee make plain.
While I the frame of bones and flesh was in
My mother gave me, all the deeds I wrought
Were fox-like and in no wise leonine.
Of every wile and hidden way I caught
The secret trick, and used them with such sleight
That all the world with fame of it was fraught.
When I perceived I had attainèd quite
The time of life when it behoves each one
To furl his sails and coil his cordage tight,
Sorrowing for deeds I had with pleasure done,
Contrite and shriven, I religious grew.
Ah, wretched me! and well it was begun

But for the Chieftain of the Pharisees new,[707]
Then waging war hard by the Lateran,
And not with Saracen nor yet with Jew;
For Christian[708] were his enemies every man,
And none had at the siege of Acre been
Or trafficked in the Empire of Soldàn.
His lofty office he held cheap, and e'en
His Sacred Orders and the cord I wore,
Which used[709] to make the wearers of it lean.
As from Soracte[710] Constantine of yore
Sylvester called to cure his leprosy,
I as a leech was called this man before
To cure him of his fever which ran high;
My counsel he required, but I stood dumb,
For drunken all his words appeared to be.
He said; "For fear be in thy heart no room;
Beforehand I absolve thee, but declare
How Palestrina I may overcome.
Heaven I unlock, as thou art well aware,
And close at will; because the keys are twin
My predecessor[711] was averse to bear."
Then did his weighty reasoning on me win
Till to be silent seemed the worst of all; And,
"Father," I replied, "since from this sin
Thou dost absolve me into which I fall—
The scant performance[712] of a promise wide
Will yield thee triumph in thy lofty stall."
Francis came for me soon as e'er I died;
But one of the black Cherubim was there

And "Take him not, nor rob me of him" cried,
"For him of right among my thralls I bear
Because he offered counsel fraudulent;
Since when I've had him firmly by the hair.
None is absolved unless he first repent;
Nor can repentance house with purpose ill,
For this the contradiction doth prevent."
Ah, wretched me! How did I shrinking thrill
When clutching me he sneered: "Perhaps of old
Thou didst not think[713] I had in logic skill."
He carried me to Minos:[714] Minos rolled
His tail eight times round his hard back; in ire
Biting it fiercely, ere of me he told:
"Among the sinners of the shrouding fire!"
Therefore am I, where thou beholdest, lost;
And, sore at heart, go clothed in such attire.'
What he would say thus ended by the ghost,
Away from us the moaning flame did glide
While to and fro its pointed horn was tossed.
But we passed further on, I and my Guide,
Along the cliff to where the arch is set
O'er the next moat, where paying they reside,
As schismatics who whelmed themselves in debt.

FOOTNOTES:

688. Consenting: See line 21.

689. One that came: This is the fire-enveloped shade of Guido of Montefeltro, the colloquy with whom occupies the whole of the Canto.

690. The Sicilian bull: Perillus, an Athenian, presented Phalaris, the tyrant of Agrigentum, with a brazen bull so constructed that when it was heated from below thecries of the victim it contained were converted into the bellowing of a bull. The first trial of the invention was made upon the artist.

691. Accurst: Not in the original. 'Rime in English hath such scarcity,' as Chaucer says.

692. As moved the tongue, etc.: The shade being enclosed in the hollow fire all his words are changed into a sound like the roaring of a flame. At last, when an opening has been worked through the crested point, the speech becomes articulate.

693. Depart, etc.: One at least of the words quoted as having been used by Virgil is Lombard. There is something very quaint in making him use the Lombard dialect of Dante's time.

694. 'Tween springs, etc.: Montefeltro lies between Urbino and the mountain where the Tiber has its source.

695. Already: Dante knew that Virgil would refer to him for an answer to Guido's question, bearing as it did on modern Italian affairs.

696. Romagna: The district of Italy lying on the Adriatic, south of the Po and east of Tuscany, of which Bologna and the cities named in the text were the principal towns. During the last quarter of the thirteenth century it was the scene of constant wars promoted in the interest of the Church, which claimed Romagna as the gift of the Emperor Rudolf, and in that of the great nobles of the district, who while using theGuelf and Ghibeline war-cries aimed at nothing but the lordship of the various cities. Foremost among these nobles was he with whose shade Dante speaks. Villani calls him 'the most sagacious and accomplished warrior of his time in Italy' (Cronica, vii. 80). He was possessed of lands of his own near Forlì and Cesena, and was lord in turnof many of the Romagnese cities. On the whole he appears to have remained true to his Ghibeline colours in spite of Papal fulminations, although once and again he was reconciled to the Church; on the last occasion in 1294. In the years immediately beforethis he had greatly distinguished himself as a wise governor and able general in the service of the Ghibeline Pisa—or rather as the paid lord of it.

697. Ravenna: Ravenna and the neighbouring town of Cervia were in 1300 underthe lordship of members of the Polenta family—the father and brothers of the ill-fatedFrancesca (Inf. v.). Their arms were an eagle, half white on an azure and half red on agold field. It was in the court of the generous Guido, son of one of these brothers, thatDante was to find his last refuge and to die.

698. Over the city, etc.: Forlì. The reference is to one of the most brilliant feats of war performed by Guido of Montefeltro. Frenchmen formed great part of an army sent in 1282 against Forlì by the Pope, Martin IV., himself a Frenchman. Guido, then lord ofthe city, led them into a trap and overthrew them with great slaughter. Like most men of his time Guido was a believer in astrology, and is said on this occasion to have acted on the counsel of Guido Bonatti, mentioned among the diviners in the Fourth Bolgia (Inf. xx. 118).

699. The Green Paws: In 1300 the Ordelaffi were lords of Forlì. Their arms were a green lion on a gold ground. During the first years of his exile Dante had to do with Scarpetta degli Ordelaffi, under whose command the exiled Florentines put themselves for a time, and there is even a tradition that he acted as his secretary.

700. The Mastiffs of Verrucchio: Verrucchio was the castle of the Malatestas, lords ofRimini, called the Mastiffs on account of their cruel tenacity. The elder was the father of Francesca's husband and lover; the younger was a brother of these.

701. Montagna: Montagna de' Parcitati, one of a Ghibeline family that contested superiority in Rimini with the Guelf Malatestas, was taken prisoner by guile and committed by the old Mastiff to the keeping of the young one, whose fangs were set inhim to such purpose that he soon died in his dungeon.

702. Cities, etc.: Imola and Faenza, situated on the rivers named in the text. Mainardo Pagani, lord of these towns, had for arms an azure lion on a white field. During his minority he was a ward of the Commonwealth of Florence. By his cunning and daring he earned the name of the Demon (Purg. xiv. 118). He died at Imola in 1302, and was buried in the garb of a monk of Vallombrosa. Like most of his neighbours he changed his party as often as his interest required. He was a Guelf in Florence and a Ghibeline in Romagna, say some.

703. Savio: Cesena, on the Savio, was distinguished among the cities of Romagna by being left more frequently than the others were to manage its own affairs. The Malatestas and Montefeltros were in turn possessed of the tyranny of it.

704. But since, etc.: The shades, being enveloped in fire, are unable to see those with whom they speak; and so Guido does not detect in Dante the signs of a living man, but takes him to be like himself a denizen of Inferno. He would not have the truth regarding his fate to be known in the world, where he is supposed to have departed life in the odour of sanctity. Dante's promise to refresh his fame he either regards as meaningless, or as one made without the power of fulfilling it. Dante leaves him in his error, for he is there to learn all he can, and not to bandy personal confessions with the shades.

705. A Cordelier: In 1296 Guido entered the Franciscan Order. He died in 1298, but where is not known; some authorities say at Venice and others at Assisi. Benvenuto tells: 'He was often seen begging his bread in Ancona, where he was buried. Many good deeds are related of him, and I cherish a sweet hope that he may have been saved.'

706. The High Priest: Boniface VIII.

707. The Pharisees new: The members of the Court of Rome. Saint Jerome calls the dignified Roman clergy of his day 'the Senate of the Pharisees.'

708. For Christian, etc.: The foes of Boniface, here spoken of, were the Cardinals Peter and James Colonna. He destroyed their palace in Rome (1297) and carriedthe war against them to their country seat at Palestrina, the ancient Præneste, then a great stronghold. Dante here bitterly blames Boniface for instituting a crusade againstChristians at a time when, by the recent loss of Acre, the gate of the Holy Land had been lost to Christendom. The Colonnas were innocent, too, of the crime of supplyingthe Infidel with munitions of war—a crime condemned by the Lateran Council of 1215, and by Boniface himself, who excluded those guilty of it from the benefits of thegreat Jubilee of 1300.

709. Which used, etc.: In former times, when the rule of the Order was faithfully observed. Dante charges the Franciscans with degeneracy in the Paradiso, xi. 124.

710. From Soracte: Referring to the well-known legend. The fee for the cure was thefabulous Donation. See Inf. xix. 115.

711. My predecessor: Celestine v. See Inf. iii. 60.

712. The scant performance, etc.: That Guido gave such counsel is related by a contemporary chronicler: 'The Pope said: Tell me how to get the better of those mine enemies, thou who art so knowing in these things. Then he answered: Promise much, and perform little; which he did.' But it seems odd that the wily and unscrupulous Boniface should have needed to put himself to school for such a simple lesson.

713. Thou didst not think, etc.: Guido had forgot that others could reason besides thePope. With regard to the inefficacy of the Papal absolution an old commentator says, following Origen: 'The Popes that walk in the footsteps of Peter have this power of binding and loosing; but only such as do so walk.' But on Dante's scheme of what fixesthe fate of the soul absolution matters little to save, or priestly curses to damnify. SeePurg. iii. 133. It is unfeigned repentance that can help a sinner even at the last; and it is remarkable that in the case of Buonconte, the gallant son of this same Guido, the infernal angel who comes for him as he expires complains that he has been cheatedof his victim by one poor tear. See Purg. v. 88, etc. Why then is no indulgence shown in Dante's court to Guido, who might well have been placed in Purgatory and made to have repented effectually of this his last sin? That Dante had any personal grudge against him we can hardly think. In the Fourth Book of the Convito (written, according to Fraticelli, in 1297), he calls him 'our most noble Guido

Montefeltrano;' and praises him as one of the wise and noble souls that refuse to run with full sails into the port of death, but furl the sails of their worldly undertakings, and, relinquishing all earthly pleasures and business, give themselves up in their old age to a religious life. Either, then, he sets Guido here in order that he may have a modern false counsellor worthy to be ranked with Ulysses; or because, on longer experience, he had come to reprobate more keenly the abuse of the Franciscan habit; or, most likely of all, that he might, even at the cost of Guido, load the hated memory of Boniface with another reproach.

714. Minos: Here we have Minos represented in the act of pronouncing judgment in words as well as by the figurative rolling of his tail around his body (Inf. v. 11).

CANTO XXVIII.

Could any, even in words unclogged by rhyme
Recount the wounds that now I saw,[715] and blood,
Although he aimed at it time after time?
Here every tongue must fail of what it would,
Because our human speech and powers of thought
To grasp so much come short in aptitude.
If all the people were together brought
Who in Apulia,[716] land distressed by fate,
Made lamentation for the bloodshed wrought
By Rome;[717] and in that war procrastinate[718]
When the large booty of the rings was won,
As Livy writes whose every word has weight;
With those on whom such direful deeds were done
When Robert Guiscard[719] they as foes assailed;
And those of whom still turns up many a bone
At Ceperan,[720] where each Apulian failed
In faith; and those at Tagliacozzo[721] strewed,
Where old Alardo, not by arms, prevailed;
And each his wounds and mutilations showed,
Yet would they far behind by those be left
Who had the vile Ninth Bolgia for abode.
No cask, of middle stave or end bereft,
E'er gaped like one I saw the rest among,
Slit from the chin all downward to the cleft.
Between his legs his entrails drooping hung;
The pluck and that foul bag were evident
Which changes what is swallowed into dung.

And while I gazed upon him all intent,
Opening his breast his eyes on me he set,
Saying: 'Behold, how by myself I'm rent!
See how dismembered now is Mahomet![722]
Ali[723] in front of me goes weeping too;
With visage from the chin to forelock split.
By all the others whom thou seest there grew
Scandal and schism while yet they breathed the day;
Because of which they now are cloven through.
There stands behind a devil on the way,
Us with his sword thus cruelly to trim:
He cleaves again each of our company
As soon as we complete the circuit grim;
Because the wounds of each are healed outright
Or e'er anew he goes in front of him.
But who art thou that peerest from the height,
It may be putting off to reach the pain
Which shall the crimes confessed by thee requite?'
'Death has not seized him yet, nor is he ta'en
To torment for his sins,' my Master said;
'But, that he may a full experience gain,
By me, a ghost, 'tis doomed he should be led
Down the Infernal circles, round on round;
And what I tell thee is the truth indeed.'
A hundred shades and more, to whom the sound
Had reached, stood in the moat to mark me well,
Their pangs forgot; so did the words astound.
'Let Fra Dolcin[724] provide, thou mayst him tell—T
hou, who perchance ere long shalt sunward go—

Unless he soon would join me in this Hell,
Much food, lest aided by the siege of snow
The Novarese should o'er him victory get,
Which otherwise to win they would be slow.'
While this was said to me by Mahomet
One foot he held uplifted; to the ground
He let it fall, and so he forward set
Next, one whose throat was gaping with a wound
,Whose nose up to the brows away was sheared
And on whose head a single ear was found,
At me, with all the others, wondering peered;
And, ere the rest, an open windpipe made,
The outside of it all with crimson smeared.
'O thou, not here because of guilt,' he said;
'And whom I sure on Latian ground did know
Unless by strong similitude betrayed,
Upon Pier da Medicin[725] bestow
A thought, shouldst thou revisit the sweet plain
That from Vercelli[726] slopes to Marcabò.
And make thou known to Fano's worthiest twain—
To Messer Guido and to Angiolel—
They, unless foresight here be wholly vain,
Thrown overboard in gyve and manacle
Shall drown fast by Cattolica, as planned
By treachery of a tyrant fierce and fell.
Between Majolica[727] and Cyprus strand
A blacker crime did Neptune never spy
By pirates wrought, or even by Argives' hand.
The traitor[728] who is blinded of an eye,

Lord of the town which of my comrades one
Had been far happier ne'er to have come nigh,
To parley with him will allure them on,
Then so provide, against Focara's[729] blast
No need for them of vow or orison.'
And I: 'Point out and tell, if wish thou hast
To get news of thee to the world conveyed,
Who rues that e'er his eyes thereon were cast?'
On a companion's jaw his hand he laid,
And shouted, while the mouth he open prised: '
'Tis this one here by whom no word is said.
He quenched all doubt in Cæsar, and advised—
Himself an outlaw—that a man equipped
For strife ran danger if he temporised.'
Alas, to look on, how downcast and hipped
Curio,[730] once bold in counsel, now appeared;
With gorge whence by the roots the tongue was ripped.
Another one, whose hands away were sheared,
In the dim air his stumps uplifted high
So that his visage was with blood besmeared,
And, 'Mosca,[731] too, remember!' loud did cry,
'Who said, ah me! "A thing once done is done!"
An evil seed for all in Tuscany.'
I added: 'Yea, and death to every one
Of thine!' whence he, woe piled on woe, his way
Went like a man with grief demented grown.
But I to watch the gang made longer stay,
And something saw which I should have a fear,
Without more proof, so much as even to say,

But that my conscience bids me have good cheer—
The comrade leal whose friendship fortifies
A man beneath the mail of purpose clear.
I saw in sooth (still seems it 'fore mine eyes),
A headless trunk; with that sad company
It forward moved, and on the selfsame wise.
The severed head, clutched by the hair, swung free
Down from the fist, yea, lantern-like hung down;
Staring at us it murmured: 'Wretched me!'
A lamp he made of head-piece once his own;
And he was two in one and one in two;
But how, to Him who thus ordains is known
.Arrived beneath the bridge and full in view,
With outstretched arm his head he lifted high
To bring his words well to us. These I knew:
'Consider well my grievous penalty,
Thou who, though still alive, art visiting
The people dead; what pain with this can vie?
In order that to earth thou news mayst bring
Of me, that I'm Bertrand de Born[732] know well,
Who gave bad counsel to the Younger King.
I son and sire made each 'gainst each rebel:
David and Absalom were fooled not more
By counsels of the false Ahithophel.
Kinsmen so close since I asunder tore,
Severed, alas! I carry now my brain
From what[733] it grew from in this trunk of yore:
And so I prove the law of pain for pain.'[734]

FOOTNOTES:

715. That now I saw: In the Ninth Bolgia, on which he is looking down, and in whichare punished the sowers of discord in church and state.

716. Apulia: The south-eastern district of Italy, owing to its situation a frequent battle-field in ancient and modern times.

717. Rome: 'Trojans' in most MSS.; and then the Romans are described as descended from Trojans. The reference may be to the defeat of the Apulians with considerable slaughter by P. Decius Mus, or to their losses in general in the course of the Samnite war.

718. War procrastinate: The second Punic war lasted fully fifteen years, and in the course of it the battle of Cannæ was gained by Hannibal, where so many Roman knights fell that the spoil of rings amounted to a peck.

719. Guiscard: One of the Norman conquerors of the regions which up to our own timeconstituted the kingdom of Naples. In Apulia he did much fighting against Lombards, Saracens, and Greeks. He is found by Dante in Paradise among those who foughtfor the faith (Par. xviii. 48). His death happened in Cephalonia in 1085, at the age of seventy, when he was engaged on an expedition against Constantinople.

720. Ceperan: In the swift and decisive campaign undertaken by Charles of Anjou against Manfred, King of Sicily and Naples, the first victory was obtained at Ceperano;but it was won owing to the treachery of Manfred's lieutenant, and not by the sword. The true battle was fought at Benevento (Purg. iii. 128). Ceperano may be named by Dante as the field where the defeat of Manfred was virtually begun, and where the Apulians first failed in loyalty to their gallant king. Dante was a year old at the time ofManfred's overthrow (1266).

721. Tagliacozzo: The crown Charles had won from Manfred he had to defend against Manfred's nephew Conradin (grandson and last representative of Frederick II. and the legitimate heir to the kingdom of Sicily), whom, in 1268, he defeated near Tagliacozzo in the Abruzzi. He made his victory the more complete by acting on the advice of Alardo or Erard de Valery, an old Crusader, to hold good part of his force inreserve. Charles wrote to the Pope that the slaughter was so great as far to exceed thatat Benevento. The feet of all the low-born prisoners not slain on the field were cut off,while the gentlemen were beheaded or hanged.

722. Mahomet: It has been objected to Dante by M. Littré that he treats Mahomet, the founder of a new religion, as a mere schismatic. The wonder would have been had hedwelt on the good qualities of the Prophet at a time when Islam still threatened Europe. He goes on the fact that Mahomet and his followers rent great part of the East and South from Christendom; and for this the Prophet is represented as being mutilated in a sorer degree than the other schismatics.

723. Ali: Son-in-law of Mahomet.

724. Fra Dolcin: At the close of the thirteenth century, Boniface being Pope, the general discontent with the corruption of the higher clergy found expression in the north of Italy in the foundation of a new sect, whose leader was Fra Dolcino. What he chiefly was—enthusiast, reformer, or impostor—it is impossible to ascertain; all we know of him being derived from writers in the Papal interest. Among other crimes he was charged with that of teaching the lawfulness of telling an Inquisitor a lie to save your life, and with prophesying the advent of a pious Pope. A holy war on a small scale was preached against him. After suffering the extremities of famine, snowed up as he was among the mountains, he was taken prisoner and cruelly put to death (1307). It may have been in order to save himself from being suspected of sympathy with him, that Dante, whose hatred of Boniface and the New Pharisees was equal to Dolcino's, provides for him by anticipation a place with Mahomet.

725. Pier da Medicin: Medicina is in the territory of Bologna. Piero is said to have stirred up dissensions between the Polentas of Ravenna and the Malatestas of Rimini.

726. From Vercelli, etc.: From the district of Vercelli to where the castle of Marcabò once stood, at the mouth of the Po, is a distance of two hundred miles. The plain is Lombardy.

727 Majolica, etc.: On all the Mediterranean, from Cyprus in the east to Majorca in the west.

728. The traitor, etc.: The one-eyed traitor is Malatesta, lord of Rimini, the Young Mastiff of the preceding Canto. He invited the two chief citizens of Fano, named in the text, to hold a conference with him, and procured that on their way they should be pitched overboard opposite the castle of Cattolica, which stood between Fano and Rimini. This is said to have happened in 1304.

729. Focara: The name of a promontory near Cattolica, subject to squalls. The victims were never to double the headland.

730. Curio: The Roman Tribune who, according to Lucan—the incident is not historically correct—found Cæsar hesitating whether to cross the Rubicon, and advised him: Tolle moras: semper nocuit differre paratis. 'No delay! when men are ready they always suffer by putting off.' The passage of the Rubicon was counted as the beginning of the Civil War.—Curio gets scant justice, seeing that in Dante's view Cæsar in all he did was only carrying out the Divine purpose regarding the Empire.

731. Mosca: In 1215 one of the Florentine family of the Buondelmonti jilted a daughter of the Amidei. When these with their friends met to take counsel touching revenge forthe insult, Mosca, one of the Uberti or of the Lamberti, gave his opinion in the proverb,Cosa fatta ha capo: 'A thing once done is done with.' The hint was approved of, and on the following Easter morning the young Buondelmonte, as, mounted on a white steed and dressed in white he rode across the Ponte Vecchio, was dragged to the groundand cruelly slain. All the great Florentine families took sides in the feud, and it soon widened into the civil war between Florentine Guelf and Ghibeline.

732. Bertrand de Born: Is mentioned by Dante in his Treatise De Vulgari Eloquio, ii.2, as specially the poet of warlike deeds. He was a Gascon noble who used his poeticalgift very much to stir up strife. For patron he had the Prince Henry, son of Henry II. of England. Though Henry never came to the throne he was, during his father's lifetime, crowned as his successor, and was known as the young King. After the deathof the Prince, Bertrand was taken prisoner by the King, and, according to the legend, was loaded with favours because he had been so true a friend to his young master. That he had a turn for fomenting discord is shown by his having also led a revolt in Aquitaine against Richard I.—All the old MSS. and all the earlier commentators read Re Giovanni, King John; Re Giovane, the young King, being a comparatively modern emendation. In favour of adopting this it may be mentioned that in his poems Bertrandcalls Prince Henry lo Reys joves, the young King; that it was Henry and not John thatwas his friend and patron; and that in the old Cento Novelle Henry is described asthe young King: in favour of the older reading, that John as well as his brother wasa rebel to Henry; and that the line is hurt by the change from Giovanni to Giovane. Considering that Dante almost certainly wrote Giovanni it seems most reasonable to suppose that he may have confounded the Re Giovane with King John.

733. From what, etc.: The spinal cord, as we should now say, though Dante may havemeant the heart.

734. Pain for pain: In the City of Dis we found the heresiarchs, those who lead othersto think falsely. The lower depth of the Malebolge is reserved for such as needlessly rend any Divinely-constituted order of society, civil or religious. Conduct counts morewith Dante than opinion—in this case.

CANTO XXIX.

The many folk and wounds of divers kind
Had flushed mine eyes and set them on the flow,
Till I to weep and linger had a mind;
But Virgil said to me: 'Why gazing so?
Why still thy vision fastening on the crew
Of dismal shades dismembered there below?
Thou didst not[735] thus the other Bolgias view:
Think, if to count them be thine enterprise,
The valley circles twenty miles and two.[736]
Beneath our feet the moon[737] already lies;
The time[738] wears fast away to us decreed;
And greater things than these await thine eyes.
'I answered swift: 'Hadst thou but given heed
To why it was my looks were downward bent,
To yet more stay thou mightest have agreed.'
My Guide meanwhile was moving, and I went
Behind him and continued to reply
,Adding: 'Within the moat on which intent
I now was gazing with such eager eye
I trow a spirit weeps, one of my kin,
The crime whose guilt is rated there so high.'
Then said the Master: 'Henceforth hold thou in
Thy thoughts from wandering to him: new things claim
Attention now, so leave him with his sin.
Him saw I at thee from the bridge-foot aim
A threatening finger, while he made thee known;

Geri del Bello[739] heard I named his name.
But, at the time, thou wast with him alone
Engrossed who once held Hautefort,[740] nor the place
Didst look at where he was; so passed he on.'
'O Leader mine! death violent and base,
And not avenged as yet,' I made reply,
'By any of his partners in disgrace,
Made him disdainful; therefore went he by
And spake not with me, if I judge aright;
Which does the more my ruth[741] intensify.'
So we conversed till from the cliff we might
Of the next valley have had prospect good
Down to the bottom, with but clearer light.[742]
When we above the inmost Cloister stood
Of Malebolge, and discerned the crew
Of such as there compose the Brotherhood,[743]
So many lamentations pierced me through—
And barbed with pity all the shafts were sped—
My open palms across my ears I drew.
From Valdichiana's[744] every spital bed
All ailments to September from July,
With all in Maremma and Sardinia[745] bred,
Heaped in one pit a sickness might supply
Like what was here; and from it rose a stink
Like that which comes from limbs that putrefy.
Then we descended by the utmost brink
Of the long ridge[746]—leftward once more we fell—
Until my vision, quickened now, could sink
Deeper to where Justice infallible,

The minister of the Almighty Lord,
Chastises forgers doomed on earth[747] to Hell.
Ægina[748] could no sadder sight afford,
As I believe (when all the people ailed
And all the air was so with sickness stored,
Down to the very worms creation failed
And died, whereon the pristine folk once more,
As by the poets is for certain held,
From seed of ants their family did restore),
Than what was offered by that valley black
With plague-struck spirits heaped upon the floor.
Supine some lay, each on the other's back
Or stomach; and some crawled with crouching gait
For change of place along the doleful track.
Speechless we moved with step deliberate,
With eyes and ears on those disease crushed down
Nor left them power to lift their bodies straight.
I saw two sit, shoulder to shoulder thrown
As plate holds plate up to be warmed, from head
Down to the feet with scurf and scab o'ergrown.
Nor ever saw I curry-comb so plied
By varlet with his master standing by,
Or by one kept unwillingly from bed,
As I saw each of these his scratchers ply
Upon himself; for nought else now avails
Against the itch which plagues them furiously.
The scab[749] they tore and loosened with their nails,
As with a knife men use the bream to strip,
Or any other fish with larger scales.

'Thou, that thy mail dost with thy fingers rip,'
My Guide to one of them began to say,
'And sometimes dost with them as pincers nip,
Tell, is there any here from Italy
Among you all, so may thy nails suffice
For this their work to all eternity.'[750]
"Latians are both of us in this disguise
Of wretchedness,' weeping said one of those;
'But who art thou, demanding on this wise?'
My Guide made answer: 'I am one who goes
Down with this living man from steep to steep
That I to him Inferno may disclose.'
Then broke their mutual prop; trembling with deep
Amazement each turned to me, with the rest
To whom his words had echoed in the heap.
Me the good Master cordially addressed:
'Whate'er thou hast a mind to ask them, say.
'And since he wished it, thus I made request:
'So may remembrance of you not decay
Within the upper world out of the mind
Of men, but flourish still for many a day,
As ye shall tell your names and what your kind:
Let not your vile, disgusting punishment
To full confession make you disinclined.'
'An Aretine,[751] I to the stake was sent
By Albert of Siena,' one confessed,
'But came not here through that for which I went
To death. 'Tis true I told him all in jest,
I through the air could float in upward gyre;

And he, inquisitive and dull at best,
Did full instruction in the art require:
I could not make him Dædalus,[752] so then
His second father sent me to the fire.
But to the deepest Bolgia of the ten,
For alchemy which in the world I wrought,
The unerring Minos doomed me.'
'Now were menE'er found,'
I of the Poet asked, 'so fraught
With vanity as are the Sienese?[753]
French vanity to theirs is surely nought.'
The other leper hearing me, to these
My words: 'Omit the Stricca,'[754] swift did shout,'
Who knew his tastes with temperance to please;
And Nicholas,[755] who earliest found out
The lavish custom of the clove-stuffed roast
Within the garden where such seed doth sprout.
Nor count the club[756] where Caccia d' Ascian lost
Vineyards and woods; 'mid whom away did throw
His wit the Abbagliato.[757] But whose ghost
It is, that thou mayst weet, that backs thee so
Against the Sienese, make sharp thine eyes
That thou my countenance mayst surely know.
In me Capocchio's[758] shade thou'lt recognise,
Who forged false coin by means of alchemy:
Thou must remember, if I well surmise,
How I of nature very ape could be.'

FOOTNOTES:

735. Thou didst not, etc.: It is a noteworthy feature in the conduct of the Poem that when Dante has once gained sufficient knowledge of any group in the Inferno he at once detaches his mind from it, and, carrying on as little arrear of pity as he can, giveshis thoughts to further progress on the journey. The departure here made from his usualbehaviour is presently accounted for. Virgil knows why he lingers, but will not seem to approve of the cause.

736. Twenty miles and two: The Ninth Bolgia has a circumference of twenty-two miles, and as the procession of the shades is slow it would indeed involve a protracted halt to wait till all had passed beneath the bridge. Virgil asks ironically if he wishesto count them all. This precise detail, taken along with one of the same kind in the following Canto (line 86), has suggested the attempt to construct the Inferno to a scale.Dante wisely suffers us to forget, if we will, that—taking the diameter of the earth at 6500 miles, as given by him in the Convito—he travels from the surface of the globe to the centre at the rate of more than two miles a minute, counting downward motion alone. It is only when he has come to the lowest rings that he allows himself to give details of size; and probably the mention of the extent of the Ninth Bolgia, which comeson the reader as a surprise, is thrown out in order to impress on the imagination somesense of the enormous extent of the regions through which the pilgrim has already passed. Henceforth he deals in exact measurement.

737. The moon: It is now some time after noon on the Saturday. The last indication of time was at Canto xxi. 112.

738. The time, etc.: Before nightfall they are to complete their exploration of the Inferno, and they will have spent twenty-four hours in it.

739. Geri del Bello: One of the Alighieri, a full cousin of Dante's father. He was guilty of encouraging dissension, say the commentators; which is to be clearly inferredfrom the place assigned him in Inferno: but they do not agree as to how he met his death, nor do they mention the date of it. 'Not avenged till thirty years after,' says Landino; but does not say if this was after his death or the time at which Dante writes.

740. Hautefort: Bertrand de Born's castle in Gascony.

741. My ruth: Enlightened moralist though Dante is, he yet shows himself man of his age enough to be keenly alive to the extremest claims of kindred; and while he condemns the vendetta by the words put into Virgil's mouth, he confesses to a feelingof meanness not to have practised it on behoof of a distant relative. There is a high art in this introduction of Geri del Bello. Had they conferred together Dante must have seemed either cruel or pusillanimous, reproaching or being reproached. As it is, all thepoetry of the situation comes out the stronger that they do not meet face to face: the threatening finger, the questions hastily put to Geri by the astonished shades, and his disappearance under the dark vault when by the law of his punishment the sinner can no longer tarry.

742. With but clearer light: They have crossed the rampart dividing the Ninth Bolgia from the Tenth, of which they would now command a view, were it not so dark.

743. The Brotherhood: The word used properly describes the Lay Brothers of a monastery. Philalethes suggests that Dante may regard the devils as the true monks of the monastery of Malebolge. The simile involves no contempt for the monastic life, but is naturally used with reference to those who live secluded and under a fixed rule. He elsewhere speaks of the College of the Hypocrites (Inf. xxiii. 91) and of Paradise as the Cloister where Christ is Abbot (Purg. xxvi.129).

744. Valdichiana: The district lying between Arezzo and Chiusi; in Dante's time a hotbed of malaria, but now, owing to drainage works promoted by the enlightened Tuscan minister Fossombroni (1823), one of the most fertile and healthy regions of Italy.

745. Sardinia: Had in the middle ages an evil reputation for its fever-stricken air. The Maremma has been already mentioned (Inf. xxv.19). In Dante's time it was almost unpeopled.

746. The long ridge: One of the ribs of rock which, like the spokes of a wheel, ran from the periphery to the centre of Malebolge, rising into arches as they crossed each successive Bolgia. The utmost brink is the inner bank of the Tenth and last Bolgia. To the edge of this moat they descend, bearing as usual to the left hand.

747. Doomed on earth, etc.: 'Whom she here registers.' While they are still on earth their doom is fixed by Divine justice.

748. Ægina: The description is taken from Ovid (Metam. vii.).

749. The scab, etc.: As if by an infernal alchemy the matter of the shadowy bodies of these sinners is changed into one loathsome form or another.

750. To all eternity: This may seem a stroke of sarcasm, but is not. Himself a shade, Virgil cannot, like Dante, promise to refresh the memory of the shades on earth, and can only wish for them some slight alleviation of their suffering.

751. An Aretine: Called Griffolino, and burned at Florence or Siena on a charge of heresy. Albert of Siena is said to have been a relative, some say the natural son, of the Bishop of Siena. A man of the name figures as hero in some of Sacchetti's novels, always in a ridiculous light. There seems to be no authentic testimony regarding the incident in the text.

752. Dædalus: Who escaped on wings of his invention from the Cretan Labyrinth hehad made and lost himself in.

753. The Sienese: The comparison of these to the French would have the more cogency as Siena boasted of having been founded by the Gauls. 'That vain people,' says Dante of the Sienese in the Purgatory (xiii. 151). Among their neighbours they still bear the reputation of light-headedness; also, it ought to be added, of great urbanity.

754. The Stricca: The exception in his favour is ironical, as is that of all the others mentioned.

755. Nicholas: 'The lavish custom of the clove' which he invented is variously described. I have chosen the version which makes it consist of stuffing pheasants withcloves, then very costly.

756. The club: The commentators tell that the two young Sienese nobles above mentioned were members of a society formed for the purpose of living luxuriously together. Twelve of them contributed a fund of above two hundred thousand gold florins; they built a great palace and furnished it magnificently, and launched out intoevery other sort of extravagance with such assiduity that in a few months their capital was gone. As that amounted to more than a hundred thousand pounds of our money, equal in those days to a million or two, the story must be held to savour of romance. That Dante refers to a prodigal's club that actually existed some time before he wrote we cannot doubt. But it seems uncertain, to say the least, whether the sonnets addressed by the Tuscan poet Folgore da Gemignano to a jovial crew in Siena can be taken as having been inspired by the club Dante speaks of. A translation of them is given by Mr. Rossetti in his Circle of Dante. (See Mr. Symonds's Renaissance, vol. iv. page 54, note, for doubts as to the date of Folgore.)—Caccia d' Ascian: Whose short and merryclub life cost him his estates near Siena.

757. The Abbagliato: Nothing is known, though a great deal is guessed, about this member of the club. It is enough to know that, having a scant supply of wit, he spent it freely.

758. Capocchio: Some one whom Dante knew. Whether he was a Florentine or a Sienese is not ascertained, but from the strain of his mention of the Sienese we may guess Florentine. He was burned in Siena in 1293.—(Scartazzini.) They had studied together, says the Anonimo. Benvenuto tells of him that one Good Friday, while in a cloister, he painted on his nail with marvellous completeness a picture of the crucifixion. Dante came up, and was lost in wonder, when Capocchio suddenly lickedhis nail clean—which may be taken for what it is worth.

CANTO XXX.

Because of Semele[759] when Juno's ire
Was fierce 'gainst all that were to Thebes allied,
As had been proved by many an instance dire;
So mad grew Athamas[760] that when he spied
His wife as she with children twain drew near,
Each hand by one encumbered, loud he cried:
'Be now the nets outspread, that I may snare
Cubs with the lioness at yon strait ground!'
And stretching claws of all compassion bare
He on Learchus seized and swung him round,
And shattered him upon a flinty stone;
Then she herself and the other burden drowned
.And when by fortune was all overthrown
The Trojans' pride, inordinate before—
Monarch and kingdom equally undone—
Hecuba,[761] sad and captive, mourning o'er
Polyxena, when dolorous she beheld
The body of her darling Polydore
Upon the coast, out of her wits she yelled,
And spent herself in barking like a hound;
So by her sorrow was her reason quelled.
But never yet was Trojan fury[762] found,
Nor that of Thebes, to sting so cruelly
Brute beasts, far less the human form to wound,
As two pale naked shades were stung, whom
I Saw biting run, like swine when they escape

Famished and eager from the empty sty.
Capocchio[763] coming up to, in his nape
One fixed his fangs, and hauling at him made
His belly on the stony pavement scrape.
The Aretine[764] who stood, still trembling, said:'
That imp is Gianni Schicchi,[765] and he goes
Rabid, thus trimming others.' 'O!' I prayed,
'So may the teeth of the other one of those
Not meet in thee, as, ere she pass from sight,
Thou freely shalt the name of her disclose.'
And he to me: 'That is the ancient sprite
Of shameless Myrrha,[766] who let liking rise
For him who got her, past all bounds of right.
As, to transgress with him, she in disguise
Came near to him deception to maintain;
So he, departing yonder from our eyes,
That he the Lady of the herd might gain,
Bequeathed his goods by formal testament
While he Buoso Donate's[767] form did feign.'
And when the rabid couple from us went,
Who all this time by me were being eyed,
Upon the rest ill-starred I grew intent;
And, fashioned like a lute, I one espied,
Had he been only severed at the place
Where at the groin men's lower limbs divide.
The grievous dropsy, swol'n with humours base,
Which every part of true proportion strips
Till paunch grows out of keeping with the face,
Compelled him widely ope to hold his lips

Like one in fever who, by thirst possessed,
Has one drawn up while the other chinward slips
.'O ye![768] who by no punishment distressed,
Nor know I why, are in this world of dool,'
He said; 'a while let your attention rest
On Master Adam[769] here of misery full.Living,
I all I wished enjoyed at will;
Now lust I for a drop of water cool.
The water-brooks that down each grassy hill
Of Casentino to the Arno fall
And with cool moisture all their courses fill—
Always, and not in vain, I see them all;
Because the vision of them dries me more
Than the disease 'neath which my face grows small.
For rigid justice, me chastising sore,
Can in the place I sinned at motive find
To swell the sighs in which I now deplore.
There lies Romena, where of the money coined[770]
With the Baptist's image I made counterfeit,
And therefore left my body burnt behind.
But could I see here Guido's[771] wretched sprite,
Or Alexander's, or their brother's, I
For Fonte Branda[772] would not give the sight.
One is already here, unless they lie—
Mad souls with power to wander through the crowd—
What boots it me, whose limbs diseases tie?
But were I yet so nimble that I could
Creep one poor inch a century, some while
Ago had I begun to take the road

Searching for him among this people vile;
And that although eleven miles[773] 'tis long,
And has a width of more than half a mile.
Because of them am I in such a throng;
For to forge florins I by them was led,
Which by three carats[774] of alloy were wrong,' '
Who are the wretches twain,' I to him said,
'Who smoke[775] like hand in winter-time fresh brought
From water, on thy right together spread?'
'Here found I them, nor have they budged a jot,
'He said, 'since I was hurled into this vale;
And, as I deem, eternally they'll not.
One[776] with false charges Joseph did assail;
False Sinon,[777] Greek from Troy, is the other wight.
Burning with fever they this stink exhale.'
Then one of them, perchance o'ercome with spite
Because he thus contemptuously was named,
Smote with his fist upon the belly tight.
It sounded like a drum; and then was aimed
A blow by Master Adam at his face
With arm no whit less hard, while he exclaimed:'
What though I can no longer shift my place
Because my members by disease are weighed!
I have an arm still free for such a case.'
To which was answered: 'When thou wast conveyed
Unto the fire 'twas not thus good at need,
But even more so when the coiner's trade
Was plied by thee.' The swol'n one: 'True indeed!
But thou didst not bear witness half so true

When Trojans[778] at thee for the truth did plead.'
'If I spake falsely, thou didst oft renew
False coin,' said Sinon; 'one fault brought me here;
Thee more than any devil of the crew.'
'Bethink thee of the horse, thou perjurer,'
He of the swol'n paunch answered; 'and that by
All men 'tis known should anguish in thee stir.'
'Be thirst that cracks thy tongue thy penalty,
And putrid water,' so the Greek replied,
'Which 'fore thine eyes thy stomach moundeth high.'
The coiner then: 'Thy mouth thou openest wide,
As thou art used, thy slanderous words to vent;
But if I thirst and humours plump my hide
Thy head throbs with the fire within thee pent
.To lap Narcissus' mirror,[779] to implore
And urge thee on would need no argument.'
While I to hear them did attentive pore
My Master said: 'Thy fill of staring take!
To rouse my anger needs but little more.'
And when I heard that he in anger spake
Toward him I turned with such a shame inspired,
Recalled, it seems afresh on me to break.
And, as the man who dreams of hurt is fired
With wish that he might know his dream a dream,
And so what is, as 'twere not, is desired;
So I, struck dumb and filled with an extreme
Craving to find excuse, unwittingly
The meanwhile made the apology supreme.
'Less shame,' my Master said, 'would nullify

A greater fault, for greater guilt atone;
All sadness for it, therefore, lay thou by.
But bear in mind that thou art not alone,
If fortune hap again to bring thee near
Where people such debate are carrying on.
To things like these 'tis shame[780] to lend an ear.'

FOOTNOTES:

759. Semele: The daughter of Cadmus, founder and king of Thebes, was beloved by Jupiter and therefore hated by Juno, who induced her to court destruction by urging thegod to visit her, as he was used to come to Juno, in all his glory. And in other instancesthe goddess took revenge (Ovid, Metam. iv.).

760. Athamas: Married to a sister of Semele, was made insane by the angry Juno, withthe result described in the text.

761. Hecuba: Wife of Priam, king of Troy, and mother of Polyxena and Polydorus. While she was lamenting the death of her daughter, slain as an offering on the tomb ofAchilles, she found the corpse of her son, slain by the king of Thrace, to whose keepingshe had committed him (Ovid, Metam. xiii.).

762. Trojan fury, etc.: It was by the agency of a Fury that Athamas was put out of his mind; but the Trojan and Theban furies here meant are the frenzies of Athamas and Hecuba, wild with which one of them slew his son, and the other scratched out the eyesof the Thracian king.

763. Capocchio: See close of the preceding Canto. Here as elsewhere sinners are made ministers of vengeance on one another.

764. The Aretine: Griffolino, who boasted he could fly; already represented as trembling (Inf. xxix. 97).

765. Gianni Schicchi: Giovanni Schicchi, one of the Cavalcanti of Florence.

766. Myrrha: This is a striking example of Dante's detestation of what may be called heartless sins. It is covered by the classification of Canto xi. Yet it is almost with a shock that we find Myrrha here for personation, and not rather condemned to some other circle for another sin.

767. Buoso Donati: Introduced as a thief in the Seventh Bolgia (Inf. xxv. 140). Buoso was possessed of a peerless mare, known as the Lady of the herd. To make some amends for his unscrupulous acquisition of wealth, he made a will bequeathing legacies to various religious communities. When he died his nephew Simon kept the fact concealed long enough to procure a personation of him as if on his death-bed by Gianni Schicchi, who had great powers of mimicry. Acting in the character of Buoso, the rogue professed his wish to make a new disposition of his means, and after specifying some trifling charitable bequests the better to maintain his assumed character, named Simon as general legatee, and bequeathed Buoso's mare to himself.

768. O ye, etc.: The speaker has heard and noted Virgil's words of explanation given in the previous Canto, line 94.

769. Master Adam: Adam of Brescia, an accomplished worker in metals, was induced by the Counts Guidi of Romena in the Casentino, the upland district of the upper Arno, to counterfeit the gold coin of Florence. This false coin is mentioned in a Chronicle as having been in circulation in 1281. It must therefore have been somewhat later that Master Adam was burned, as he was by sentence of the Republic, upon the road which led from Romena to Florence. A cairn still existing near the ruined castle bears the name of the 'dead man's cairn.'

770. The money coined, etc.: The gold florin, afterwards adopted in so many countries, was first struck in 1252; 'which florins weighed eight to the ounce, and bore the lily on the one side, and on the other Saint John.'—(Villani, vi. 54.) The piece was thus of about the weight of our half-sovereign. The gold was of twenty-four carats; that is, it had no alloy. The coin soon passed into wide circulation, and to maintain its purity became for the Florentines a matter of the first importance. Villani, in the chapter bove cited, tells how the King of Tunis finding the florin to be of pure gold sent for some of the Pisans, then the chief traders in his ports, and asked who were the Florentines that they coined such money. 'Only our Arabs,' was the answer; meaning that they were rough country folk, dependent on Pisa. 'Then what is your coin like?' he asked. A Florentine of Oltrarno named Pera Balducci, who was present, took the opportunity of informing him how great Florence was compared with Pisa, as was shown by that city having no gold coinage of its own; whereupon the King made the Florentines free of Tunis, and allowed them to have a factory there. 'And this,' adds Villani, who had himself been agent abroad for a great Florentine house of business, 'we had at first hand from the aforesaid Pera, a man worthy of credit, and with whom we were associated in the Priorate.'

771. Guido, etc.: The Guidi of Romena were a branch of the great family of the Counts Guidi. The father of the three brothers in the text was grandson of the old Guido that married the Good Gualdrada, and cousin of the Guidoguerra met by Dante in the Seventh Circle (Inf. xvi. 38). How the third brother was called is not settled, nor which of the three was already dead in the beginning of 1300. The Alexander of Romena, who for some time was captain of the banished

Florentine Whites, was, most probably, he of the text. A letter is extant professing to be written by Dante to two of Alexander's nephews on the occasion of his death, in which the poet excuses himself for absence from the funeral on the plea of poverty. By the time he wrote the Inferno he may, owing to their shifty politics, have lost all liking for the family, yet it seems harsh measure that is here dealt to former friends and patrons.

772. Fonte Branda: A celebrated fountain in the city of Siena. Near Romena is a spring which is also named Fonte Branda; and this, according to the view now most in favour, was meant by Master Adam. But was it so named in Dante's time? Or was it not so called only when the Comedy had begun to awaken a natural interest in the old coiner, which local ingenuity did its best to meet? The early commentators know nothing of the Casentino Fonte Branda, and, though it is found mentioned under the date of 1539, that does not take us far enough back. In favour of the Sienese fountain is the consideration that it was the richest of any in the Tuscan cities; that it was a great architectural as well as engineering work; and that, although now more than half a century old, it was still the subject of curiosity with people far and near. Besides, Adam has already recalled the brooks of Casentino, and so the mention of the paltry spring at Romena would introduce no fresh idea like that of the abundant waters of the great fountain which daily quenched the thirst of thousands.

773. Eleven miles: It will be remembered that the previous Bolgia was twenty-two miles in circumference.

774. Three carats: Three carats in twenty-four being of some foreign substance.

775. Who smoke, etc.: This description of sufferers from high fever, like that of Master Adam with his tympanitis, has the merit, such as it is, of being true to the life.

776. One, etc.: Potiphar's wife.

777. Sinon: Called of Troy, as being known through his conduct at the siege. He pretended to have deserted from the Greeks, and by a false story persuaded the Trojans to admit the fatal wooden horse.

778. When Trojans, etc.: When King Priam sought to know for what purpose the wooden horse was really constructed.

779. Narcissus' mirror: The pool in which Narcissus saw his form reflected.

780. 'Tis shame: Dante knows that Virgil would have scorned to portray such a scene of low life as this, but he must allow himself a wider licence and here as elsewhere refuses nothing, even in the way of mean detail, calculated to convey to his readers 'a full experience of the Inferno' as he conceived of it—the place 'where all the vileness of the world is cast.'

CANTO XXXI.

The very tongue that first had caused me pain,
Biting till both my cheeks were crimsoned o'er,
With healing medicine me restored again.
So have I heard, the lance Achilles[781] bore,
Which earlier was his father's, first would wound
And then to health the wounded part restore.
From that sad valley[782] we our backs turned round,
Up the encircling rampart making way
Nor uttering, as we crossed it, any sound.
Here was it less than night and less than day,
And scarce I saw at all what lay ahead;
But of a trumpet the sonorous bray—
No thunder-peal were heard beside it—led
Mine eyes along the line by which it passed,
Till on one spot their gaze concentrated.
When by the dolorous rout was overcastT
he sacred enterprise of Charlemagne
Roland[783] blew not so terrible a blast.
Short time my head was that way turned, when plain
I many lofty towers appeared to see.
'Master, what town is this?' I asked. 'Since fain
Thou art,' he said, 'to pierce the obscurity
While yet through distance 'tis inscrutable,
Thou must of error needs the victim be.
Arriving there thou shalt distinguish well
How much by distance was thy sense betrayed;

Therefore to swifter course thyself compel.'
Then tenderly[784] he took my hand, and said: '
Ere we pass further I would have thee know,
That at the fact thou mayst be less dismayed,
These are not towers but giants; in a row
Set round the brink each in the pit abides,
His navel hidden and the parts below.'
And even as when the veil of mist divides
Little by little dawns upon the sight
What the obscuring vapour earlier hides;
So, piercing the gross air uncheered by light,
As I step after step drew near the bound
My error fled, but I was filled with fright.
As Montereggion[785] with towers is crowned
Which from the walls encircling it arise;
So, rising from the pit's encircling mound,
Half of their bodies towered before mine eyes—
Dread giants, still by Jupiter defied
From Heaven whene'er it thunders in the skies.
The face of one already I descried,
His shoulders, breast, and down his belly far,
And both his arms dependent by his side.
When Nature ceased such creatures as these are
To form, she of a surety wisely wrought
Wresting from Mars such ministers of war.
And though she rue not that to life she brought
The whale and elephant, who deep shall read
Will justify her wisdom in his thought;
For when the powers of intellect are wed

To strength and evil will, with them made one,
The race of man is helpless left indeed.
As large and long as is St. Peter's cone[786]
At Rome, the face appeared; of every limb
On scale like this was fashioned every bone.
So that the bank, which covered half of him
As might a tunic, left uncovered yet
So much that if to his hair they sought to climb
Three Frisians[787] end on end their match had met;
For thirty great palms I of him could see,
Counting from where a man's cloak-clasp is set.
Rafel[788] mai amech zabi almi!
Out of the bestial mouth began to roll,
Which scarce would suit more dulcet psalmody.
And then my Leader charged him: 'Stupid soul,
Stick to thy horn. With it relieve thy mind
When rage or other passions pass control.
Feel at thy neck, round which the thong is twined
O puzzle-headed wretch! from which 'tis slung;
Clipping thy monstrous breast thou shalt it find.'
And then to me: 'From his own mouth is wrung
Proof of his guilt. 'Tis Nimrod, whose insane
Whim hindered men from speaking in one tongue.
Leave we him here nor spend our speech in vain;
For words to him in any language said,
As unto others his, no sense contain.'
Turned to the left, we on our journey sped,
And at the distance of an arrow's flight
We found another huger and more dread.

By what artificer thus pinioned tight
I cannot tell, but his left arm was bound
In front, as at his back was bound the right,
By a chain which girt him firmly round and round;
About what of his frame there was displayed
Below the neck, in fivefold gyre 'twas wound.
'Incited by ambition this one made
Trial of prowess 'gainst Almighty Jove,'
My Leader told, 'and he is thus repaid. '
Tis Ephialtes,[789] mightily who strove
What time the giants to the gods caused fright:
The arms he wielded then no more will move.'
And I to him: 'Fain would I, if I might,
On the enormous Briareus set eye,
And know the truth by holding him in sight.'
'Antæus[790] thou shalt see,' he made reply,'
Ere long, and he can speak, nor is in chains.
Us to the depth of all iniquity
He shall let down. The one thou'dst see[791] remains
Far off, like this one bound and like in make,
But in his face far more of fierceness reigns.'
Never when earth most terribly did quake
Shook any tower so much as what all o'er
And suddenly did Ephialtes shake.
Terror of death possessed me more and more;
The fear alone had served my turn indeed,
But that I marked the ligatures he wore.
Then did we somewhat further on proceed,
Reaching Antæus who for good five ell,[792]

His head not counted, from the pit was freed.
'O thou who from the fortune-haunted dell[793]—
Where Scipio of glory was made heir
When with his host to flight turned Hannibal—
A thousand lions didst for booty bear
Away, and who, hadst thou but joined the host
And like thy brethren fought, some even aver
The victory to earth's sons had not been lost,
Lower us now, nor disobliging show,
To where Cocytus[794] fettered is by frost.
To Tityus[795] nor to Typhon make us go.
To grant what here is longed for he hath power,
Cease them to curl thy snout, but bend thee low.
He can for wage thy name on earth restore;
He lives, and still expecteth to live long,
If Grace recall him not before his hour.'
So spake my Master. Then his hands he swung
Downward and seized my
Leader in all haste— Hands in whose grip even
Hercules once was wrung.
And Virgil when he felt them round him cast Said:
'That I may embrace thee, hither tend,'
And in one bundle with him made me fast.
And as to him that under Carisend[796]
Stands on the side it leans to, while clouds fly
Counter its slope, the tower appears to bend;
Even so to me who stood attentive by
Antæus seemed to stoop, and I, dismayed,
Had gladly sought another road to try.

But us in the abyss he gently laid,

Where Lucifer and Judas gulfed remain;

Nor to it thus bent downward long time stayed,

But like a ship's mast raised himself again.

FOOTNOTES:

781. Achilles: The rust upon his lance had virtue to heal the wound.

782. From that sad valley: Leaving the Tenth and last Bolgia they climb the inner bank of it and approach the Ninth and last Circle, which consists of the pit of the Inferno.

783. Roland: Charles the Great, on his march north after defeating the Saracens at Saragossa, left Roland to bring up his rear-guard. The enemy fell on this in superior strength, and slew the Christians almost to a man. Then Roland, mortally wounded, sat down under a tree in Roncesvalles and blew upon his famous horn a blast so loud thatit was heard by Charles at a distance of several miles.—The Chansons de Geste were familiarly known to Italians of all classes.

784. Then tenderly, etc.: The wound inflicted by his reproof has been already healed,but Virgil still behaves to Dante with more than his wonted gentleness. He will have him assured of his sympathy now that they are about to descend into the 'lowest depthof all wickedness.'

785. Montereggioni: A fortress about six miles from Siena, of which ample ruins stillexist. It had no central keep, but twelve towers rose from its circular wall like spikes from the rim of a coronet. They had been added by the Sienese in 1260, and so were comparatively new in Dante's time.—As the towers stood round Montereggioni so thegiants at regular intervals stand round the central pit. They have their foothold within the enclosing mound; and thus, to one looking at them from without, they are hidden by it up to their middle. As the embodiment of superhuman impious strength and pride they stand for warders of the utmost reach of Hell.

786. St. Peter's cone: The great pine cone of bronze, supposed to have originally crowned the mausoleum of Hadrian, lay in Dante's time in the forecourt of St Peter's.When the new church was built it was removed to the gardens of the Vatican, whereit still remains. Its size, it will be seen, is of importance as helping us to a notionof the stature of the giants; and, though the accounts of its height are strangely at variance with one another, I think the measurement made specially for Philalethes may be accepted as substantially correct. According to that, the cone is ten palms long—about six feet. Allowing something for the neck, down to 'where a man clasps his cloak' (line 66), and taking the thirty palms as eighteen feet, we get twenty-six feetor so for half his height. The giants vary in bulk; whether they do so in height is not clear. We cannot be far mistaken if we assume them to stand from fifty to sixty feet high. Virgil and Dante must throw their heads well back to look up into the giant's face; and Virgil must raise his voice as he speaks.—With regard to the height of the cone it may be remarked that Murray's Handbook for Rome makes it eleven feet high;Gsell-Fels two and a half metres, or eight feet and three inches. It is so placed as to bedifficult of measurement.

787. Three Frisians: Three very tall men, as Dante took Frisians to be, if standing oneon the head of the other would not have reached his hair.

788. Rafel, etc.: These words, like the opening line of the Seventh Canto, have, to noresult, greatly exercised the ingenuity of scholars. From what follows it is clear that Dante meant them to be meaningless. Part of Nimrod's punishment is that he who brought about the confusion of tongues is now left with a language all to himself. It seems strange that commentators should have exhausted themselves in searching fora sense in words specially invented to have none.—In his De Vulg. El., i. 7, Dante enlarges upon the confusion of tongues, and speaks of the tower of Babel as having been begun by men on the persuasion of a giant.

789. Ephialtes: One of the giants who in the war with the gods piled Ossa on Pelion.

790. Antæus: Is to be asked to lift them over the wall, because, unlike Nimrod, he canunderstand what is said to him, and, unlike Ephialtes, is not bound. Antæus is free- handed because he took no part in the war with the gods.

791. The one thou'dst see: Briareus. Virgil here gives Dante to know what is the truthabout Briareus (see line 97, etc.). He is not, as he was fabled, a monster with a hundredhands, but is like Ephialtes, only fiercer to see. Hearing himself thus made light of Ephialtes trembles with anger, like a tower rocking in an earthquake.

792. Five ell: Five ells make about thirty palms, so that Antæus is of the same stature as that assigned to Nimrod at line 65. This supports the view that the 'huger' of line 84may apply to breadth rather than to height.

793. The fortune-haunted dell: The valley of the Bagrada near Utica, where Scipio defeated Hannibal and won the surname of Africanus. The giant Antæus had, accordingto the legend, lived in that neighbourhood, with the flesh of lions for his food and his dwelling in a cave. He was son of the Earth, and could not be vanquished so long as he was able to touch the ground; and thus ere Hercules could give him a mortal hug he needed to swing him aloft. In the Monarchia, ii. 10, Dante refers to the combat between Hercules and Antæus as an instance of the wager of battle corresponding to that between David and Goliath. Lucan's Pharsalia, a favourite authority with Dante, supplies him with these references to Scipio and Antæus.

794. Cocytus: The frozen lake fed by the waters of Phlegethon. See Canto xiv. at theend.

795. Tityus, etc.: These were other giants, stated by Lucan to be less strong than Antæus. This introduction of their names is therefore a piece of flattery to the monster.A light contemptuous turn is given by Virgil to his flattery when in the following sentence he bids Antæus not curl his snout, but at once comply with the demand for aid. There is something genuinely Italian in the picture given of the giants in this Canto, as of creatures whose intellect bears no proportion to their bulk and brute strength. Mighty hunters like Nimrod, skilled in sounding the horn but feeble in reasoned speech, Frisians with great thews and long of limb, and German men-at-arms who traded in their rude valour, to the subtle Florentine in whom the ferment of the Renaissance was beginning to work were all specimens of Nature's handicraft that hadbetter have been left unmade, were it not that wiser people could use them as tools.

796. Carisenda: A tower still standing in Bologna, built at the beginning of the twelfth century, and, like many others of its kind in the city, erected not for strength but merelyin order to dignify the family to whom it belonged. By way of further distinction to theirowners, some of these towers were so constructed as to lean from the perpendicular. Carisenda, like its taller neighbour the Asinelli, still supplies a striking feature to the near and distant views of Bologna. What is left of it hangs for more than two yards offthe plumb. In the half-century after Dante's time it had, according to Benvenuto, lost something of its height. It would therefore as the poet saw it seem to be bending downeven more than it now does to any one standing under it on the side it slopes to, whena cloud is drifting over it in the other direction.

CANTO XXXII.

Had I sonorous rough rhymes at command,
Such as would suit the cavern terrible
Rooted on which all the other ramparts stand,
The sap of fancies which within me swell
Closer I'd press; but since I have not these,
With some misgiving I go on to tell.
For 'tis no task to play with as you please,
Of all the world the bottom to portray,
Nor one that with a baby speech[797] agrees.
But let those ladies help me with my lay
Who helped Amphion[798] walls round Thebes to pile,
And faithful to the facts my words shall stay.
O 'bove all creatures wretched, for whose vile
Abode 'tis hard to find a language fit,
As sheep or goats ye had been happier! While
We still were standing in the murky pit—
Beneath the giant's feet[799] set far below—
And at the high wall I was staring yet,
When this I heard: 'Heed to thy steps[800] bestow,
Lest haply by thy soles the heads be spurned
Of wretched brothers wearied in their woe.'
Before me, as on hearing this I turned,
Beneath my feet a frozen lake,[801] its guise
Rather of glass than water, I discerned.
In all its course on Austrian Danube lies
No veil in time of winter near so thick,

Nor on the Don beneath its frigid skies,
As this was here; on which if Tabernicch[802]
Or Mount Pietrapana[803] should alight
Not even the edge would answer with a creak.
And as the croaking frog holds well in sight
Its muzzle from the pool, what time of year[804]
The peasant girl of gleaning dreams at night;
The mourning shades in ice were covered here,
Seen livid up to where we blush[805] with shame.
In stork-like music their teeth chattering were.
With downcast face stood every one of them:
To cold from every mouth, and to despair
From every eye, an ample witness came.
And having somewhat gazed around me there
I to my feet looked down, and saw two pressed
So close together, tangled was their hair,
'Say, who are you with breast[806] thus strained to breast?'
I asked; whereon their necks they backward bent,
And when their upturned faces lay at rest
Their eyes, which earlier were but moistened, sent
Tears o'er their eyelids: these the frost congealed
And fettered fast[807] before they further went.
Plank set to plank no rivet ever held
More firmly; wherefore, goat-like, either ghost
Butted the other; so their wrath prevailed.
And one who wanted both cars, which the frost
Had bitten off, with face still downward thrown, Asked:
'Why with us art thou so long engrossed?
If who that couple are thou'dst have made known—

The vale down which Bisenzio's floods decline
Was once their father Albert's[808] and their own.
One body bore them: search the whole malign
Caïna,[809] and thou shalt not any see
More worthy to be fixed in gelatine;
Not he whose breast and shadow equally
Were by one thrust of Arthur's lance[810] pierced through:
Nor yet Focaccia;[811] nor the one that me
With his head hampers, blocking out my view,
Whose name was Sassol Mascheroni:[812] well
Thou must him know if thou art Tuscan too.
And that thou need'st not make me further tell—
I'm Camicion de' Pazzi,[813] and Carlin[814]
I weary for, whose guilt shall mine excel.'
A thousand faces saw I dog-like grin,
Frost-bound; whence I, as now, shall always shake
Whenever sight of frozen pools I win.
While to the centre[815] we our way did make
To which all things converging gravitate,
And me that chill eternal caused to quake;
Whether by fortune, providence, or fate,
I know not, but as 'mong the heads I went
I kicked one full in the face; who therefore straight'
Why trample on me?' snarled and made lament, '
Unless thou com'st to heap the vengeance high
For Montaperti,[816] why so virulent
'Gainst me?' I said: 'Await me here till I
By him, O Master, shall be cleared of doubt;[817]
Then let my pace thy will be guided by.'

My Guide delayed, and I to him spake out,
While he continued uttering curses shrill:
'Say, what art thou, at others thus to shout?'
'But who art thou, that goest at thy will
Through Antenora,[818] trampling on the face Of others? '
Twere too much if thou wert still
In life.' 'I live, and it may help thy case,'
Was my reply, 'if thou renown wouldst gain,
Should I thy name[819] upon my tablets place.'
And he: 'I for the opposite am fain.
Depart thou hence, nor work me further dool;
Within this swamp thou flatterest all in vain.'
Then I began him by the scalp to pull,
And 'Thou must tell how thou art called,'
I said,'Or soon thy hair will not be plentiful.'
And he: 'Though every hair thou from me shred
I will not tell thee, nor my face turn round;
No, though a thousand times thou spurn my head.'
His locks ere this about my fist were wound,
And many a tuft I tore, while dog-like wails
Burst from him, and his eyes still sought the ground.
Then called another: 'Bocca, what now ails?
Is't not enough thy teeth go chattering there,
But thou must bark? What devil thee assails?'
'Ah! now,' said I, 'thou need'st not aught declare,
Accursed traitor; and true news of thee
To thy disgrace I to the world will bear.'
'Begone, tell what thou wilt,' he answered me;
'But, if thou issue hence, not silent keep[820]

Of him whose tongue but lately wagged so free.
He for the Frenchmen's money[821] here doth weep.
Him of Duera saw I, mayst thou tell,
Where sinners shiver in the frozen deep.
Shouldst thou be asked who else within it dwell—
Thou hast the Beccheria[822] at thy side;
Across whose neck the knife at Florence fell.
John Soldanieri[823] may be yonder spied
With Ganellon,[824] and Tribaldell[825] who threw
Faenza's gates, when slept the city, wide.
'Him had we left, our journey to pursue,
When frozen in a hole[826] a pair I saw;
One's head like the other's hat showed to the view.
And, as their bread men hunger-driven gnaw,
The uppermost tore fiercely at his mate
Where nape and brain-pan to a junction draw.
No worse by Tydeus[827] in his scornful hate
Were Menalippus' temples gnawed and hacked
Than skull and all were torn by him irate.
'O thou who provest by such bestial act
Hatred of him who by thy teeth is chewed,
Declare thy motive,' said I, 'on this pact—
That if with reason thou with him hast feud,
Knowing your names and manner of his crime
I in the world[828] to thee will make it good;
If what I speak with dry not ere the time.'

FOOTNOTES:

797. A baby speech: 'A tongue that cries mamma and papa' For his present purpose, he complains, he has not in Italian an adequate supply of rough high-sounding rhymes; but at least he will use only the best words that can be found. In another work (De Vulg. El. ii. 7) he instances mamma and babbo as words of a kind to be avoided by allwho would write nobly in Italian.

798. Amphion: Who with his music charmed rocks from the mountain and heaped them in order for walls to Thebes.

799. The giant's feet: Antæus. A bank slopes from where the giants stand inside the wall down to the pit which is filled with the frozen Cocytus. This is the Ninth and inmost Circle, and is divided into four concentric rings—Caïna, Antenora, Ptolomæa, and Judecca—where traitors of different kinds are punished.

800. Thy steps: Dante alone is addressed, the speaker having seen him set heavily down upon the ice by Antæus.

801. A frozen lake: Cocytus. See Inf. xiv. 119.

802. Tabernicch: It is not certain what mountain is here meant; probably Yavornick near Adelsberg in Carniola. It is mentioned, not for its size, but the harshness of its name.

803. Pietrapana: A mountain between Modena and Lucca, visible from Pisa: Petra Apuana.

804. Time of year: At harvest-time, when in the warm summer nights the wearied gleaner dreams of her day's work.

805. To where we blush: The bodies of the shades are seen buried in the clear glassyice, out of which their heads and necks stand free—as much as 'shows shame,' thatis, blushes.

806. With breast, etc.: As could be seen through the clear ice.

807. Fettered fast: Binding up their eyes. In the punishment of traitors is symbolised thehardness and coldness of their hearts to all the claims of blood, country, or friendship.

808. Their father Albert's: Albert, of the family of the Counts Alberti, lord of the upper valley of the Bisenzio, near Florence. His sons, Alexander and Napoleon, slew one another in a quarrel regarding their inheritance.

809. Caïna: The outer ring of the Ninth Circle, and that in which are punished those treacherous to their kindred.—Here a place is reserved for Gianciotto Malatesta, the husband of Francesca (Inf. v. 107).

810. Arthur's lance: Mordred, natural son of King Arthur, was slain by him in battle as a rebel and traitor. 'And the history says that after the lance-thrust Girflet plainly saw a ray of the sun pass through the hole of the wound.'—Lancelot du Lac.

811. Focaccia: A member of the Pistoiese family of Cancellieri, in whose domestic feuds the parties of Whites and Blacks took rise. He assassinated one of his relatives and cut off the hand of another.

812. Sassol Mascheroni: Of the Florentine family of the Toschi. He murdered his nephew, of whom by some accounts he was the guardian. For this crime he was punished by being rolled through the streets of Florence in a cask and then beheaded.Every Tuscan would be familiar with the story of such a punishment.

813. Camicion de' Pazzi: To distinguish the Pazzi to whom Camicione belonged fromthe Pazzi of Florence they were called the Pazzi of Valdarno, where their possessionslay. Like his fellow-traitors he had slain a kinsman.

81*4. Carlin:* Also one of the Pazzi of Valdarno. Like all the spirits in this circle Camicione is eager to betray the treachery of others, and prophesies the guilt of his still living relative, which is to cast his own villany into the shade. In 1302 or 1303 Carlino held the castle of Piano de Trevigne in Valdarno, where many of the exiled Whites ofFlorence had taken refuge, and for a bribe he betrayed it to the enemy.

815. The centre: The bottom of Inferno is the centre of the earth, and, on the system of Ptolemy, the central point of the universe.

8*16. Montaperti*: See Inf. x. 86. The speaker is Bocca, of the great Florentine familyof the Abati, who served as one of the Florentine cavaliers at Montaperti. When the enemy was charging towards the standard of the Republican cavalry Bocca aimed a blow at the arm of the knight who bore it and cut off his hand. The sudden fall of the flag disheartened the Florentines, and in great measure contributed to the defeat.

817. Cleared of doubt: The mention of Montaperti in this place of traitors suggests toDante the thought of Bocca. He would fain be sure as to whether he has the traitor at his feet. Montaperti was never very far from the thoughts of the Florentine of that day.It is never out of Bocca's mind.

818. Antenora: The second ring of the Ninth Circle, where traitors to their country arepunished, named after Antenor the Trojan prince who, according to the belief of the middle ages, betrayed his native city to the Greeks.

819. Should I thy name, etc.: 'Should I put thy name among the other notes.' It is the last time that Dante is to offer such a bribe; and here the offer is most probably ironical.

820. Not silent keep, etc.: Like all the other traitors Bocca finds his only pleasure in betraying his neighbours.

821. The Frenchmen's money: He who had betrayed the name of Bocca was Buoso of Duera, one of the Ghibeline chiefs of Cremona. When Guy of Montfort was leading an army across Lombardy to recruit Charles of Anjou in his war against Manfred in 1265 (Inf. xxviii. 16 and Purg. iii.), Buoso, who had been left to guard the passage of the Oglio, took a bribe to let the French army pass.

822. Beccheria: Tesauro of the Pavian family Beccheria, Abbot of Vallombrosa and legate in Florence of Pope Alexander IV. He was accused of conspiring against the Commonwealth along with the exiled Ghibelines (1258). All Europe was shocked to hear that a great churchman had been tortured and beheaded by the Florentines. The city was placed under Papal interdict, proclaimed by the Archbishop of Pisa from the tower of S. Pietro in Vincoli at Rome. Villani seems to think the Abbot was innocent of the charge brought against him (Cron. vi. 65), but he always leans to the indulgent view when a priest is concerned.

823. Soldanieri: Deserted from the Florentine Ghibelines after the defeat of Manfred.

824. Ganellon: Whose treacherous counsel led to the defeat of Roland at Roncesvalles.

825. Tribaldello: A noble of Faenza, who, as one account says, to revenge himself forthe loss of a pig, sent a cast of the key of the city gate to John of Apia, then prowling about Romagna in the interest of the French Pope, Martin IV. He was slain at the battleof Forlì in 1282 (Inf. xxvii. 43).

826. Frozen in a hole, etc.: The two are the Count Ugolino and the Archbishop Roger.

827. Tydeus: One of the Seven against Thebes, who, having been mortally woundedby Menalippus the Theban, whom he slew, got his friends to bring him the head of hisfoe and gnawed at it with his teeth. Dante found the incident in his favourite author Statius (Theb. viii.).

828. I in the world, etc.: Dante has learned from Bocca that the prospect of having their memory refreshed on earth has no charm for the sinners met with here. The bribehe offers is that of loading the name of a foe with ignominy—but only if from the taleit shall be plain that the ignominy is deserved.

CANTO XXXIII.

His mouth uplifting from the savage feast,
The sinner[829] rubbed and wiped it free of gore
On the hair of the head he from behind laid waste;
And then began: 'Thou'dst have me wake once more
A desperate grief, of which to think alone,
Ere I have spoken, wrings me to the core.
But if my words shall be as seed that sown
May fructify unto the traitor's shame
Whom thus I gnaw, I mingle speech[830] and groan
.Of how thou earnest hither or thy name
I nothing know, but that a Florentine[831]
In very sooth thou art, thy words proclaim.
Thou then must know I was Count Ugolin,
The Archbishop Roger[832] he. Now hearken well
Why I prove such a neighbour. How in fine,
And flowing from his ill designs, it fell
That I, confiding in his words, was caught
Then done to death, were waste of time[833] to tell.
But that of which as yet thou heardest nought
Is how the death was cruel which I met:
Hearken and judge if wrong to me he wrought.
Scant window in the mew whose epithet
Of Famine[834] came from me its resident,
And cooped in which shall many languish yet,
Had shown me through its slit how there were spent
Full many moons,[835] ere that bad dream

I dreamedWhen of my future was the curtain rent.
Lord of the hunt and master this one seemed,
Chasing the wolf and wolf-cubs on the height[836]
By which from Pisan eyes is Lucca hemmed.
With famished hounds well trained and swift of flight,
Lanfranchi[837] and Gualandi in the van,
And Sismond he had set. Within my sight
Both sire and sons—nor long the chase—began
To grow (so seemed it) weary as they fled;
Then through their flanks fangs sharp and eager ran.
When I awoke before the morning spread
I heard my sons[838] all weeping in their sleep—
For they were with me—and they asked for bread.
Ah! cruel if thou canst from pity keep
At the bare thought of what my heart foreknew;
And if thou weep'st not, what could make thee weep?
Now were they 'wake, and near the moment drew
At which 'twas used to bring us our repast;
But each was fearful[839] lest his dream came true.
And then I heard the under gate[840] made fast
Of the horrible tower, and thereupon I gazed
In my sons' faces, silent and aghast.
I did not weep, for I to stone was dazed:
They wept, and darling Anselm me besought:
"What ails thee, father? Wherefore thus amazed?"
And yet I did not weep, and answered not
The whole day, and that night made answer none,
Till on the world another sun shone out.
Soon as a feeble ray of light had won

Into our doleful prison, made aware
Of the four faces[841] featured like my own,
Both of my hands I bit at in despair;
And they, imagining that I was fain
To eat, arose before me with the prayer:
"O father, 'twere for us an easier pain
If thou wouldst eat us. Thou didst us array
In this poor flesh: unclothe us now again."
I calmed me, not to swell their woe.
That dayAnd the next day no single word we said.
Ah! pitiless earth, that didst unyawning stay!
When we had reached the fourth day,
Gaddo, spreadOut at my feet, fell prone; and made demand:
"Why, O my father, offering us no aid?"
There died he. Plain as I before thee stand
I saw the three as one by one they failed,
The fifth day and the sixth; then with my hand,
Blind now, I groped for each of them, and wailed
On them for two days after they were gone.
Famine[842] at last, more strong than grief, prevailed,'
When he had uttered this, his eyes all thrown
Awry, upon the hapless skull he fell
With teeth that, dog-like, rasped upon the bone.
Ah, Pisa! byword of the folk that dwell
In the sweet country where the Si[843] doth sound,
Since slow thy neighbours to reward thee well
Let now Gorgona and Capraia[844] mound
Themselves where Arno with the sea is blent,
Till every one within thy walls be drowned.

For though report of Ugolino went
That he betrayed[845] thy castles, thou didst wrong
Thus cruelly his children to torment.
These were not guilty, for they were but young,
Thou modern Thebes![846] Brigata and young Hugh,
And the other twain of whom above 'tis sung.
We onward passed to where another crew[847]
Of shades the thick-ribbed ice doth fettered keep;
Their heads not downward these, but backward threw.
Their very weeping will not let them weep,
And grief, encountering barriers at their eyes,
Swells, flowing inward, their affliction deep;
For the first tears that issue crystallise,
And fill, like vizor fashioned out of glass,
The hollow cup o'er which the eyebrows rise.
And though, as 'twere a callus, now my face
By reason of the frost was wholly grown
Benumbed and dead to feeling,
I could trace (So it appeared), a breeze against it blown,
And asked: 'O Master, whence comes this? So low
As where we are is any vapour[848] known?' And he replied:
'Thou ere long while shalt go
Where touching this thine eye shall answer true,
Discovering that which makes the wind to blow.'
Then from the cold crust one of that sad crew
Demanded loud: 'Spirits, for whom they hold
The inmost room, so truculent were you,
Back from my face let these hard veils be rolled,
That I may vent the woe which chokes my heart,

Ere tears again solidify with cold.'
And I to him: 'First tell me who thou art
If thou'dst have help; then if I help not quick
To the bottom[849] of the ice let me depart.'
He answered: 'I am Friar Alberic[850]—
He of the fruit grown in the orchard fell—
And here am I repaid with date for fig.'
'Ah!' said I to him, 'art thou dead as well?'
'How now my body fares,' he answered me,
'Up in the world, I have no skill to tell;
For Ptolomæa[851] has this quality—
The soul oft plunges hither to its place
Ere it has been by Atropos[852] set free.
And that more willingly from off my face
Thou mayst remove the glassy tears, know, soon
As ever any soul of man betrays
As I betrayed, the body once his own
A demon takes and governs until all
The span allotted for his life be run.
Into this tank headlong the soul doth fall;
And on the earth his body yet may show
Whose shade behind me wintry frosts enthral.
But thou canst tell, if newly come below:
It is Ser Branca d'Oria,[853] and complete
Is many a year since he was fettered so.'
'It seems,' I answered, 'that thou wouldst me cheat,
For Branca d'Oria never can have died:
He sleeps, puts clothes on, swallows drink and meat.' '
Or e'er to the tenacious pitchy tide

Which boils in Malebranche's moat had come
The shade of Michael Zanche,' he replied,
'That soul had left a devil in its room
Within its body; of his kinsmen one[854]
Treacherous with him experienced equal doom.
But stretch thy hand and be its work begun
Of setting free mine eyes.' This did not I.
Twas highest courtesy to yield him none.[855]
Ah, Genoese,[856] strange to morality!
Ye men infected with all sorts of sin!
Out of the world 'tis time that ye should die.
Here, to Romagna's blackest soul[857] akin
,I chanced on one of you; for doing ill
His soul o'erwhelmed Cocytus' floods within,
Though in the flesh he seems surviving still.

NOTE ON THE COUNT UGOLINO.

Ugolino della Gherardesca, Count of Donoratico, a wealthy noble and a man fertile in political resource, was deeply engaged in the affairs of Pisa at a critical period ofher history. He was born in the first half of the thirteenth century. By giving one of his daughters in marriage to the head of the Visconti of Pisa—not to be confounded with those of Milan—he came under the suspicion of being Guelf in his sympathies; the general opinion of Pisa being then, as it always had been, strongly Ghibeline. When driven into exile, as he was along with the Visconti, he improved the occasion by entering into close relations with the leading Guelfs of Tuscany, and in 1278 afree return for him to Pisa was made by them a condition of peace with that city. He commanded one of the divisions of the Pisan fleet at the disastrous battle of Meloria in 1284, when Genoa wrested from her rival the supremacy of the Western Mediterranean, and carried thousands of Pisan citizens into a captivity which lasted many years. Isolated from her Ghibeline allies, and for the time almost sunk in despair, the city called him to the government with wellnigh dictatorial powers; and by dint of crafty negotiations in detail with the members of the league formed against Pisa, helped as was believed by lavish bribery, he had the glory of saving the Commonwealth from destruction though he could not wholly save it from loss. This was in 1285. He soon came to be suspected of being in a secret alliance with Florence and of being lukewarm in the negotiations for the return of the prisoners in Genoa, all with a view to depress the Ghibeline element in the city that he might establish himself as an absolute tyrant with the greater ease. In order still further to strengthen his position he entered into a family compact with his Guelf grandson Nino (Purg. viii. 53), now at the head of the Visconti. But without the support of the people it was impossible for him to hold his ground against the Ghibeline nobles, who resented the arrogance of his manners and were embittered by the loss of their own share in the government; and these contrivedthat month by month the charges of treachery brought against him should increasein virulence. He had, by deserting his post, caused the defeat at Meloria, it was said; and had bribed the other Tuscan cities to favour him, by ceding to them distant Pisan strongholds. His fate was sealed when, having quarrelled with his grandson Nino, he sought alliance with the Archbishop Roger who now led the Ghibeline opposition. With Ugo's connivance an onslaught was planned upon the Guelfs. To preserve an appearance of impartiality he left the city for a neighbouring villa. On returning to enjoy his riddance from a rival he was invited to a conference, at which he resisteda proposal that he should admit partners with him in the government. On this the Archbishop's party raised the cry of treachery; the bells rang out for a street battle,in which he was worsted; and with his sons he had to take refuge in the Palace of the People. There he stood a short siege against the Ghibeline families and the angry mob; and in the same palace he was kept prisoner for twenty days. Then, with his sons and grandsons, he was carried in chains to the tower of the Gualandi, which stood where seven ways met in the heart of Pisa. This was in July 1288. The imprisonment lasted for months, and seems to have been thus prolonged with the view of extorting a heavyransom. It was only in the following March that the Archbishop ordered his victims to be starved to death; for, being a churchman, says one account, he would not shed blood. Not even a confessor was allowed to Ugo and his sons. After the door of the tower had been kept closed for eight days it was opened, and the corpses, still fettered,were huddled into a tomb in the Franciscan church.—The original authorities are far from being agreed as to the details of Ugo's overthrow and death.—For the matter of this note I am chiefly indebted to the careful epitome of the Pisan history of that time by Philalethes in his note on this Canto (Göttliche Comödie).

FOOTNOTES:

829. The sinner: Count Ugolino. See note at the end of the Canto.

830. Mingle speech, etc.: A comparison of these words with those of Francesca (Inf. v. 124) will show the difference in moral tone between the Second Circle of Inferno and the Ninth.

831. A Florentine: So Farinata (Inf. x. 25) recognises Dante by his Florentine speech.The words heard by Ugo are those at xxxii. 133.

832. The Archbishop Roger: Ruggieri, of the Tuscan family of the Ubaldini, to whichthe Cardinal of Inf. x. 120 also belonged. Towards the end of his life he was summonedto Rome to give an account of his evil deeds, and on his refusal to go was declared a rebel to the Church. Ugolino was a traitor to his country; Roger, having entered into some sort of alliance with Ugolino, was a traitor to him. This has led some to supposethat while Ugolino is in Antenora he is so close to the edge of it as to be able to reachthe head of Roger, who, as a traitor to his friend, is fixed in Ptolomæa. Against this view is the fact that they are described as being in the same hole (xxxii. 125), and alsothat in Ptolomæa the shades are set with head thrown back, and with only the face appearing above the ice, while Ugo is described as biting his foe at where the skull joins the nape. From line 91 it is clear that Ptolomæa lay further on than where Rogeris. Like Ugo he is therefore here as a traitor to his country.

833. Were waste, etc.: For Dante knows it already, all Tuscany being familiar with the story of Ugo's fate.

834. Whose epithet of Famine: It was called the Tower of Famine. Its site is now builtover. Buti, the old Pisan commentator of Dante, says it was called the Mew because the eagles of the Republic were kept in it at moulting-time. But this may have been anafter-thought to give local truth to Dante's verse, which it does at the expense of the poetry.

835. Many moons: The imprisonment having already lasted for eight months.

836. The height, etc.: Lucca is about twelve miles from Pisa, Mount Giuliano rising between them.

837. Lanfranchi, etc.: In the dream, these, the chief Ghibeline families of Pisa, are thehuntsmen, Roger being master of the hunt, and the populace the hounds. Ugo and his sons and grandsons are the wolf and wolf-cubs. In Ugo's dream of himself as a wolf there may be an allusion to his having engaged in the Guelf interest.

838. My sons: According to Dante, taken literally, four of Ugo were imprisoned withhim. It would have hampered him to explain that two were grandsons—Anselmuccio and Nino, called the Brigata at line 89, grandsons by their mother of

King Enzo, natural son of Frederick II.—the sons being Gaddo and Uguccione, the latter Ugo's youngest son.

839. Each was fearful, etc.: All the sons had been troubled by dreams of famine. Had their rations been already reduced?

840. The under gate, etc.: The word translated made fast (chiavare) may signify either to nail up or to lock. The commentators and chroniclers differ as to whether the door was locked, nailed, or built up. I would suggest that the lower part of the tower was occupied by a guard, and that the captives had not been used to hear the main door locked. Now, when they hear the great key creaking in the lock, they know that the tower is deserted.

841. The four faces, etc.: Despairing like his own, or possibly that, wasted by famine, the faces of the young men had become liker than ever to Ugo's own time-worn face.

842. Famine, etc.: This line, quite without reason, has been held to mean that Ugo was driven by hunger to eat the flesh of his children. The meaning is, that poignant though his grief was it did not shorten his sufferings from famine.

843. Where the Si, etc.: Italy, Si being the Italian for Yes. In his De Vulg. El., i.8, Dante distinguishes the Latin languages—French, Italian, etc.—by their words of affirmation, and so terms Italian the language of Si. But Tuscany may here be meant, where, as a Tuscan commentator says, the Si is more sweetly pronounced than in any other part of Italy. In Canto xviii. 61 the Bolognese are distinguished as the people who say Sipa. If Pisa be taken as being specially the opprobrium of Tuscany the outburst against Genoa at the close of the Canto gains in distinctness and force.

844. Gorgona and Capraia: Islands not far from the mouth of the Arno.

845. That he betrayed, etc.: Dante seems here to throw doubt on the charge. At the height of her power Pisa was possessed of many hundreds of fortified stations in Italy and scattered over the Mediterranean coasts. The charge was one easy to make and difficult to refute. It seems hard on Ugo that he should get the benefit of the doubt only after he has been, for poetical ends, buried raging in Cocytus.

846. Modern Thebes: As Thebes was to the race of Cadmus, so was Pisa to that of Ugolino.

847. Another crew: They are in Ptolomæa, the third division of the circle, and that assigned to those treacherous to their friends, allies, or guests. Here only the faces of the shades are free of the ice.

848. Is any vapour: Has the sun, so low down as this, any influence upon the temperature, producing vapours and wind? In Dante's time wind was believed to be the exhalation of a vapour.

849. To the bottom, etc.: Dante is going there in any case, and his promise is nothingbut a quibble.

850. Friar Alberic: Alberigo of the Manfredi, a gentleman of Faenza, who late in life became one of the Merry Friars. See Inf. xxiii. 103. In the course of a dispute with his relative Manfred he got a hearty box on the ear from him. Feigning to have forgiven the insult he invited Manfred with a youthful son to dinner in his house, having first arranged that when they had finished their meat, and he called for fruit, armed men should fall on his guests. 'The fruit of Friar Alberigo' passed into a proverb. Here he s repaid with a date for a fig—gets more than he bargained for.

851. Ptolomœa: This division is named from the Hebrew Ptolemy, who slew his relatives at a banquet, they being then his guests (1 Maccab. xvi.).

852. Atropos: The Fate who cuts the thread of life and sets the soul free from the body.

853. Branca d'Oria: A Genoese noble who in 1275 slew his father-in-law Michael Zanche (Inf. xxii. 88) while the victim sat at table as his invited guest.—This mentionof Branca is of some value in helping to ascertain when the Inferno was finished. He was in imprisonment and exile for some time before and up to 1310. In 1311 he was one of the citizens of Genoa heartiest in welcoming the Emperor Henry to their city. Impartial as Dante was, we can scarcely think that he would have loaded with infamy one who had done what he could to help the success of Henry, on whom all Dante's hopes were long set, and by their reception of whom on his descent into Italy he continued to judge his fellow-countrymen. There is considerable reason to believe that the Inferno was published in 1309; this introduction of Branca helps to prove that at least it was published before 1311. If this was so, then Branca d'Oria lived long enough to read or hear that for thirty-five years his soul had been in Hell.—It is significant of the detestation in which Dante held any breach of hospitality, that it is as a treacherous host and not as a treacherous kinsman that Branca is punished—in Ptolomæa and not in Caïna. Cast as the poet was on the hospitality of the world, any disloyalty to its obligations came home to him. For such disloyalty he has invented oneof the most appalling of the fierce retributions with the vision of which he satisfied hiscraving for vengeance upon prosperous sin.—It may be that the idea of this demon- possession of the traitor is taken from the words, 'and after the sop Satan entered intoJudas.'

854. Of his kinsmen one: A cousin or nephew of Branca was engaged with him in themurder of Michael Zanche. The vengeance came on them so speedily that their souls were plunged in Ptolomæa ere Zanche breathed his last.

855. To yield him none: Alberigo being so unworthy of courtesy. See note on 117. But another interpretation of the words has been suggested which saves Dante from the charge of cruelty and mean quibbling; namely, that he did not clear the ice from the sinner's eyes because then he would have been seen to be a living man—one who could take back to the world the awful news that Alberigo's body was the dwelling- place of a devil.

856. Ah, Genoese, etc.: The Genoese, indeed, held no good character. One of their annalists, under the date of 1293, describes the city as suffering from all kinds of crime.

857. Romagna's blackest soul: Friar Alberigo.

CANTO XXXIV.

'Vexilla[858] Regis prodeunt Inferni
Towards where we are; seek then with vision keen,'
My Master bade, 'if trace of him thou spy.'
As, when the exhalations dense have been,
Or when our hemisphere grows dark with night,
A windmill from afar is sometimes seen,
I seemed to catch of such a structure sight;
And then to 'scape the blast did backward draw
Behind my Guide—sole shelter in my plight.
Now was I where[859] (I versify with awe)
The shades were wholly covered, and did show
Visible as in glass are bits of straw.
Some stood[860] upright and some were lying low,
Some with head topmost, others with their feet;
And some with face to feet bent like a bow.
But we kept going on till it seemed meet
Unto my Master that I should behold
The creature once[861] of countenance so sweet
.He stepped aside and stopped me as he told:
'Lo, Dis! And lo, we are arrived at last
Where thou must nerve thee and must make thee bold,'
How I hereon stood shivering and aghast,
Demand not, Reader; this I cannot write;
So much the fact all reach of words surpassed.
I was not dead, yet living was not quite:
Think for thyself, if gifted with the power,

What, life and death denied me, was my plight.
Of that tormented realm the Emperor
Out of the ice stood free to middle breast;
And me a giant less would overtower
Than would his arm a giant. By such test
Judge then what bulk the whole of him must show,[862]
Of true proportion with such limb possessed.
If he was fair of old as hideous now,
And yet his brows against his Maker raised,
Meetly from him doth all affliction flow.
O how it made me horribly amazed
When on his head I saw three faces[863] grew!
The one vermilion which straight forward gazed;
And joining on to it were other two,
One rising up from either shoulder-bone,
Till to a junction on the crest they drew.
'Twixt white and yellow seemed the right-hand one;
The left resembled them whose country lies
Where valleywards the floods of Nile flow down.
Beneath each face two mighty wings did rise,
Such as this bird tremendous might demand:
Sails of sea-ships ne'er saw I of such size.
Not feathered were they, but in style were planned
Like a bat's wing:[864] by them a threefold breeze—
For still he flapped them—evermore was fanned,
And through its depths Cocytus caused to freeze.
Down three chins tears for ever made descent
From his six eyes; and red foam mixed with these.
In every mouth there was a sinner rent

By teeth that shred him as a heckle[865] would;
Thus three at once compelled he to lament.
To the one in front 'twas little to be chewed
Compared with being clawed and clawed again,
Till his back-bone of skin was sometimes nude.[866]'
The soul up yonder in the greater pain
Is Judas 'Scariot, with his head among
The teeth,' my Master said, 'while outward strain
His legs. Of the two whose heads are downward hung,
Brutus is from the black jowl pendulous:
See how he writhes, yet never wags his tongue.
The other, great of thew, is Cassius:[867]
But night is rising[868] and we must be gone;
For everything hath now been seen by us.'
Then, as he bade, I to his neck held on
While he the time and place of vantage chose;
And when the wings enough were open thrown
He grasped the shaggy ribs and clutched them close,
And so from tuft to tuft he downward went
Between the tangled hair and crust which froze.
We to the bulging haunch had made descent,
To where the hip-joint lies in it; and then
My Guide, with painful twist and violent,
Turned round his head to where his feet had been,
And like a climber closely clutched the hair:
I thought to Hell[869] that we returned again.
'Hold fast to me; it needs by such a stair,'
Panting, my Leader said, like man foredone,
'That we from all that wretchedness repair.'

Right through a hole in a rock when he had won,
The edge of it he gave me for a seat
And deftly then to join me clambered on.
I raised mine eyes, expecting they would meet
With Lucifer as I beheld him last,
But saw instead his upturned legs[870] and feet.
If in perplexity I then was cast,
Let ignorant people think who do not see
What point[871] it was that I had lately passed.
'Rise to thy feet,' my Master said to me;
'The way is long and rugged the ascent,
And at mid tierce[872] the sun must almost be.'
'Twas not as if on palace floors we went:
A dungeon fresh from nature's hand was this;
Rough underfoot, and of light indigent
.'Or ever I escape from the abyss,
O Master,' said I, standing now upright,
'Correct in few words where I think amiss.
Where lies the ice?
How hold we him in sightSet upside down?
The sun, how had it skill
In so short while to pass to morn from night?'[873]
And he: 'In fancy thou art standing, still,
On yon side of the centre, where I caught
The vile worm's hair which through the world doth drill.
There wast thou while our downward course I wrought;
But when I turned, the centre was passed by
Which by all weights from every point is sought.
And now thou standest 'neath the other sky,

Opposed to that which vaults the great dry ground
And 'neath whose summit[874] there did whilom die
The Man[875] whose birth and life were sinless found.
Thy feet are firm upon the little sphere,
On this side answering to Judecca's round.
'Tis evening yonder when 'tis morning here;
And he whose tufts our ladder rungs supplied.
Fixed as he was continues to appear.
Headlong from Heaven he fell upon this side;
Whereon the land, protuberant here before,
For fear of him did in the ocean hide,
And 'neath our sky emerged: land, as of yore[876]
Still on this side, perhaps that it might shun
His fall, heaved up, and filled this depth no more.'
From Belzebub[877] still widening up and on,
Far-stretching as the sepulchre,[878] extends
A region not beheld, but only known
By murmur of a brook[879] which through it wends
Declining by a channel eaten through
The flinty rock; and gently it descends.
My Guide and I, our journey to pursue
To the bright world, upon this road concealed
Made entrance, and no thought of resting knew.
He first, I second, still ascending held
Our way until the fair celestial train
Was through an opening round to me revealed:
And, issuing thence, we saw the stars[880] again.

FOOTNOTES:

858. Vexilla, etc.: 'The banners of the King of Hell advance.' The words are adaptedfrom a hymn of the Cross used in Holy Week; and they prepare us to find in Lucifer the opponent of 'the Emperor who reigns on high' (Inf. i. 124). It is somewhat odd thatDante should have put a Christian hymn into Virgil's mouth.

859. Now was I where: In the fourth and inner division or ring of the Ninth Circle. Here are punished those guilty of treachery to their lawful lords or to their benefactors.From Judas Iscariot, the arch-traitor, it takes the name of Judecca.

860. Some stood, etc.: It has been sought to distinguish the degrees of treachery of the shades by means of the various attitudes assigned to them. But it is difficult to make more out of it than that some are suffering more than others. All of them are the worst of traitors, hard-hearted and cold-hearted, and now they are quite frozen in the ice, sealed up even from the poor relief of intercourse with their fellow-sinners.

861. The creature once, etc.: Lucifer, guilty of treachery against the Highest, at Purg.25 described as 'created noble beyond all other creatures.' Virgil calls him Dis, thename used by him for Pluto in the Æneid, and the name from which that of the City ofUnbelief is taken (Inf. viii. 68).

862. Judge then what bulk: The arm of Lucifer was as much longer than the stature ofone of the giants as a giant was taller than Dante. We have seen (Inf. xxxi. 58) that the giants were more than fifty feet in height—nine times the stature of a man. If a man'sarm be taken as a third of his stature, then Satan is twenty-seven times as tall as a giant,that is, he is fourteen hundred feet or so. For a fourth of this, or nearly so—from the middle of the breast upwards—he stands out of the ice, that is, some three hundred and fifty feet. It seems almost too great a height for Dante's purpose; and yet on the calculations of some commentators his stature is immensely greater—from three to five thousand feet.

863. Three faces: By the three faces are represented the three quarters of the world from which the subjects of Lucifer are drawn: vermilion or carnation standing for Europe, yellow for Asia, and black for Africa. Or the faces may symbolise attributes opposed to the Wisdom, Power, and Love of the Trinity (Inf. iii. 5). See also note on line 1.

864. A bat's wing: Which flutters and flaps in dark and noisome places. The simile helps to bring more clearly before us the dim light and half-seen horrors of the Judecca.

865. A heckle: Or brake; the instrument used to clear the fibre of flax from the woody substance mixed with it.

866. Sometimes nude: We are to imagine that the frame of Judas is being for ever renewed and for ever mangled and torn.

867. Cassius: It has been surmised that Dante here confounds the pale and lean Cassiuswho was the friend of Brutus with the L. Cassius described as corpulent by Cicero in the Third Catiline Oration. Brutus and Cassius are set with Judas in this, the deepest room of Hell, because, as he was guilty of high treason against his Divine Master, so they were guilty of it against Julius Cæsar, who, according to Dante, was chosen and ordained by God to found the Roman Empire. As the great rebel against the spiritual authority Judas has allotted to him the fiercer pain. To understand the significance of this harsh treatment of the great Republicans it is necessary to bear in mind that Dante's devotion to the idea of the Empire was part of his religion, and far surpassed in intensity all we can now well imagine. In the absence of a just and strong Emperorthe Divine government of the world seemed to him almost at a stand.

868. Night is rising: It is Saturday evening, and twenty-four hours since they enteredby the gate of Inferno.

869. I thought to Hell, etc.: Virgil, holding on to Lucifer's hairy sides, descends the dark and narrow space between him and the ice as far as to his middle, which marks thecentre of the earth. Here he swings himself round so as to have his feet to the centre ashc cmerges from the pit to the southern hemisphere. Dante now feels that he is being carried up, and, able to see nothing in the darkness, deems they are climbing back to the Inferno. Virgil's difficulty in turning himself round and climbing up the legs of Lucifer arises from his being then at the 'centre to which all weights tend from every part.' Dante shared the erroneous belief of the time, that things grew heavier the nearerthey were to the centre of the earth.

870. His upturned legs: Lucifer's feet are as far above where Virgil and Dante are as was his head above the level of the Judecca.

871. What point, etc.: The centre of the earth. Dante here feigns to have been himselfconfused—a fiction which helps to fasten attention on the wonderful fact that if we could make our way through the earth we should require at the centre to reverse our posture. This was more of a wonder in Dante's time than now.

872. Mid tierce: The canonical day was divided into four parts, of which Tierce was the first and began at sunrise. It is now about half-past seven in the morning. The nightwas beginning when they took their departure from the Judecca: the day is now asfar advanced in the southern hemisphere as they have spent time on the passage. The journey before them is long indeed, for they have to ascend to the surface of the earth.

873. To morn from night: Dante's knowledge of the time of day is wholly derived from what Virgil tells him. Since he began his descent into the Inferno he has not seenthe sun.

874. 'Neath whose summit: Jerusalem is in the centre of the northern hemisphere— an opinion founded perhaps on Ezekiel v. 5: 'Jerusalem I have set in the midst of the nations and countries round about her.' In the Convito, iii. 5, we find Dante's belief regarding the distribution of land and sea clearly given: 'For those I write for it is enough to know that the Earth is fixed and does not move, and that, with the ocean, it isthe centre of the heavens. The heavens, as we see, are for ever revolving around it as a centre; and in these revolutions they must of necessity have two fixed poles. Of these one is visible to almost all the dry land of the Earth; and that is our north pole [star].The other, that is, the south, is out of sight of almost all the dry land.'

875. The Man: The name of Christ is not mentioned in the Inferno.

876. Land, as of yore, etc.: On the fall of Lucifer from the southern sky all the dry land of that hemisphere fled before him under the ocean and took refuge in the other; that is, as much land emerged in the northern hemisphere as sank in the southern. But the ground in the direct line of his descent to the centre of the earth heaped itself up into theMount of Purgatory—the only dry land left in the southern hemisphere. The Inferno was then also hollowed out; and, as Mount Calvary is exactly antipodal to Purgatory, we may understand that on the fall of the first rebels the Mount of Reconciliation for the human race, which is also that of Purification, rose out of the very realms of darkness and sin.—But, as Todeschini points out, the question here arises of whether the Inferno was not created before the earth. At Parad. vii. 124, the earth, with the air and fire and water, is described as 'corruptible and lasting short while;' but the Inferno is to endure for aye, and was made before all that is not eternal (Inf. iii. 8).

877. Belzebub: Called in the Gospel the prince of the devils. It may be worth mentioning here that Dante sees in Purgatory (Purg. viii. 99) a serpent which he says may be that which tempted Eve. The identification of the great tempter with Satan is aMiltonic, or at any rate a comparatively modern idea.

878. The sepulchre: The Inferno, tomb of Satan and all the wicked.

879. A brook: Some make this to be the same as Lethe, one of the rivers of the EarthlyParadise. It certainly descends from the Mount of Purgatory.

880. The stars: Each of the three divisions of the Comedy closes with 'the stars.' These, as appears from Purg. i. are the stars of dawn. It was after sunrise when they began their ascent to the surface of the earth, and so nearly twenty-four hours have been spent on the journey—the time it took them to descend through Inferno. It is now the morning of Easter Sunday—that is, of the true anniversary of the Resurrection although not of the day observed that year by the Church.

9 789358 480450

Printed at Repro India Ltd.